Becoming-Social in a Networked Age

"This is the book on post-documentary technologies that I've been waiting for: an understandable, but also deep and critical explanation of the philosophical assumptions, the form and functions, and the political implications and possibilities of recent new media technologies."
—*Ronald E. Day, Indiana University at Bloomington*

"This book proves that critical consideration of the processes of subjectivity belong in the foreground of media, technology and software studies. Vanquishing the shallow presumptions of subjecthood and identity that linger in accounts of social computing, Neal Thomas expands the philosophical space currently available for the investigation of how sociality is constituted and a post-individual subjectivity is structured by a-signifying machinic relations."
—*Gary Genosko, University of Ontario Institute of Technology*

This book examines the semiotic effects of protocols and algorithms at work in popular social media systems, bridging philosophical conversations in human-computer interaction (HCI) and information systems (IS) design with contemporary work in critical media, technology and software studies. Where most research into social media is sociological in scope, Neal Thomas shows how the underlying material-semiotic operations of social media now crucially define what it means to be social in a networked age. He proposes that we consider social media platforms as computational processes of collective individuation that produce, rather than presume, forms of subjectivity and sociality.

Neal Thomas is Assistant Professor of Media and Technology Studies in the Department of Communication Studies at the University of North Carolina at Chapel Hill, USA.

Routledge Studies in New Media and Cyberculture

For a full list of titles in this series, please visit www.routledge.com.

30 Girls' Feminist Blogging in a Postfeminist Age
   Jessalynn Keller

31 Indigenous People and Mobile Technologies
   Edited by Laurel Evelyn Dyson, Stephen Grant, and Max Hendriks

32 Citizen Participation and Political Communication in a Digital World
   Edited by Alex Frame and Gilles Brachotte

33 Feminism, Labour and Digital Media
   The Digital Housewife
   Kylie Jarrett

34 The Politics of Ephemeral Digital Media
   Permanence and Obsolescence in Paratexts
   Edited by Sara Pesce and Paolo Noto

35 Studying Digital Media Audiences
   Perspectives from Australasia
   Edited by Craig Hight and Ramaswami Harindranath

36 Between the Public and Private in Mobile Communication
   Edited by Ana Serrano Tellería

37 Performing Digital Activism
   New Aesthetics and Discourses of Resistance
   Fidèle A. Vlavo

38 Online Activism in Latin America
   Edited by Hilda Chacón

39 Becoming-Social in a Networked Age
   Neal Thomas

Becoming-Social in a Networked Age

Neal Thomas

Routledge
Taylor & Francis Group

LONDON AND NEW YORK

First published 2018 by Routledge

2 Park Square, Milton Park, Abingdon, Oxfordshire OX14 4RN
52 Vanderbilt Avenue, New York, NY 10017

Routledge is an imprint of the Taylor & Francis Group, an informa business

First issued in paperback 2019

Library of Congress Cataloging-in-Publication Data
CIP data has been applied for.

ISBN: 978-1-138-71902-6 (hbk)
ISBN: 978-0-367-88843-5 (pbk)

Typeset in Sabon
by codeMantra

Contents

Acknowledgements   vii

1 On the Notion of a Formatted Subject   1

2 The Epistemically Formatted Subject   31

3 The Performatively Formatted Subject   64

4 The Signaletically Formatted Subject   96

5 The Allagmatically Formatted Subject   125

6 Conclusion: Toward an Enunciative Informatics   158

Works Cited   177
Index   187

Acknowledgements

Though now well in the rear-view mirror, this work represents a (seemingly endless) mutation, extension, and updating of my doctoral thesis. First and foremost then, I am grateful to my original PhD project advisor Darin Barney, who was the consummate mentor. Jonathan Sterne also had an important if punctuated influence on my time as a doctoral student at McGill. Along with Darin's seminar on technology, Jonathan's seminar on repetition introduced me to thinkers and theories that will forever color my scholarship.

More recently, I am grateful to the many people who've offered support and guidance as I worked to finish the book. Ronald Day is a tireless promoter of my work and ideas, and conversations with him over email in the past few years have helped to buoy my spirits in anxious times. Roy Bendor has similarly been a long-time sounding board and friend. I am grateful to Sarah Sharma and Ken Hillis for being early mentors upon my arrival to UNC, and to Michael Palm for listening to me complain in abstruse ways about the manuscript while carpooling. All three of them have helped me acclimate to academic life in the United States. I am especially grateful to Ken for his early advice as a mentor, and for keeping my service responsibilities manageable while he was department chair. I owe a similar debt of thanks to our current chair Pat Parker, who has been continuously supportive of me as deadlines loomed, and to Lawrence Grossberg, for reading the full final draft.

UNC's Department of Communication is an incredibly stimulating and rewarding place to work, not least because I get to interact with graduate students, who regularly inspire me with their enthusiasm and subtlety of thought. I was especially glad to have arrived while Bryan Behrenshausen was a doctoral candidate; his intellectual curiosity and theoretical acumen were a model for pursuing my own ideas. I am also grateful for having discovered fellow-travelers in the School of Library and Information Science's ORG reading group—including Ryan Shaw, Melanie Feinberg, and their thoughtful graduate students. Conversations with Stephen Wiley and participants in his graduate seminar on Guattari, Deleuze, and Media Theory at NC State were immensely helpful in honing my understanding of the Deleuzoguattarian universe.

I must also acknowledge that this book would not have been completed, were it not for Kumi Silva's regular encouragement, and her semi-frequent harangues to finish, already. She and David Monje read early drafts of chapters, as well as the book's proposal, graciously casting a critical eye whenever necessary.

Finally, I extend the greatest acknowledgements to my family, for supporting me on a personal level throughout. Whether they know it or not, my brothers Bryan and Hugh have each served as sounding boards for my perspective, helping to adjust my ideas to the forces and realities of contemporary life. Most importantly, my parents, Paul and Roberta, remain a lifelong source of encouragement and support.

Please note that a section of chapter three, and a portion of chapter six adapts material from a 2015 article, "Choice or disparation? Theorizing the social in social media systems", published in the Westminster Papers on Communication and Culture, Volume 10, Issue 1.

1 On the Notion of a Formatted Subject

Technology at present is covert philosophy; the point is to make it openly philosophical.

—Philip E. Agre, *Computation and Human Experience* (1997)

How should we make sense of the global, social computing apparatus that now frames and permeates our lives? Any response we offer to the question will be complicated simultaneously by the intense enthusiasms and persistent anxieties that we harbor toward the technology. Through it, we enjoy instant connection to friends and public figures on social media, the fluid circulation of culture and ideas, and unforeseen opportunities for trade and collaboration. But these benefits call forth real concerns in the very same breath: the demise of privacy, intellectual de-skilling, and the potential for massive layoffs thanks to automation, as well as pernicious new forces of economic exclusion, political repression, and interpersonal alienation, which come along with our new transparency to one another. Real-time sentiment analysis of social media now modulates public opinion, political possibility, and consumer affect to an ever-finer degree. There is talk of social network activity becoming a factor in the extension of financial credit, and meanwhile, a sensor-enabled Internet of Things is on the march, complicating the relationship between our computer devices and the infrastructural technologies and systems that make up our built environment. The philosopher Bernard Stiegler diagnoses the situation as an industrialization of all things, which he fears is leading to the widespread *disfiguration* of the individual.[1]

Thinking through the consequences of these technological "innovations" as they were emerging back in 2010, inventor of the World Wide Web Sir Tim Berners-Lee and his coauthor James Hendler described the situation in which we now find ourselves in the more pragmatic terms of a rise of *social machines*, which had begun to connect and process knowledge together through a computational medium that they called *global graphs*.[2] It is relatively easy to recognize our phones and their attendant infrastructures as social machines; but what exactly is a global graph? The first, but as we shall see by no means last, way of answering this question is that graphs are both a way of structuring data and acting algorithmically on that data, using a set of practices called graph theory to mathematically model *pairwise relations*. Global graphs materialize in information systems (IS) the vast representational webs of relation that social computing platforms require in order to automate knowledge about the world and our roles in it.

If the central motivation of this book is to begin to see these global graphs as a collectivizing medium, then we might start from a basic premise of Friedrich Nietzsche, fondly quoted by the German media theorist Friedrich Kittler, that "our writing tools are also working on our thoughts."[3] What I take him to mean is that like every other writing technology before it, social computing, via global graphs, functions according to certain logico-representational techniques, which organize and generalize the conditions for thinking and communicating in particular ways. Unavoidably, their techniques must therefore foreground certain intellectual commitments, modes of engagement, and effects on collective judgment, which we adopt in using the technology to represent our daily lives. Examining the functional mixture of network science, human-computer interaction (HCI), protocols, and algorithms that make social computing possible, this work will be attempting to triangulate our enthusiasms and anxieties in relation to global graphs. It will follow Stiegler, Hendler, Berners-Lee, and others, in contending that social computing platforms now amount to a kind of *philosophical engineering* of societies.[4] More specifically, it will describe some of the ways in which creative formalizations of mathematical networks blend with philosophical and social-theoretical ideas about language, meaning, and cognition to produce the techniques of protocol, algorithm, and interface that make social computing possible. The idea here is that it is only by engaging with the technology across these multiple registers that will we be able to properly come to grips with our collective anxieties around the rise of social machines, and their future role in our lives.

In part because Hendler and Berners-Lee's notion of the global graph now travels under a variety of different names—social graph, knowledge graph, enterprise graph, taste graph, and others besides—those outside of computer science may not yet be especially familiar with the term. But most certainly will have a sense of how computer networks in general, and their global conglomeration into the Internet and Web, have reshaped Westernized life over the past half-century. We know that collaborations between diverse institutional actors—the US military, university research labs, and transnational corporations—were originally responsible for the physical infrastructure of the Internet. Baseline principles for packet-switched networks, diffused into practice through these institutions, opened up the possibilities for social computing in the first place.[5] In the intervening decades, Berners-Lee's development of the Hypertext Transfer Protocol specification, and its global implementation through organizations like the World Wide Web Consortium, slowly layered more human-centric, semantic protocols over top of these original network transport protocols. Built on top of sophisticated strategies for machine-to-machine data exchange in the original Internet, the World Wide Web enabled a subsequent flourishing of human-to-human communication and knowledge exchange. Where the Transmission Control Protocol/Internet Protocol and the Domain Name System organized data packets and destination servers at the level of transport, in today's social web of platforms, emphasis continues to shift toward circulating networks of *content-objects* and *named data*. Global graphs are the conceptual basis upon which this has occurred.

Along the way, networks have gone from being a specialized topic for telecoms engineers and computer scientists to become a wholesale social imaginary. Global hardware and software networks have substantially reconfigured the conditions of cultural production, while also deeply altering the distributive relays between and within state economies. Network science has restructured knowledge practices across academia and is reshaping life in urban centers through its application to traffic flows, crime, economic risk, and other forms of population management. In a more intimate register, teens and tweens unwittingly make sense of their protean identities according to global graph-based scores of 'relevance', computed on social media platforms. All of these developments have further cemented the Internet's centrality as a communications infrastructure. Where 20 years ago the dominant paradigm was the retrieval of a simple web page, today's circulating units in social computing are much more likely to represent the world in terms of named software-objects that correspond to *things* and *people* in the world, conceptually linked together through the representational networks of global graphs.

A basic effect is that our manipulation of data has moved into a 'post-documentary' phase, taking on a much more entity- or object-oriented quality.[6] And it is here that we can start to better understand the deeper significance of Hendler and Berners-Lee's ideas about social machines and global graphs. Merging the technical capacities of networks with their epistemological potential, we now speak less of interconnected pages than of interconnected, structured, or linked data-objects. Whether at work, in scientific practice, or in support of interpersonal relations, these post-documentary-objects are modeling the epistemic and communicative relations between social actors, actions, and concepts at a much finer-grained level of detail. As Berners-Lee described it early on,

> The Net and the Web may both be shaped as something mathematicians call a Graph, but they are at different levels. The Net links computers, the Web links documents. Now, people are making another mental move. There is realization now, 'It's not the documents,

it is the things they are about which are important'. Obvious, really.
Biologists are interested in proteins, drugs, genes. Businesspeople
are interested in customers, products, sales. We are all interested in
friends, family, colleagues, and acquaintances.[7]

Beyond any device, platform, or programming language then, the central power of today's social computing platforms is to be building out
from the Internet's original network structures, to establish second- and
third-order foundations for the efficient, collective manipulation of
knowledge, expression, and, most importantly, interrelationship through
distributed naming strategies that follow a network form. The consequences of this are hinted at when the information architect Andrew
Hinton writes, for example, that,

> The spirit of the hyperlink means everything can be connected out
> of context to everything else. We can link enterprise resource management platforms with loading docks, map software with automobiles, and radio frequency ID (RFID) chips injected into pet dogs
> that include the dog's records in licensing databases.[8]

All of these developments are provoking new forms of communication—
and new possibilities for social *reasoning*—as humans and machines
become enmeshed together in an increasingly subtle, socio-semantic register of use.

If we accept this admittedly caricatured, big picture view of digital
networks as they've changed over time, then it is also important to consider how the role of the *user* has evolved alongside it. Thinking around
how to define the user can be divided into roughly three overlapping
eras, which have seen HCI variously as (1) information processing,
(2) the initiative of agents pursuing projects, and (3) socially and materially embedded in rich contexts.[9] HCI design sees each of these eras as
a "convergence of scientific opportunity and application need" that is
broadly motivated along two lines of inquiry.[10] With every technological
innovation, designers and developers grapple with pragmatic issues conceived in light of the specific requirements of a given system. They ask
empirically minded questions, like what's the most effective or optimal
approach to help a user achieve their goals? How does one algorithmic
technique offer better results than another? Should decisions about a
system compel users to adapt to certain kinds of designed behavior in a
'top-down' way, or should users themselves be setting the agenda of an
evolving design?

Researchers and practitioners who follow these lines of inquiry understand their work primarily in terms of testing and iterating an application through social-scientific experimentation. Strong correlation
between economic profitability and a platform's uptake by large numbers

of users means that innovation and optimization in this evidence-based way can become an intense and ongoing concern. Whether architecting an entire operating system through peer production, like Linux, or more commercially in the case of an app or platform like Gmail, developers rely heavily on users in the wild to steer the ongoing development of their systems. This dynamic of social computing design is often captured by the tongue-in-cheek moniker of a service being in 'perpetual beta'; constantly testing, tweaking, and improving software in response to user input, designers wind up defining the user as part research subject and part co-developer.

But another mode of inquiry around the user brackets this intensely pragmatic approach of "realized instrumentality"[11] to ask after the user more philosophically, as a subject. With an ear to ongoing debates in cognitive science, philosophy, and social theory, research in this vein asks a different set of questions: as a matter of disciplinary commitment and a societal ethics of design, how should we approach the conceptual relationship between user and system in general? Should it be in terms of a scientific model of cognition, or more ethnologically as an individual working in a cultural context? Under what ontological terms of reference should we define, enable, and constrain user capacity, and how might these definitions need to change over time as they reflexively circulate between users and designers?[12] Working toward deeper and more generalizable assumptions about the user in this way punctuates the fields of HCI and IS design over the long term, inevitably provoking tensions and debates between paradigms. The latter have developed in the past out of such diverse disciplinary perspectives as cognitive science, semiotics, ethnomethodology, phenomenology, economics, critical theory, the philosophy of science, and science and technology studies.

Given the field's aforementioned focus on actual working systems though, any ideas imported from philosophy into technique will need to take stock of how such theories fit together with the material capacities of a computer. Formalization, as a semiotic moment of making-object, is at the very heart of this fitting together. Philosophy acts as a conceptual scaffold upon which human-computer and human-human relations in software may be theorized; but any isomorphic relation claimed between computers and the user as philosophical subject will need to be carefully articulated to the logical structures of software. Again, at one time or another, empiricist, cognitive, phenomenological, economic, sociolinguistic, and affective conceptualizations of the user have achieved this fit, taking IS in new and different directions, even while still hewing to the basic material constraints of computing through their formalizing procedures.

Between these two modes of inquiry—steady empirical experimentation with ongoing systems and more speculative, but still materially grounded, debates concerning the deeper philosophical roots of the user—discussion here will fall mostly into the second mode. Straddling a disciplinary boundary between IS theory and critical-materialist digital media studies, which intriguingly seems to be becoming more porous by the year, the book is frankly concerned with elaborations of the user as philosophical subject. To be more specific, it is my hope that the book will contribute to ongoing debates around the conceptual foundations of social computing and global graphs from a media studies perspective by critically engaging with their formalizing approaches in terms of what Michel Foucault called modes and mechanisms of 'subjectification'.[13]

It may help to pose a few rhetorical questions that gesture to the book's overall framing on these terms: how do philosophical theories of the subject structure informational processes at both the level of interface and system design, to produce the collectivizing and individualizing functions that we come to call 'social'? As I have been suggesting, if the subject is somehow now being 'objectivized' differently following a turn to global graphs, then which elements of thinking, communication, and creativity are being foregrounded, and which remain latent or obscure? How should we understand these formalizing moments I have begun to describe as conjoined to wider political and economic processes and projects, expressed in the increasing promotion and adoption of social computing platforms across societies? And ultimately, if a desirable goal is to foster greater public control over this type of technology, so that it might better function as a more frankly political platform for global collective judgment—something we can firmly say that it both does and fails to do—then how might representational and formalizing strategies need to change? From where would we draw philosophical impetus in support of such changes? These are some of the book's main motivating concerns.

Defining a Formatted Subject

To capture the particular space of ideas I have in mind, in place of 'user', I will be adopting the term *formatted subject*. When something is formatted, it is structured by design to elicit reliable routine functioning and an assured effectivity. But it is not just our information or data-objects that are being formatted; the promise of social computing is also about a smooth interoperability between ourselves and the world in our practices, as we accede to being formatted across a variety of socio-technical assemblages. In other words, embracing the representational strategies of social computing means that worlds, things, and people will be *formed by them*. Our affects, dispositions, identities, and interactions will receive structure as their semiotic content, as the platforms promise in return to help us manage everyday relations in a context of social action.

These relations and interactions are most typically framed in terms of heading off 'information overload', setting the conceptual stage to be about social computing, making our lives more convenient, efficient, and effective. Organizational studies management and decision sciences, and process optimization represent more specialized but important points of reference here, which further frame the subject as related to processes of modern bureaucracy, business administration, and knowledge management. But I will not be focusing on these literatures, and will instead be looking more exclusively at the formatted subject in terms of its operational, semiotic relation to the information technology itself. My rationale is media-theoretical; to say that it is at this operational level that social computing systems infrastructurally organize the production of meaning. Too often, this aspect tends to be understood in the functionalistic language of social systems theory, where people are portrayed as individual elements of a system that draw functional distinctions from its environment. My thinking is instead guided by critical approaches in materialist media and software studies, which treat IS and the wider contexts in which they participate in operational terms, but start from a much more cultural perspective.[14]

To take up just one of these authors, Mark Hansen's account can help to initially characterize the global graph techniques that I will be interrogating here. Thanks to an increasing reliance on algorithmic and statistical techniques for generating subject-object relations using networks, Hansen argues that shared symbolic reference between human beings is giving way to what he calls *machinic* reference. The 'feed-forward' circuits enabled by machine learning technologies, for example, increasingly structure subjectivity through what he calls the "indirect presentification of the operationality of sensibility."[15] By this, he means that as network and social media systems increasingly structure our practical judgment in the everyday, they remain themselves "fundamentally opaque" to more traditional accounts of subjectivity based in the intentional grasping of a human being in a social context, because they operate below our threshold of perception and attention, at the level of high-speed calculation.[16] In a sense, the graph techniques examined in what follows will trace the trajectory of this development, as representation in social computing shifts from traditional epistemological interpretations of a subject with egocentric intentionality toward more 'post-positivist' techniques that format populations of people as bundles of signals, again, typically framed in terms of the functional reproduction of a system in its environment.

Besides developing operational formatting as a theme in this way, I follow a contemporary line of Foucauldian thinkers in software studies who are concerned with the relationship between the subject, computer technology, and power. I will, however, be relying more on the subsequent development of Foucault's ideas at the hands of Gilles Deleuze and Félix Guattari. In his theorization of power-knowledge apparatuses, one of Foucault's most powerful insights was to conceptualize subjectivity beyond its traditional definition as a structural consequence of ideological, economic, experiential, or linguistic-grammatical forces. For him, these forces were always present but circulated in a more capillary way, according to underlying *processes of individualization*. Power relations combine with communicative relations in the establishment of what he called the 'finalized activities' of power, like an educated populace or the production of goods in a workshop.[17] Individualization through a power relation was ambiguous for him in that it did not just involve a one-way relation of domination.

Rather, he wrote that

> what defines a relationship of power is that it is a mode of action which does not act directly and immediately on others. Instead it acts upon their actions: an action upon an action, on existing actions or on those which may arise in the present or the future.[18]

Social computing platforms are an important contemporary site where such a power relationship is established. Insofar as design strategies motivate a philosophical approach to the subject by embedding certain precepts about agency and the communication of knowledge into software process, two terms emerge from Foucault's work that will be relevant to understanding what I am getting at with my use of the term formatted subject: subjectivation and subjectification. If subjectivation concerns individuals becoming themselves in the crucible of life, through agonal relations that afford the possibility of achieving self-authority (the Greeks were Foucault's archetype here), then subjectification involves the organization of those relations for the purposes of managing populations in a more stratified, or static, way, through a collective relation to self that is produced by some dominant knowledge relation.[19]

One way to understand the motivation of what follows then is a desire to measure the distance between subjectivation and subjectification when it comes to the major relational approaches to structured data and global graphs deployed in social computing. In his book on Foucault, Deleuze writes that subjectification on the one hand "involves being 'subject to someone else by control and dependence', with all the processes of individuation and modulation which power installs, acting on the daily life and the interiority of those it calls its subjects."[20] On the other, it makes the subject "'tied to his own identity by a conscience or self-knowledge', through all the techniques of moral and human sciences that go to make up a knowledge of the subject."[21] These features of Foucault's work form an important basis upon which I want to analyze the representational techniques at work in social computing. With subjectivation serving as a desirable, more open comparative ideal to forms of subjectification, the terms together refer to how power operates through the production of subjectivity, according to what Foucault called 'governmentality', or the conduct of conduct.

Subjectivation and subjectification are helpful to understand our relationship to social computing in two ways. First, as we bring the technology's totalizing and individualizing functions further into social relations at work, at home, and in the circulation of public ideas, social computing platforms are becoming a de facto means for the 'government of all and of each'. Second, social computing is a governmental technology in that it achieves this totalizing functionality under the declared terms of free agency. Through their interactive affordances, services like Twitter, Google, and Facebook become representational mechanisms for political and economic sovereignty, and are often held up as such, as an important universal means for both making a living and 'having a voice'. Analogous to Colin Gordon's explanation of governmentality, their technical power lies in taking "freedom itself and the 'soul of the citizen', the life and life-conduct of the ethically free subject, as in some sense the correlative-object of its own suasive capacity."[22]

In a passage that should resonate with our basic sense of social computing's power to continuously feed back upon collective interests, steering us toward and away from information-objects, ideas, and one another, Foucault writes that "to 'conduct' is at the same time to 'lead' others (according to mechanisms of coercion which are, to varying degrees, strict) and a way of behaving within a more or less open field of possibilities."[23] Keeping all of these ideas in mind, I therefore want the term formatted subject to denote the technical effect of a structuring, subjectifying nexus, developed at the level of code and semiotic technique, and intellectually justified according to some account of the subject-object relation in philosophy, which has also somehow been operationally aligned to the quantification of meaning as *information*.

Through combinations of interface, protocol, and algorithm, the formatted subject develops first and foremost on the basis of some form of objectivity, but one that will inevitably come to also define a relation for conducting oneself in the world as it gets taken up into collective practice. Today, we define this relation much too generically in terms of *information retrieval*; as we shall see, underneath the metaphor of retrieval lies a set of deeper relationalities that have been structured at different points by rationalist, phenomenological, linguistic, and ethnomethodological theories of the sign at the level of interface, as well as more epistemically and economically styled theories of meaningful agency at the level of protocol and algorithm. To put it in a way that observes our basic intuitions about the difference between interface and program, or 'front end' and 'back end', philosophical notions of an interpretive, embodied, and affective subject typically inform interface design strategies in rich ways; but following the material necessities of computation, these also hook up to more formalized techniques for staging agency and system reproduction at the level of information processing. The latter tend toward more functionalistic accounts of the subject, relying on positivist social science, economics, and other fields that use statistics and mathematics to model populations.

To borrow Hansen's terminology, it is these two sides that come together to "indirectly presentify" an operation of sensibility, by guiding communicative conduct through a governmental relation that frames our experience of and through the technology. To anticipate the book's conclusion, in the final chapter, I come to rely on work by the philosopher of technology Gilbert Simondon, as offering a way to think through how the sides might start to be reconceived, in terms of an ideal for what Guattari would call a transversal 'subjectivation'. For now, let us just say that any formatted subject can be produced only according to some relational distinction between entitative or referential signs that point to people, things, and events in knowledge representation (KR), and a free relation to self-action and expression, coupled together in what Hansen calls a 'system-environment hybrid'.[24]

Taking on board the productive ways in which social theories—including the social construction of technology, symbolic interactionism, phenomenological sociology, ethnomethodology, and the sociology of knowledge—have shaped the conversation in social computing around the production of such hybrids, it is also important to look beyond dominant approaches. In asking what Foucault, Deleuze, and Guattari have to tell us about social computing as a medium, the counterintuitive gambit here is that there are theoretical gains to be had by setting aside sociological approaches to social computing. Asking after alternatives in what follows, humanistic and sociologically based theories of the subject figure in the discussion, but most often as a contrasting foil to a less warm-blooded perspective, to which I now turn.

Semiosis and the Constitution of the Social

Acknowledging the centrality of intersubjectivity and constructionist thinking in so many theories of the social, the approach taken here will be less humanistic and more impersonally processual. In both their separate and collaborative works, Deleuze and Guattari sought to destabilize our understanding of a traditional reasoning subject holding sway over the world through linguistic signification by prioritizing the connections between matter, form, and organizational structure that produce linguistically framed signs in the first place. For them, life's immanent field of forces resolves into meaningful subject-object relations only according to the ways in which power transects and organizes them into stable significance. Their emphasis on the constitution of subjectivity on these terms offers a compelling counter-narrative to the ways that we typically think about our relationship to social computing. The account that follows will rely heavily on Deleuze and Guattari's understanding of signs as a way of recalibrating our sense of the social: away from intersubjectivity as a natural or assumed ground and toward the more elementary, material-semiotic patternings of nature and life, including the role that signs play with respect to habit and desire.

Linguistically focused accounts of signification typically ground our relation to the world in terms of consensus over semantics, reproduced and coordinated according to the shifting social circumstances of a community of speakers embedded, as Ludwig Wittgenstein famously described, in language games. As Deleuze and Guattari see it, this seemingly commonsensical approach winds up too quickly conforming the pragmatics of signs to intersubjective recognition, at the expense of understanding how the nondiscursive, transformative elements of a particular material-semiotic system might *also* significantly structure language use. In their lingo, Deleuze and Guattari instead place an emphasis on the effects of the wider *collective assemblages of enunciation* in which a sign manifests, arguing that these effects, multiply discursive and materially incorporeal, are just as important as any sign's uptake by speakers and hearers in a community. For a variety of historical and technical reasons to do with how information theory came to intersect with views of social communication—most famously in Warren Weaver's reconfiguration of Claude Shannon's work on information to 'reinsert' human beings into engineering accounts of communication—software design theory continues to focus too heavily on rules and consensus around symbols.[25]

Intersubjective pragmatics are clearly at work in the IS design literature when Clarisse de Souza proposes, for example, that "The encoding of both the problem situation and the corresponding solutions is fundamentally linguistic (i.e., based on a system of symbols—verbal, visual, aural, or other—that can be interpreted by consistent semantic rules)."[26] For Deleuze and Guattari, the problem with anticipating the pragmatics of signs in this manner is that it cements a kind of linguistic psychologism. When signs get preemptively accounted for in the universalized manner of their already being given in individual minds as *reference*, simultaneously, problems of difference—between ideas, circumstances, individuals, and systems—wind up defined in terms of a distinction between opinion and knowledge, in the consensual matching of causal means to ends among subjects. The pragmatic achievement, but also the overriding assumption, becomes one of signs conceived as already-formed *units*, 'transmitted' between minds as a kind of epistemic or social substance. Specific to documentation and IS, Ronald E. Day diagnoses the general approach as perpetually suffering from an overly simplified "conduit metaphor."[27]

It's important to gainsay this criticism against the fact that semiotic engineering strategies are also influenced by phenomenology, which sees embodied experience as wrapped up with language, in a more fundamental ground for sign relations. Phenomenologists conceive of signs less in terms of a clear separation of semantics from pragmatics, and more in terms of an existential event, a singular 'coming-to-reference' for human beings in a life context. Greater heed is, thus, paid to the genesis of meaning, in terms of the subject realizing themselves as a unique and mortal human being through their marking of semiotic difference in the world. To the extent that interface and system designers have been influenced by phenomenology, social computing has lately been an important technical means through which this deeper relationship is disclosed. The philosopher Martin Heidegger, for example, did not presume meaning to be attached phonematically or informationally to signs; rather, we always find ourselves 'being amidst' equipment in an interrelated, referential context. Signs are particular to this equipmentality, and thus to the orientation of our being in a particular environment, or *Welt*.

Though computers may at base be soulless calculating machines, Heidegger's perspective on the sign has certainly been influential among HCI practitioners, and the phenomenological sociologists upon which they rely. Through affordances developed in their coding and design, modern social platforms open up a space in which one's embodied concern may dwell, collectively mediating our comportment in the world in important ways. The phenomenological perspective reminds us not to take the abstractions of semiotic engineering too far, to the point where social action amounts to semantically exchangeable symbols in a cognitive mode, divorced from the emerging and changing pragmatic contexts in which these symbols are produced. The now-ubiquitous 'hashtag' plays a dual and pragmatic role, for example, in enabling both phenomenologically shared expression and analytically optimized retrieval, as it organizes the content around a dynamic and shifting consensus of reference. Information retrieval, communication, and experience increasingly mix together in real time online, as users cluster, communicate, and dissipate around tags, indicating that 'this' is 'about that' in formal-semantic terms, while also being able to mark that some collectively constituted '*we*' cares about some sign as a matter of concern.

To Deleuze's way of thinking, however, even Heidegger's attempt to situate the sign more radically in terms of phenomenal life fails to shed certain individualistic biases of the Western philosophical tradition, pointing to a basic 'image of thought' that time and again recurs. Under its terms, thinking gets perpetually construed according to a difference between common sense—established thanks to some stable, unifying relation between subject and object that is grounded in an individual's faculties—and *good* sense, as coordinated by the particular 'me' who dynamically judges indeterminate objects in the world by differentiating them according to that common sense.[28] Establishing conditions for thought in this way, he argues, surreptitiously comes to define things in the world as *entirely conditioned by thought*, leaving no possibility for things to possess their *own* conditions of genesis, nor their own signification. Accordingly, people, things, and the relations under which they are subsumed cannot be *self-caused* in any meaningful way.

Under constraint of introduction for the moment, we can sum up by saying that philosophical engineering achieved by way of interface, protocol, and algorithm in social computing relies on philosophically transcendental commitments to both analytically framed epistemological constructivism and more Continentally framed theories of phenomenality, language, and embodiment. This is so in spite of the fact that Deleuze's 'image of thought' haunts the technology in both of these allegiances, in a manner to be specified in later chapters.

To say a bit more about their mixture in computing, Wittgenstein's analytic philosophy helped to set the stage for the automation of reasoning in computing, for example; first, in early and influential dialogue with Gottlob Frege and the logical empiricists around propositional representation and the normativity of logic in his 'picture theory' of meaning, and then later, with his more pragmatically formulated ideas about language games in forms of life. In dialogue with both Heidegger and Wittgenstein's work, Jürgen Habermas tried to square the circle of logic and culture through his account of communicative rationality, which was subsequently influential in the development of computer-supported cooperative work environments. Already mentioned, Heidegger's, but also Husserl's, work in phenomenology has been equally influential in the development of social computing, especially through Peter L. Berger and Thomas Luckmann's reliance on Alfred Schütz's social phenomenology. Important to also mention are certain crosscutting systems theories, which have borrowed from both the analytic and Continental traditions to articulate a second-order cybernetics—works by Humberto Maturana and Francisco Varela, Heinz von Foerster, and Niklas Luhmann are all relevant here.

These various perspectives find common ground for debate in the basic assertion that subjects (users) and objects (devices, platforms, information-objects, and other users) are *co-constructed* by the social contexts in which they circulate. Another way to say this is that computer technologies are philosophically engineered to meet the pragmatic conditions of contextual validity that accompany subjectification by the knowledge practices of scientific, economic, bureaucratic, and legal life. As Paul Dourish writes of ubiquitous computing, for example, the inscription of contextual cues into the technology forms a key basis for interactive control in complex societies, taking on their meaning or relevance "through their relationship to forms of practice; that is, it is engaged action around artifacts and information that make those artifacts meaningful and relevant to people."[29] As these contexts all seem to be converging and merging on the Internet, we might say that social computing represents a kind of technological pinnacle of this constructivist insight; originally the sedate province of corporate and state bureaucracies and large libraries, services like Google and Facebook now coordinate a permanent and ongoing *social rationality*, which operates at a collectively vast, and yet uncannily intimate, scale.

It is here that Deleuze and Guattari can offer us a different vocabulary for thinking through just what we *mean* by social rationality, in their radical conceptualization of signs as involving more than just a shared phenomenological context of communicative exchange and meaning making. Against a rationalist legacy in analytic philosophy that has received much scrutiny, we can assert that signs also involve more than just logical denotation in a symbolic context. While clearly delineated, subject-object relations retain an important power in Deleuze and Guattari's so-called 'mixed semiotic', they are never the whole story; neither subject nor object exhaustively defines the role of signs in the production of sociality. Instead, signs produced in so-called 'assemblages of enunciation' carry a generative and ordering 'third-person' perspective, which *stages* coherent subject-object relations at the level of indirect discourse, habitual repetitions involving the unconscious, involvements with matter, and, at base, an eternity of impersonal events that simultaneously shift and incorporate a vast, virtual field of sense relations in signification.

With conceptual details to follow episodically in later chapters, it is according to this deeper relation to impersonal events, modulated through the territorializations and deterritorializations of enunciative assemblages, that we receive (1) an orientation and disposition toward our becoming a 'fractured self', (2) a metaphysical account of identity and difference among things in the world, (3) a temporalizing sense of before and after, and, most importantly, (4) a *logic of the social*, which (re)produces the conditions for collective sense making. The idea is that by taking such an a-humanistic perspective on board, we will achieve a greater critical attunement to the interplay between philosophical approaches to IS, both analytic and phenomenological. The mixed semiotic view insists that above and beyond a role for the constituted user as subject, we must also account for the organized matter relations upon which the technology *produces* this subjectifying process and social substance in the first place.

To paraphrase their cowritten work on signs in *A Thousand Plateaus*, Deleuze and Guattari, in other words, help us to problematize the semantic/pragmatic distinction at the heart of social computing by

- Undercutting the common assumption that language is subjectively some kind of representational code peeled off from concrete material existence;
- Making it impossible to conceive of speech and writing as merely the communication of information as signal; and

- Bringing back into view the effectuating act dimension of concrete language use, making it "impossible to define semantics, syntactics, or even phonematics as scientific zones of language independent of pragmatics."[30]

Ironically, with its emphasis on information as signal, social computing technology is novel precisely for its increased reliance upon this effectuating act dimension of concrete language use, both at the level of interface and in the machine layer. To be personally useful and therefore economically value producing, social computing depends on the real-time *manifestation* of signs from particular users in an ongoing fashion—whether clicking a link, inputting a hashtag, befriending someone, or otherwise constantly making choices between options on devices.

The point here will be that the political valence and collective functioning of signs in this constant solicitation of effectuating acts is not especially well captured by social-constructionist accounts of communication and mediation. Energies of the singular resist easy capture by the more traditional subject-object semantics of a relational database, for example, where significance in real-time social computing becomes far more prone to constant shifting and reorganization according to what Deleuze calls the 'manifester' of the 'I'. This is not to say that informational techniques have failed to shift accordingly; no longer the purview of taxonomy experts, significance is now induced from an ongoing, collective churn of the singular, recursed using predictive-analytic strategies to stabilize the identity of post-documentary units like hashtags, comments, consumer goods, and pages for public events. Hansen describes the situation aptly when he states that twenty-first-century media *"broker human access to* a domain of sensibility since every individual act of access is itself a new datum of sensation that will expand the world incrementally but in a way that intensifies human sensibility."[31]

Questioning the paradigmatic forms of philosophical engineering that now structure our lives via social computing can therefore open us up to seeing how the technology does much more than ground us in communicative consensus. Social software platforms now structure and involve pre-personal layers of mood, roles at work, political regimes, layers of infrastructural system, singular bodies, mimetic rationality, and again impersonal events—as all of these erupt and collide over time in milieus large and small. It is certainly true that designers have been adjusting their thinking around systems to better account for these layers, retheorizing the user to place greater emphasis on embodiment, affect, and the practical, contextual reasoning of groups.[32] Under the auspices of discovering different styles of formatted subject, the point in pursuing a mixed semiotic view alongside such work is to further hone and challenge exactly what we mean when we talk about users.

With some important exceptions, Deleuze and Guattari's ideas have yet to receive much direct consideration in this regard.[33] Constructivist accounts of semiosis as intersubjective exchange continue to play a dominant role in driving creative IS design. Yet, the resulting conceptual vocabulary has tended to overemphasize socially styled interface designs, while neglecting the underlying processes of datafication as equally carefully designed, underplaying the ways in which lower level algorithmic and protocological techniques produce sociality. This is especially true in terms of their creative reliance upon mathematically and statistically formatted network signals, upon which the sociable user is given form. In other words, beneath the affordances that make social relations explicit through interface is a set of *machinic* relations that must also be accounted for. These two facets of social computing generally meet under the semiotic terms of networked KR.

Networked Knowledge Representation

Artificial intelligence and big data are probably the two most well-known umbrella terms for networked KR. If artificial intelligence concerns the capacity of computers to reason in a fully- or quasi-autonomous fashion, then network-based KR is the conceptual strategy through which these systems are developed. Similarly, if big data is about an infrastructural capacity to model the complex correlations of bureaucracies, marketers, and scientists, then KR is a blueprint for organizing this infrastructure. A key feature of KR theory that cries out for examination in the terms of assemblage theory is its propensity to bracket concerns over the nature of the subject and instead focus on people and things in terms of their mixed *rational agency*. In KR-based systems, human beings are but one actant in the overall arrangement of a system of rational-objects.

As we've already seen, at the level of interface, users seek out and exchange these rational-objects on the basis of communicative and shared concern; but at the level of technique, underlying those interactions are strategies that conceive of what's sought and exchanged much more impersonally. The relationship, or better, the *hierarchy*, between these two modes is most often illustrated using what's called the DIKW pyramid, a somewhat hoary and contested diagram for describing the stages of our semiotic relation to the world as a kind of bootstrapping operation: from an impersonal base of *data*, to syntactical *information*, on to semantic *knowledge*, and culminating in collective *wisdom*. With help especially from Guattari's work, it will be another goal of this book to complicate and reconfigure the pyramid in substantial ways.

Following its schema, data is information *as* reality; any phenomenon that suggests some lack of uniformity in the world, minimally inferable by empirical experience—like tree rings or fluctuations in an electrical current.[34] Semantic information is information *for* reality, as when an observer subjectively selects some cross section of this data, holding it to be plausibly meaningful. Finally, knowledge is well-formed or *valid* information that is capable of being demonstrably true or false to someone in a collective, conventionally defined world of meaning—what Wittgenstein called a 'form of life', like being an economist or a mechanic.[35] Implied in the difference between data and information is a distinction between syntax and semantics, between the raw, combinatorial contingencies of reality and our subjective interpretations of that reality. Implied in the difference between information and knowledge is the aforementioned distinction between semantics and pragmatics that we seek to problematize: one between our subjective notions of reality and the externalizing codes that we collectively impose upon them in the determination of a social context.

Key to the impersonal or immanent sense of rationality presumed in KR is the notion that the world *itself* is composed of wider biological, physical, and psychic phenomena (*data*) that are intrinsically rational but have yet to receive uniform human measure. Modeling the world through the lens of information theory, this immanent difference, or lack of uniformity, gets inscribed and put to work in the formal distinctions that make up the DIKW pyramid in KR, organizing the emissions of immanent rational process in the world in ways that induce a rational *individualization* of measurable entities, including our social selves. As Luciano Floridi writes, data is simply "x being distinct from y, where x and y are two uninterpreted variables and the relation of 'being distinct', as well as the domain, are left open to further interpretation."[36] He goes on to note that "The actual *format, medium,* and *language* in which data, and hence information, are encoded is often irrelevant and disregardable."[37]

Much of what follows here will involve retrieving this encoding moment from information science, to insist that we consider it more carefully and critically in its operational contours, given how much it now contributes to the production of sociality and subjectivity in contemporary societies. It is also worth saying at the outset that Deleuze and Guattari's mixed semiotic bears some resemblances, but also crucial differences in semiotic approach, to the DIKW pyramid; the point will be to develop them alongside one another, especially to see where power manifests in construing the sign in different ways.

A simple starting point for their comparison is that in the construction of impersonal, distinction-drawing data processes that bootstrap us into shared meaning and knowledge, social platforms comprise the perpetual reconciliation of two perspectives on information. As I have been introducing so far, social rationality at the level of interface design presumes individuals who enact an exchange of meaning on the basis of intersubjective convention, as users communicate and help each other find correct answers, the right document, the useful web link, or the relevant person. But this exchange must always be somehow fitted together using representational elements in computing that rely on the more immanent, inter*objective* rationality of symbolic logic and statistical process, applied to the world conceived as data. Depending on the goals of the platform, approaches in KR achieve this fit differently in social networking systems, search engines, and other emerging social machine platforms, like Apple's Siri. For our purposes, the point is that each, thus, brings with it a particular *form of subjectification*—structuring through data technique how we think with computers, offering rational schemas for what we should be *doing* with computers, and setting the terms of our performative capacities to *encounter* and interact with one another semiotically through their affordances.

Common to every strategy though is that set of techniques from mathematics mentioned earlier: graph theory. With roots in eighteenth-century mathematics, especially in seminal work done by the Swiss mathematician Leonhard Euler, graphs are at the very basis of both modern network science and computing itself. Not to be mistaken with the 'charts and graphs' of a scientific or annual report, graphs are a sophisticated way to treat the geometry of position and relations between pairwise-entities. In computer science they are a fundamental representational abstraction, which at its most basic involves the formalization of points, lines, and, in the case of directed graphs, arrows, which, respectively, indicate position, relation, and orientation. To get at the basic premise of graphs, picture a set of dots strewn randomly across a blank page.

To represent a knowledge graph, for example, each dot on the page would be labeled to represent an individual entity—some place, thing, person, or event—about which one might want to stipulate a *fact*. Next, imagine drawing arrows from dot to dot, with each arrow expressing semantic *predication*—the assertion of a fact, capable of being logically computed as valid or invalid knowledge among the accumulating facts of a given form of life; all of the relevant qualities, states, or actions among entities that are worth noting. A tiny web of knowledge concerning Canada might be diagrammed by connecting the dots as follows: Justin Trudeau (dot) "is a" (predication, or arrow to) prime minister (dot). Justin Trudeau (dot) "is prime minister of" (predication, or arrow to) Canada (dot). Canada (dot) "is a" (predication, or arrow to) constitutional monarchy (dot), a point from which we might begin to follow lines of inference into knowledge about Australia, for example. In KR lingo, the graph's points are called *nodes* or *vertices*, with the lines or arrows expressing their predicate relations named *edges*. The resulting lattice of nodes and edges depicts what is colloquially known as *structured*, or when speaking of knowledge between organizations, *linked* or *joined-up* data in social computing.

Directed graphs of the type just described form the foundation of many large-scale big data, machine learning, and social networking services and platforms. As of 2012, Google maintained 18 billion predicate facts, structured around 570 million data-objects in their knowledge graph, which now sits squarely at the center of their future expansion.[38] Developing an account of knowledge graphs at length in the next chapter, in subsequent ones I will be navigating two other approaches to directed graphs—social and predictive-analytic, both of which work in concert with knowledge graphs to form the conceptual basis for social computing in general. In all three cases, I will be seeking out some of the intellectual roots of their core technical commitments, unearthing moments where social-theoretical, social-scientific, and related philosophical influences are significantly at play in their interfaces, algorithms, and protocols. Though they may overlap in practice, I develop and clarify differences between each approach to bolster my claim that each style of graph helps to constitute a formatted subject in different ways; throughout, I will gesture to popular platforms as a way to make the role and impact of graphs more concrete.

Knowledge graphs, for example, produce a rational basis for sociality and a kind of formatted subject by constructing interconnected *systems of fact* about the context in which people are embedded. Organizing collective thinking into interconnected webs of atomic propositions, they preserve understanding between things and people as networks of logical inference. Social graphs operate in a similar way but treat *people*, with their attitudinal investments, goals, and relationships as they address one another as speaker and hearer, as the substantial units to be computed. Finally, predictive-analytic graphs are so named in light of increasingly sophisticated, generically empirical approaches to the relationship between graph technique and the world's purportedly immanent rationality, mentioned earlier. Strategies of this kind subsume knowledge and social graphs to take a more thorough-going, post-individualistic approach: with roots in both citation indexing and neural network theory, they place greater emphasis on what is known as Bayesian, or probabilistic, reasoning. Predictive-analytic graphs treat rational information less as a feature of individual knowers or social groupings and more in terms of the generic, stochastic emissions of a complex adaptive system.

In other words, taking the DIKW pyramid on faith, predictive-analytic graphs eschew theories of the subject so as to produce social knowledge according to *any* sensed relation that might pragmatically serve as a source of agentic patterning—whatever aspects of a context or environment that system designers have access to, or opt to capture as data, in some ongoing fashion. Existing stores of prior user activity, geographic location, native tongue, or even the jiggling of a computer mouse are all potential fodder for inducing contextual distinction and, thus, rational significance, simply in their functioning in the mode of information as reality, or as an *index of computable difference*. As these differential input streams get organized into a predictive-analytic graph, individual user behavior blurs together with digital entity relations, combining machine learning and collective judgment into a powerful feedback loop that the computer scientist Alex Pentland has taken to simply calling "reality mining."[39]

To summarize, by combination of interface, protocol, and algorithm, the formatted subject in modern social computing negotiates difference between post-documentary entities in one of three interactive ways: (1) through *something factually being or not being the case*, as when a user seeks out (or creatively contributes to) chains of inferential reasoning about a person, place, or thing by relying on a **knowledge** graph; (2) through *someone knowing, being known by*, or *not knowing* someone else, whether intentionally or through degree of affiliation, in the establishment of identity through public performance in a **social** graph; or (3) through the generic, behavioral emission of *decision signals*, as one simply goes about daily life using social machines that emit and rely upon some designed set of indexed differences, in the production of a **predictive-analytic** graph. These days, computer scientists are quick to collapse (1) and (2) into (3), but for our purposes, there is merit in keeping them analytically separate, at least until the concluding chapters of the book.

The Valuation of Graphs

As social platforms entice users to seek out, share, communicate, and retrieve signs through the creative embedding of these different styles of KR, global graphs become an increasingly important locus not just for user subjectification, but also for the production of economic value. As Alexandre Monnin argues, knowledge in a knowledge economy "[...] no longer denotes to any norm or domain of knowledge, but rather betokens a broad assimilation to a commodity essentially cultivated in order to sustain growth."[40] It's no secret that commercial social computing platforms generate enormous returns through the capture and steering of consumer behavior, as the companies observe the personal interests, opinions, and tastes of their users in order to sell targeted advertising. Altering the face of global commerce in subtle and not-so subtle ways, platforms like Google and Facebook now act as powerful semiotic feedback loops for a post-Fordist economy, exploiting the public expression and retrieval of signs as a way of optimizing cycles of production and consumption.[41]

That said, it's important to also understand how social computing generates value well beyond targeted advertising. Karl Marx held more broadly that under conditions of the so-called 'general intellect', capitalism develops to such a degree that social knowledge *itself* becomes a direct force of production. Here, the creation of wealth comes to depend "not on the direct expertise of labour time in production, but on two interrelated factors: technological expertise—'scientific labour'—and organization—'social combination'."[42] As they link machine learning and artificial intelligence-style KR schemes up to the continuous social exchange of their platforms, companies like Google, Facebook, and Microsoft accumulate capital not just through consumer targeting, but also by laying down material foundations for the future automation of intellectual labor itself. Their various graph schemes are designed to facilitate the organization and production of value in the broadest terms of mass intellectuality, under circumstances that some call cognitive capitalism, and others, semiocapitalism.[43] Examining the actual formal operations in KR that recursively transform expressive signs into informational ones in pleasurable and meaningful ways will help to show, at an improved level of detail, just how value is generated by users in the ongoing production of *metadata*.

Graphs are a key semiotic formalism here, a kind of logico-semantic blueprint for organizing signs into an ever-more refined machine intelligence. They are the figurative basis upon which signs are made durable and exchangeable, as material trace on computer servers, and more to the point, as fixed capital on commercial platforms. Simultaneously, they remain crucial social sites for the ongoing global registration of informational need and expressive concern, as an open system for extracting value from the not-yet-seen and the not-yet-said. As the dominant form for embedding rules that apportion the expression of signs in everyday life to their calculable equivalence as stored content in this way, it behooves us to explain and critique how global graphs work, and to explore how they might work otherwise. That said, what follows is definitely not a work of political economy. In punctuated moments of critique, however, Deleuze and Guattari's mixed semiotic does articulate to Marxist theory and, in this respect, will prove useful for reverse engineering the DIKW pyramidal hierarchy upon which most ideas about IS are now based.

Instead of treating patterned data as a simple empirical phenomenon, extracted and made amenable to intersubjective signification through syntax and semantics, the mixed semiotic approach insists that we foreground the pragmatic intellectual contexts of knowledge power in which such syntaxes can arise. Divorced from a socioeconomic context, knowledge graph technique treats syntax under the basic intellectual and semiotic terms of deductive reasoning, for example, following certain key debates about the relationship between language, logic, and rationality in twentieth-century logical empiricism, as well as the work of the American logician Charles Sanders Peirce. Predictive-analytic graphs take a more inductive view, following ideas from cognitive science, cybernetic theory, and the philosophy of science; meanwhile, social graphs follow lines of reasoning from symbolic interactionism, sociometry, speech-act philosophy, and ethnomethodology. The strength of a mixed semiotic approach is to help us see all of these various commitments from a kind of meta-modeling perspective, which includes a modern economic context; to observe and interrogate moments of stereotypification from a certain remove, as concepts borrowed from philosophy and social science make their way into HCI and systems design. Each approach to global graphs foregrounds certain aspects and capacities of a social subject in technical relation to an information-object, while pushing others into the background.

The upshot in all three cases is for a formatted subject to be constituted in such a way that information retrieval becomes the generic paradigm for significance and sociability. In concluding chapters, I argue that this has important intellectual and political ramifications for networked societies. But we can start to see the stakes in thumbnail with a basic question: when all utterances—whether they involve personal conversation, some book passage, information-seeking behavior, or the expressions of friendship and taste—resolve to fit a transactional paradigm of individualized choice that is styled like a market, do these tools for thought not bring about, over and above a productive social rationality, a qualitatively different horizon for the rationalization of meaning itself? When sociability is conceived by design in terms of a negotiation of abstract 'relevance' between two economically styled agents, social communication inevitably starts to exhibit the qualities of what Habermas calls "formally-organized action domains," in a manner he believed ought not to occur.[44] On this front, it remains to say a bit more about why it is worth critically unpacking all of these practices, in the various ways that I have so far outlined.

Why Does This Project Matter?

Alongside technologies like artificial intelligence and algorithmic finance, social computing features prominently in speculations about the very future of economic and democratic life; Andrew McAfee and Erik Brynjolfsson refer to our contemporary moment as a "Second Machine Age," for example.[45] With social machines already supporting a significant portion of interpersonal, consumer, and work life, social coordination through graphs is poised to reorganize health care, education, political representation, and many other aspects of life in the global West. Eager to be the continuing institutional infrastructure upon which these shifts will take place, companies like Facebook, Google, and Microsoft fund think tank organizations, like the Machine Intelligence Research Institute and Santa Fe Institute, to promote ubiquitous social computing and machine learning as the inevitable future foundation for economic valorization. Their ideas are often laid out against the backdrop of a technological sublime, which their high priest futurist Ray Kurzweil calls "the coming Singularity."[46]

Narrating connections between species evolution, labor, collective intellectuality, social belonging, and machines, these corporate think tanks imagine a particular future for the global economy and those working in it. It is one where radical changes and disintermediation by machines are perpetually just around the corner, as computers equipped with vastly distributed and ubiquitous graph intelligence begin to outpace human beings in tasks requiring a degree of intellectuality that up to now we've thought immune to automation. For devotees of the coming Singularity, Ken Jennings' 2011 defeat at the hands of IBM's Watson was an early omen: we are living, so the story goes, in an era of autonomous machines that will soon vault past human beings in their capacity to reason and think. It can be instructive to examine some of these more high-flown, often incredibly deterministic accounts of what's to come.

The Future of Life Institute, for example, includes a variety of luminaries in science, engineering, and mathematics—from Elon Musk and Stephen Hawking to the Oxford philosopher Nick Bostrom. Concerned about what they call the "intelligence explosion," provoked by widespread informationalization, its members write in an open letter that

> There is now a broad consensus that AI research is progressing steadily, and that its impact on society is likely to increase. The potential benefits are huge, since everything that civilization has to offer is a product of human intelligence; we cannot predict what we might achieve when this intelligence is magnified by the tools AI may provide, but the eradication of disease and poverty are not unfathomable. Because of the great potential of AI, it is important to research how to reap its benefits while avoiding potential pitfalls.[47]

Technology guru Kevin Kelly is more frank in his discussions of the mercantile connections between social computing and industrial-scale artificial intelligence, pointing out in *WIRED* magazine, for example, that

> At first glance, you might think that Google is beefing up its AI portfolio to improve its search capabilities, since search contributes 80 percent of its revenue. But I think that's backward. Rather than use AI to make its search better, Google is using search to make its AI better. Every time you type a query, click on a search-generated link, or create a link on the web, you are training the Google AI. When you type "Easter Bunny" into the image search bar and then click on the most Easter Bunny-looking image, you are teaching the AI what an Easter bunny looks like.[48]

Both remarks propose and promote certain outcomes, around how technology will function politically and economically, as social computing becomes more deeply entwined with the production of value via knowledge automation. Across the political spectrum, different thinkers are weighing in with their sense of how labor processes will alter with such a concentration of intellectual capital in ways that will thoroughly redefine what we mean by value.

For those who take an optimistic view, the future holds great promise for increasing efficiency at work, as social computing strategies help to unfetter collective potential. Pentland's account of 'social physics' is a good example here. When employees work in teams tracked and logged by mobile badges keyed to a social graph, more explicit emphasis can be paid to optimizing how an individual's personality fits together with different groupings in an organization. The result is to give management and workers a more transparent sense of productivity and greater leeway around improving the bottom line on social terms. Applied to the workforce, Pentland writes that networked social science facilitated by global graphs can help us to "understand how ideas flow from person to person through the mechanism of social learning," thereby enabling us to "predict the productivity of small groups, of departments within companies, and even of entire cities. It also helps us tune communication networks so that we can reliably make better decisions and become more productive."[49]

Some rightly see a neo-Tayloristic impulse at work in Pentland's ideas, and instead seek to read social computing in more explicitly Marxist terms, contributing to shifts in the forces and relations of production. Symbolic exchange in communication has become a driving force of value, especially in the intensifying financialisation of the economy; Christian Marazzi writes, for example, that financial liquidity is a function of money that

> embodies the action of public opinion on the multiplicity of subjects participating in the economy of the financial markets. To function as a lever of choices/decisions of investors, public opinion must equip itself with a convention or interpretive model considered by everyone as "true," or *dominant*. [...] In the New Economy the convention (social *and* financial) has been expressed as a technological linguistic-communicative paradigm.[50]

Increasingly organized by way of social computing, the production and distribution of information in the service of public opinion and attention become key levers of the economy here, especially in providing a technical ground for the big data analysis of consumer behavior. Keying in to earlier discussions around the real-time manifestation of singularity in social computing, Vincent Mosco explains that

> IBM refers to the latter as "the data of desire" because it registers popular expressions of sentiment and feeling, such as likes/dislikes, about products and services. This gives its cloud customers the

ability to correlate sales records with social-media postings, thereby linking behavioral data with information about customer feelings to provide a deeper view of customer sentiment—not just which customers are buying, but why.[51]

Other thinkers diagnose the relation more bluntly as the straightforward commodification of sociality itself. Ulises Mejias writes, for example, that

> If certain social functions before were performed in the public sphere and they are facilitated by for-profit digital networks now, or if new social functions emerge that can only be facilitated by for-profit digital networks, it means those social functions have been commodified, or transformed into something people are willing to exchange in a market.[52]

As these ideas relate to my project of articulating a formatted subject, still other writers have already thoroughly considered these commodified conditions, where the subsumption of everyday life by market logic means that personal and collective participation in networked *publics* gets commodified right along with everything else.[53] In developing the notion of a formatted subject then, I will be more concerned to understand the specific technical means by which KR graphs produce representations of the social, connecting information processing by way of protocol and algorithm up to the wider intersubjective processes of capitalistic valorization that these writers rightfully criticize.

To suggest a final broad influence upon my choice of the term formatted subject, unpacking the representational strategies deployed in social computing platforms can give us a sense of how they promote or fail to promote what the philosopher of technology Andrew Feenberg calls operational *autonomy*. To his understanding, this is a freedom accorded to powerful institutional actors in technocratic societies, to define organizational practices according to managerial interests at the expense of subordinate actors and community values. I remain mindful of his criticisms of the ethical limits imposed by any technical code designed for such operational autonomy. As he writes, we employ any modern technology "with limitations that are due not only to the state of our knowledge but also to the power structures that bias this knowledge and its applications. This really existing contemporary technology favors specific ends and obstructs others."[54]

It is an admonition that I carry forward into the rest of this book. As it becomes a basic substrate for the general intellect and sociality, social computing is altering our relationship to machines and power in ways that complicate traditional political-economic modes of critique. As Matteo Pasquinelli writes, criticisms of networked thinking "cannot be established simply on the predictable narrative of the good networks against the evil monopolies. A political response can be imagined only if the nature of the molecular *dispositif* that produces the *network value* is understood."[55] That is, the techniques, algorithms, and protocols of social computing do not *in themselves* explain anything. Rather, they must themselves be explained "as manifestations and configurations of more profound processes" involving the circulation of power.[56] It is in this wider spirit of developing creative political responses to our current networked media environment that the book focuses, perhaps rather single-mindedly, on the philosophical, epistemic, and ontological commitments that underlie techniques of the social in computing.

Structure of the Book

The account of knowledge graphs developed in the next chapter speaks largely to their capacity for the rational organization of sense and reference, through techniques that have roots in twentieth-century analytic philosophy, especially in the development of the predicate calculus and propositional form of assertions. Based in ideas from philosophers like Frege, Bertrand Russell, Charles Sanders Peirce, and Wittgenstein, knowledge engineering involves an underlying commitment to logic as a transcendental substance for correspondence between subject and object. The resulting diagnosis in Chapter 2 is of an *epistemically* formatted subject, whose technical environment is defined socially and psychically according to the retrieval of empirical facts, which mediate thought according to the so-called 'backward- and forward-chaining' movements of inferential reasoning. The remainder of the chapter is devoted to introducing some basic critiques of this vision, with some help from Deleuze and Guattari's mixed semiotic perspective.

Chapter 3 examines social graphs. Here, the focus is less on fact retrieval and more on situated roles in the production of a *performatively* formatted subject. Through the concept of illocutionary force, philosophers J.L. Austin and John Searle built out from the positivist accounts of language and logic of Russell, Peirce, and Frege, reconfiguring them to better account for social context, promissory power, and everyday practical action. Over time, especially early on in the field of computer-supported cooperative work, social computing designs turned toward their ideas as a way of operationalizing intersubjective accountability in IS. The chapter discusses Terry Winograd and Fernando Flores' Language-Action Perspective as a significant milestone in this respect, as well as Lucy Suchman's important challenges to their view. Suchman, among others, was pivotal in recasting social computing more in terms of conversation analysis and ethnomethodology, using the work of the sociologists Erving Goffman, Harvey Sacks, and Harold Garfinkel to foreground the importance of local practice and context to any formalizing strategy for social order.

Social graph technologies have since incorporated these ideas at both the level of interface and the level of protocol. As we shall see, platforms like Facebook and Twitter embed a mixture of illocutionary force, lived practice, and other deontic dimensions of social life into the heart of their systems. On the one hand, this produces a free communicative relation between users who express their personal identity, beliefs, desires, and affinities according to constraints of status, esteem, and social sanction, organized via the retrieval relation. On the more processual side of algorithm and protocol, sociometry and social network analysis theory help to quantify the relation in ways that generate economic value by transforming the labor of social interaction into statistical correlations and recursive feedback loops. The latter increase a platform's operational autonomy by translating illocutionary force out in the world into the *locutionary* value of stored knowledge assertions. As with the other chapters, this arrangement gets interrogated from a mixed semiotic perspective.

Chapter 4 moves on to give a critical account of predictive-analytic graphs and their conceptual development from a mixture of neuroscience, computing, psychology, and complex systems theory. Having more fully elaborated the mixed semiotic perspective at the end of Chapter 3, this chapter strives to show how predictive-analytic graphs represent a more thoroughgoing 'machinic' approach to social computing—a term central to Deleuze and Guattari's conceptual apparatus. More a product of computer science and the philosophy of science than philosophy writ large, predictive-analytic approaches still tacitly rely on certain markers of subjectivity, especially rationality. But it is a rationality permanently skeptical of its own grounds and, in this respect, tends to most closely follow the philosophical ideas of British empiricist David Hume. Supported by information, cybernetic, and neural network theory, as well as other representational strategies from artificial intelligence like multi-agent modeling, rationality and social subjectivity in a predictive-analytic graph have a probabilistic basis, and so do not observe the usual, intentionally styled boundaries between subject and object. The result is what I call a signaletically formatted subject: partly empirical, partly behavioristic, participating in mixtures of what Hansen calls a *superjective* agency.[57]

Having considered these three main ways of conceptualizing graphs in social computing, Chapter 5 builds on the insights of Chapter 4 to *invert* the critical-analytic relationship established between the mixed semiotic perspective and our dominant, individualistic views of the social. That is, rather than continuing to critique extant approaches, emphasis turns to systematically laying out the compatibilities and contrasts between each style of graph, with a view to speculating on a hybrid alternative to our current understanding of the retrieval relation in the concluding chapter. Consonant with the epigraph from Phillip E. Agre at the beginning of the chapter, if the traditional retrieval relation commits us to a particular metaphysics of the sign, then how might we start to move away from it and toward a more expressive, or processual, position? Starting from Deleuze and Guattari's concept of collective assemblages of enunciation, this chapter compares strategies with an eye to asking, what would it mean to rely on a mixed semiotic account of signs from the *ground up*, or as a design principle for future social software systems? How might graph technologies intersect with new forms of superjective agency on this basis?

Drawing on their conceptualizations of difference, individuation, and so-called 'machinic hetero-genesis', Chapter 5 finds affinities between predictive-analytic graphs and Deleuze and Guattari's understanding of processes of subjectivation. Using their work, I return to the basic practices of each graph style and gather them together under the concept of an *allagmatically* formatted subject, as a way to stage an altered understanding of what it means to be social in the final chapter. Borrowed from Simondon's philosophy, the Greek term *allagmatic* means change, but also *that which can be given or taken in exchange*. Through it, I mean to focus on how, with each approach to social computing, the force of systematic, real-time rational change tends to be defined and controlled by an individual *platform*, whether based in backward-chaining reason, social norms, or the probabilistic signals of choice. Starting from Simondon's position of an allagmatically formatted individual, I hold, is a potentially novel way to rethink how the real-time semiotic forces of metaphysical identity and difference might be defined and orchestrated differently, at the level of both mixed-semiotic form and semiological content online.

Rather than assuming some account of epistemic change as elaborated on the basis of transcendental logic, transcendental sociality, or the empirically styled signaling of a neuronal system, what would an operationally *heteronomous* social change look like, expressed in formal-pragmatic technique? Would it be possible for social computing, at the level of infrastructure, memory strategy, and organizational impetus, to be about something other than a retrieval relation? Would it be possible to be, at the level of technique, about an expressive ontogenetic relation that is styled as a collision of antagonistic givens to constitute sociality in a way that simply does not admit of some universalizing principle of knowing? Wrapping up in the concluding chapter, I try to give a basic example of Simondon's notion of individuation, as a potentially different way to think about our relationship to post-documentary signs.

Notes

1 Stiegler, *Symbolic Misery—Volume 1*, 46.
2 Hendler and Berners-Lee, "From the Semantic Web to Social Machines," 157.
3 Kittler, *Gramophone, Film, Typewriter*, 203.
4 See Halpin and Monnin, *Philosophical Engineering*.
5 See Abbate, *Inventing the Internet*.

6 Day, "Sense in Documentary Reference."

7 Berners-Lee, "Giant Global Graph | Decentralized Information Group (DIG) Breadcrumbs."

8 Hinton, *Understanding Context*, 13–14.

9 Carroll, "Human Computer Interaction—Introduction."

10 Ibid.

11 Fuller, *Software Studies*, 3.

12 See Mackay et al., "Reconfiguring the User" and Woolgar, "Configuring the User," for example.

13 Foucault, "The Subject and Power."

14 See, for example, Hansen, *Feed-Forward*; Galloway, *The Interface Effect*; Parikka, "New Materialism as Media Theory"; Chun, *Programmed Visions*; Mackenzie, *Cutting Code*.

15 Hansen, *Feed-Forward*, 8.

16 Ibid.

17 Dreyfus, Foucault, and Rabinow, *Michel Foucault, beyond Structuralism and Hermeneutics*, 218.

18 Ibid.

19 Genosko, *Deleuze and Guattari*, 1315.

20 Deleuze and Hand, *Foucault*, 85.

21 Ibid.

22 Burchell et al., *The Foucault Effect*, 5.

23 Dreyfus, Foucault, and Rabinow, *Michel Foucault, beyond Structuralism and Hermeneutics*, 220–21.

24 Hansen, *Feed-Forward*, 115.

25 See, for example, Behrenshausen, "Information in Formation."

26 De Souza, *The Semiotic Engineering of Human-Computer Interaction*, 10.

27 Day, *Indexing It All*, 38.

28 Deleuze, *Difference and Repetition*, 137.

29 Dourish, "What We Talk about When We Talk about Context," 11.

30 Deleuze and Guattari, *A Thousand Plateaus*, 77.

31 Hansen, *Feed-Forward*, 6.

32 See, for example, Donath, *The Social Machine*; Dourish, *Where the Action Is*; Dourish and Bell, *Divining a Digital Future*; Picard, *Affective Computing*; Suchman, *Human-Machine Reconfigurations*; Suchman, "Subject Objects."

33 See, for example, Poster and Savat, *Deleuze and New Technology*; Frohmann, *Deflating Information*; Behrenshausen, "Information in Formation: Power and Agency in Contemporary Informatic Assemblages."

34 Floridi, *Information*, 23–24.

35 Mingers, "Prefiguring Floridi's Theory of Semantic Information," 396.

36 Floridi, *Information*, 23.

37 Ibid.

38 Kosner, "Diffbot Bests Google's Knowledge Graph to Feed the Need for Structured Data."

39 Pentland, *Social Physics*, 9.

40 Monnin, "Digitality, (Un)knowledge and the Ontological Character of Non-Knowledge," 2.

41 See for example Dean, *Democracy and Other Neoliberal Fantasies*; JESSOP*, "Critical Semiotic Analysis and Cultural Political Economy."

42 Dyer-Witheford, *Cyber-Marx*, 487.

43 See, respectively, Lazzarato, *Signs and Machines*; Moulier Boutang and Emery, *Cognitive Capitalism*; Hardt and Negri, *Multitude*; and Genosko and Bouissac, *Critical Semiotics*; Berardi, *Precarious Rhapsody*; Guattari, *The Three Ecologies*.

44 Habermas, *The Theory of Communicative Action*, 403.
45 Brynjolfsson and McAfee, *The Second Machine Age*.
46 Kurzweil, *The Singularity Is Near*.
47 "FLI—Future of Life Institute | AI Open Letter."
48 Kelly, "The Three Breakthroughs That Have Finally Unleashed AI on the World."
49 Pentland, *Social Physics*, 4.
50 Marazzi, Conti, and Hardt, *Capital and Language*, 56.
51 Mosco, *To the Cloud*, 178.
52 Mejias, *Off the Network*, 6.
53 See for example Dean, *Democracy and Other Neoliberal Fantasies*; Schiller, *Digital Depression*; Fuchs, *Culture and Economy in the Age of Social Media*.
54 Feenberg, "Critical Theory of Technology," 54.
55 Pasquinelli, "The Number of the Collective Beast," 9.
56 Pasquinelli, *Alleys of Your Mind*, 2.
57 Hansen, *Feed-Forward*, 118.

2 The Epistemically Formatted Subject

It becomes clear from the preceding investigations about structural definite descriptions that each object name which appears in a scientific statement can in principle (if enough information is available) be replaced by a structural definite description of the object, together with an indication of the object domain to which the description refers.
—Rudolf Carnap, *The Logical Structure of the World and Pseudoproblems in Philosophy*

The next time you find yourself using Apple's digital assistant, try posing it the question "Siri, what planes are above me right now?" Combining sophisticated natural language processing with your GPS coordinates, and querying Wolfram Alpha's knowledge graph database, the software agent will cheerfully inform you of various flights overhead, including their altitude and slant distance from the nearest radar. Giving answers to a question that most would never even think to ask, the clever trick provokes a kind of informational sublime, ideologically powerful in its pointless factuality. The underlying knowledge representation techniques that make the world understandable in this near-magical way may seem academic or mundane by comparison, but going behind the scenes to understand them is key to what I refer to in this chapter as an epistemically formatted subject. At the heart of its production is a twentieth-century *logicist* perspective on the sign and subjectivity.

I begin the chapter by describing some of the historical roots of relational database theory, outlining how early practices in the field borrowed from analytic philosophies of meaning and language to coordinate collective knowledge production in a scientific way. Subsequent debates over meaning and validity in philosophy eventually precipitated new formal approaches to data, which I describe as a shift from relational databases to knowledge graph databases. The latter now sit at the conceptual center of many large-scale commercial social computing platforms—like Siri, Google's knowledge graph, and Wolfram Alpha's Computational Knowledge Engine. In the second half of the chapter, I turn my focus to problems with the logicist idealization of meaning relative to other fields, even as it remains a dominant pragmatic approach behind-the-scenes in information systems (IS) design.

Using early criticisms of Sir Tim Berners-Lee's pioneering and utopian concept of a worldwide knowledge graph called the Semantic Web as a foil to stage a broader critical discussion, I address the relationship between the knowing subject, the social, and technical formatting in general. I do so with help from Continental philosophers who've offered sophisticated critiques of analytic theories of meaning, Gilles Deleuze and Félix Guattari's mixed semiotic among them. The chapter concludes with an exposition of knowledge graphs in relation to their ideas, beginning to lay down the basis of critique for the remainder of the book.

The Philosophy of Relational Databases

Anyone familiar with the inner workings of computers will recognize the seminal roles played by American telecommunications engineer Claude Shannon, and British logician-mathematician Alan Turing. In their attempts to engineer the symbolic operations of logic into machines, these men laid down key material foundations for computing. Pursuing ways to maintain the fidelity of communication signals, Shannon's central insight was to embed Boolean algebra (as conceived by nineteenth-century logician George Boole) into systems of electromagnetically switched circuits. Modern computing remains at least conceptually based on the 'logic gates' he originally devised, which encoded formal truth and falsity into electromechanical relays, which eventually gave way to the electronic representation of zeroes and ones in modern computers. Following his stint during World War II as Britain's leading cryptographic code breaker, Turing imagined a theoretical machine, later realized, that could represent *all machines*, and by some accounts, intelligence and the entire universe, based on just a handful of logical operations, tracked on an infinite spool of paper ruled with horizontal squares—the universal Turing machine.

Shannon's and Turing's ideas developed against a wider intellectual backdrop of the early twentieth century where innovations in the philosophy of mathematics were laying new ground both for the representation of numbers via logic and for our understanding of the relationship between logic and linguistic meaning. Important related thinkers here include the nineteenth-century logicians Boole and co-inventor of predicate calculus Gottlob Frege; the semiotician-logician Charles Sanders Peirce, who also constructed a predicate calculus, as well as early representations of logic by way of graph diagram; the originator of set theory Georg Cantor; Bertrand Russell and Alfred North Whitehead, responsible for the *Principia Mathematica*; their crucial interlocutor Kurt Gödel, who laid the groundwork for computer science with his revolutionary theories of self-referential formal systems; and the philosopher of language Ludwig Wittgenstein. I recognize that with this list of just a few key intellectual figures; I am leaving out much of the dizzyingly complex origins of the computer, which, in any case, are much better documented elsewhere.[1]

For the purposes of an audience interested in computing primarily as a material medium for sociality, I will import just some of the core concepts from logic and mathematics to frame this chapter, the goal being to simply show that as these thinkers were constructing models of truth-functional operation for mathematics, logic, and language, they were also developing certain foundational semiotic practices and, by extension, forms of objectivity that to this day still frame our ideas about meaning, rationality, and the role of computers in everyday life. Anyone who uses exclusion operators for a search (as in "jaguar-speed car") will recognize, for example, how Boole's nineteenth-century work in logic expresses in theory what is now a basic affordance of digital devices; the algebraic manipulation of sets and classes. Boole writes:

> Thus, if x = black and y = sheep, then xy represents the class of black sheep. Similarly, $(1 - x)$ would represent the class obtained by the operation of selecting all things in the world except black things; $x(1 - y)$ represents the class of all things that are black but not sheep; and $(1 - x) \bullet (1 - y)$ would give us all things that are neither sheep nor black.[2]

Relational data schemes of this type, involving the interactive inclusion and exclusion of conceptual classes, perform a fundamental mediation of IS, effectively forming "... the ontology of the world according to a computer."[3] An introductory textbook on the subject of databases writes more prosaically that they "... provide shared, reusable, and efficient services for the definition, capture, organization, and manipulation of data."[4] For more than half a century now, databases have acted as rational models for all manner of collective activity, from airline reservations and government bureaucracies to a structure for scientific practice and library systems of reference. Relational databases offer a powerful ordering disposition for human activity in the sense that differing *subjective* expectations for what each individual might need, do, or say in a given knowledge context can be coordinated from an *objectifying* perspective of analytic remove.

Underlying this impetus for order are certain philosophical blueprints for meaning, which, applied in computing, stage our technological relationship to signs. Continuing a multi-millennial tradition from Aristotle and William of Ockham to people like Boole, I have already mentioned two major figures responsible for describing this relationship between logic and meaning in a modern idiom: Frege and Peirce. In famously arguing that signs have two dimensions of *sense* and *reference*, Frege sought a universal account of how concepts, logic, numbers, and meaning could be combined. For Frege, sense is the way that a term refers subjectively to an object, while reference is to the actual *object* to which that term refers, as an identity secured in logic. Peirce is an equally important thinker in this regard who arrived at similar conclusions but took a more pragmatic, intuitive stance toward logic. Peirce understood the sign relation to be not only between a sign and its object, but also between a sign, its object, and that object's *interpretant*—an effect upon someone, analogous to Frege's notion of sense. Unlike Frege's scheme, however, the interpretant was not so easily delineated as subjective, but rather stood in a permanently triadic relationship with a sign and its object in the world.

We might say then that where Frege adopted a universalistic view of language with respect to logic, Peirce took a more pragmatic stance toward the location of meaning in the world. Amazingly, these two thinkers developed their systems for quantificational logic and predicate calculus—which now form the intellectual basis for today's database technologies—entirely separately from one another, although their ideas later intertwined in notational practice. As this is not a treatise on logic, I will be focusing somewhat generically on the semiotic structures for logic that they proposed, omitting considerable detail. That said, I concentrate on Frege's work, as it demonstrates the basic action of traditional relational databases, and then turn my attention to Peirce's work as part of the subsequent discussion of graph databases.

Frege

Frege's work involved aligning mathematics and the meaning of language to the principles of logic. He argued that while things in life might appear to have stable corresponding reference in everyday talk, in reality, objects had varying aspects of sense whose reference could only be properly coordinated from outside of ourselves. His tool in this regard was a special form of writing he developed called *Begriffschrift*, or Concept Script. It was an early example of a formal-symbolic system that stripped language down to its bare capacity for expressing logical and mathematical proofs. Although Peirce's notation beat out Frege's in terms of elegance and economy of expression, Frege's ideas have nevertheless had an enormous impact on thinking about meaning and validity, in both philosophy and IS, especially in what became known as the rationalistic tradition in computing.

As Julian Roberts writes, Frege developed his truth-theoretic approach to language in three ways: through "the separation of the empirical from the logical structure of the judgment, separation of the predicate from its 'subject', and separation of statements about things from statements about concepts."[5] These features culminated in his theory of sense and reference, which came as a critical response to the more psychologically justified accounts of his era. To put it simply, Frege was seeking a formalizable distinction between 'making representations' and 'thinking'. A crucial weakness in psychological explanations of judgment of the time was that they were too focused on the mere 'association of ideas' and, thus, failed to account for when someone believed an assertion to be true without it actually *being* true. Unless one appealed to logic outside of the individual, there was no way to tell the difference; so Frege based his process of correct thinking on the intersubjective accessibility of representations in language instead. Representations in the mind, he argued, were like *possible thoughts*; they needed to be subjected to the epistemological conditions of truth in logical statements in order to *become* thoughts that actually refer.

He especially had in mind the model of one person answering the question of another, as Wolfgang Carl writes: "Asking a propositional question is 'a demand for making a judgment', whereas making an assertion is meeting this demand by acknowledging the truth of the thought expressed by the propositional question or of its negation."[6] Applied at the level of the sentence, logical inference sat external to the individual as a 'law of thought' so that the truth or falsity of a linguistic statement would not depend on the person uttering it. A person's mind (and, as the library sciences later sought scientific interpretations of knowledge, a *document*) had representations of judgeable content, which could be 'advanced into thought' by testing their truth value through his assertoric approach to meaning. As we shall see, this basic schema for characterizing thought deeply informs our conceptualizations of knowledge representation and retrieval.

Frege's second strategy of sharply separating the subject of a sentence from its predicate is connected to his empirical/logical distinction. He found traditional views on the relationship between subject and predicate to be erroneously based in grammar where the subject was held to be merely what the sentence was 'about' while the predicate correspondingly told something about it, as in "The tree is green" or "The cat is asleep." Grammatical approaches to subject and predicate were muddled, he held, thanks again (1) to their basis in the private thoughts of individuals, (2) on a problematic reliance upon demonstrative pronouns, and (3) in overall communicative, rather than logical, criteria. He writes, for example, that "By combining subject and predicate, one reaches only a thought, never passes from sense to reference, never from a thought to its truth value."[7] How could one better organize thoughts so as to orient them toward demonstrably truthful statements?

Frege's response was to establish a more sophisticated distinction between the subject and predicate of a sentence: the subject was more accurately an *argument about an object*, whereas the predicate was more accurately *a function that signified a concept*. By basing the analysis of sentences in the abstracted form of an empty, one-place predicate statement (as in, "_____ is _____"), arguments and functions could act as abstract 'slots' that divided sentences more cleanly into their logically predicable components, turning them into testable statements with analytic content. To establish the sense and reference of a sentence, one fills the indexically indeterminate first slot with the thing, explicating it in the second slot via some conceptual class to which it belongs, in order to judge whether the sentence correctly refers.

Like chemical atoms bonding, concepts are unsaturated blanks to be filled in, and objects in the world fill in those blanks, as functions of a range of possible reference to classes of objects overall. Encoded into relational and graph database technologies in different ways in the modern era, this remains how our relationship to information, meaning, and one another in social computing is governed at the level of technique. Making judgments via various social interfaces, these days, we 'fill in the slots' together in the production of data and metadata in order to establish and maintain socio-semantic relations with one another for various purposes and practices, while also conditioning meaning to be rational for the material purposes of storage, retrieval, and communicative coordination.

Where certain theories of reference of his era (such as the one put forward by John Stuart Mill) argued that names corresponded directly to the designation of people and things in the world, Frege believed that names were rather a connotative 'mode of presentation'. Proper names encapsulated the sense of a sentence, but this sense could in principle differ while still denotatively referring to the same object. His classic example is captured in the slogan "Hesperus is Phosphorus", or "the morning star is the evening star"—both are otherwise known as the planet Venus:

> If we now replace one word of the sentence by another having the same reference, but a different sense, this can have no bearing upon the reference of the sentence. Yet we can see that in such a case the thought changes; since, e.g., the thought in the sentence 'The morning star is a body illuminated by the Sun' differs from that in the sentence 'The evening star is a body illuminated by the Sun.' Anybody who did not know that the evening star is the morning star might hold the one thought to be true, the other false. The thought, accordingly, cannot be the reference of the sentence, but must rather be considered as the sense.[8]

It was necessary to subject representations to thought in this way, Frege argued, because one could utter a sentence that had sense (representational content) but no actual reference, as in the case of making statements about a fictional character like Santa Claus.

In the later hands of the logical empiricists, Frege's account of meaning took on a more doctrinaire form of linguistic analysis called verificationism, which insisted that in order to be meaningful, *any* statement whatsoever had to have literal significance. Russell called these statements *definite descriptions*: only by testing whether an object belonged to a general concept could one could secure valid reference to some thing.[9] To make an assertion is to reach out beyond the particular case of some individually named thing, and with the risk that the assertion will be false, judge that the object logically belongs under the umbrella of some general concept. Formalizing an object to matter only according to its conceptual implication is what drives Frege's third basic strategy. The relation "_____ is asleep" has a denoted symbol ("the cat") inserted into it, as an intensional-object that falls under the extensional definition of the concept: the organized set of 'things that are asleep'.

Refined over the twentieth century into an entire medium for collective expression in informatics, Frege's ideas offer a powerful set of compositional rules for soliciting and coordinating judgment. On a variety of fronts outside of logic, however, Frege's account has long since been deemed inadequate: our linguistic utterances are simply not solely governed by the disembedded conditions of sense and reference. Though they remain a historical cornerstone of rationalist approaches to language, Frege's ideas have been subject to much critique and extension by his enthusiastic interpreters, many of who were concerned with how the underlying ordinary language *context* or *situation* of meaning seems to disappear in his account. In other words, critiques came from both the analytic tradition in philosophy, via people like Wittgenstein, and later J.L. Austin and John Searle, and also from more Continental voices, like Martin Heidegger, the social theorist Jürgen Habermas, and specific to artificial intelligence, the Heideggerean pragmatist Hubert Dreyfus.

Peirce

Work by Peirce, the founder of philosophical pragmatism and modern semiotics, has been equally influential upon the designs of both relational and graph data technologies. Peirce held that the underlying algebraic logic they demonstrate was key to organizing the world scientifically, on the basis of its observable patterns of resemblance. Building on the work of Boole, Peirce approached the world critically through algebraic logic because doing so offered the power to constructively speculate upon, determine, and further refine its patterns of resemblance. Like Frege, he understood these to emerge through a set of rigorous, and importantly, impersonal or anti-psychologistic procedures. Following Kamini Vellodi's account, Peirce saw the relational role of what he then called existential graphs as "… generator of the laws that permit the determination of the future with increasingly greater clarity, to aid the movement of logic from the vague (particulars) to the definite (general), the movement of thought's 'self-controlling' toward its ultimate destination: truth."[10]

In other words, Peirce's work on graphs was about devising powerful semiotic strategies in support of inductive, deductive, and abductive reasoning. Unlike his European counterpart, Peirce's ideas were not so thoroughly framed in terms of an idealizing relationship between symbolic logic, quantification, and language. They also had an important basis in pictorial, phenomenological, and diagrammatic ways of thinking, linking logic and reason to experience. Signs for Peirce famously involve a triadic relation between a sign (what Peirce called a *representamen*, more simply some kind of *sign-vehicle*), an object, and an interpretant, or relation of understanding. The sign-vehicle of smoke on the horizon acts as an interpretant of the sign's object (fire), for example, by drawing our focus to the physical relation between smoke and fire, thereby 'translating' or developing the fire as a sign through inference, perhaps moving us to communicate with others in pointing out the fire's significance in a longer chain of signs. Knowledge graphs play a similar role in associating a particular thing in the world with a datafied symbol that can be deductively chained along in the wider semiotic relations of a given community of knowers.

The power of knowledge graphs lies in their capacity to do this consistently and efficiently; to move us quickly from potentially vague or erroneous thinking about things in the world toward the automatic realization of their correct reference. It's in this sense that knowledge graphs quite literally mediate between social and technological determination. In one direction, graph entities face human beings as interpretants, or indices of actual things in the world, allowing for a chaining together of multiple interpretants along deductive and inductive lines, while also making allowances for the initial affective investments of indiscernible presence. In the other direction, graph entities are formal interpretants at the level of logic and code, able to move across various meta-levels of symbolic reference in software, before eventually hitting semiotic bedrock as asignifying pulses of electricity in the computer's hardware.

To get into the weeds of his theory just a bit more, Peirce developed a sophisticated, multi-level typology of signs that bootstrapped his ideas about sensation and experience up into the more formal dimensions of reference, logical proposition, and predication. Computers function in the most conventional realm of his typology, manipulating symbols that Peirce called *legisigns*. Importantly though, legisigns are like every other sign in the world in that they may be classified into one of three types: rhema, dicents, and arguments. To take these terms one at a time, when a symbol's interpretant role is to focus our understanding on the qualitative features that a thing *may* possess, then it is called a rheme in Peirce's system, or in the plural, rhema.[11]

In ways similar to Frege's account of sense and reference, rhema formalize the mere possibility that some *x* could have some feature—to be a purebred dog, to have starred in a movie with Nicholas Cage, or to share a border with Romania. Peirce writes that a rheme is " … any sign that is not true nor false."[12] A rheme is really an overly vague sign in the sense of exhibiting one's belief, but not yet the objective reference that would accompany *testing* that belief; it has connotation but not organization into a definite class—it is like 'some dog', 'some actor', or 'some country'. If you're familiar with the children's template word game Mad Libs, rhema are signs in the sense of a universe of unsaturated predicates (the aforementioned 'slots' in Frege's work) that await a 'filling in', as in "_____ is a purebred dog," "_____ starred with _____ in _____," or "_____ shares a border with _____." Platforms like Google and Wolfram Alpha can be understood as a perpetual, constructivist game of knowledge production in this respect. User and platform each gain epistemic value from the game as it progresses: the platform satisfies questions with the rhema it has encountered and stored, even as its tenders work to build out the system by including new rhema in its ontology, as these are communicated by frustrated users.

Next, a symbol is *dicentic* when it actually determines an interpretant. This happens by " … focusing our understanding of the sign upon the existential features it employs in signifying an object."[13] Dicentic signs move a rheme into judgment—they fill in its slot or slots or, more formally, saturate its empty predicates with a subject, as in "this small dog is a beagle," or "Holly Hunter starred with Nicholas Cage in *Raising Arizona*." In Peirce's telling, a dicentic sign is

> … an exhibition of the fact that one subjects oneself to the penalties visited on a liar if the proposition asserted is not true. An act of judgment is the self-recognition of a belief; and a belief consists in the deliberate acceptance of a proposition as a basis for conduct.[14]

The effect of a dicentic sign is to force one to commit to a certain relation of an object being real in order to express hypothetical or categorical propositions that may be collectively judged true or false.

Finally, there are special legisigns for inferring conclusions and lawlike connections between these rhematic and dicentic signs; Peirce calls them *arguments*. They are best thought of as a kind of mediating process for interpretants, and it's this process that we increasingly delegate to knowledge graphs. James Liszka writes that "In the argument, the propositions which serve as premises not only convey their own particular information but lead to another piece of information not stated by either premise but, of course, expressed by the proposition in the conclusion."[15] In other words, arguments change and improve our thinking by producing *new* information, as when someone asserts that "This small dog resembles a beagle, and this dog has papers attesting to its being purebred, *therefore* this dog is a purebred beagle." Or, drifting again into the approach taken by social graphs, "Holly Hunter starred with Nicholas Cage in *Raising Arizona*, therefore Holly Hunter *knows* Nicholas Cage."

Those who deal professionally with IS will have taken the conceptual aspects of data that I have just outlined as a given, and may well have found their exposition tedious. But I focus on Peirce's foundational work for a reason; while his ideas have been foundational for the way that we think about relational data, they have also been subject to substantial reconfiguration at the hands of other philosophers. Taking up his claim that logic is the primary means by which a knowledge community thinks together in a 'self-controlling' way, the philosopher of language Horst Ruthrof has sought to reverse Peirce's emphasis, for example. Ruthrof argues that an unjustified equivocation occurs when we separate judgment grounded in logic from judgment grounded in shared social experience, allowing the former to define the latter. When we take valid reference to be secured by what Ruthrof calls Peirce's *homo-semiotic* relations of analytic sense, we obscure the role that signs actually play in the variegated materialities, bodies, languages, and shifting social orders that constitute our semantic understanding. Ruthrof argues that we must, therefore, think of reference as secured instead by the *hetero-semiotic* relations of a community in question. Reference, he writes, is not a matter of sufficient *reason;* it is a matter of sufficient *semiosis:*

> Whereas sufficient reason has traditionally been employed to handle synthetic judgments as if they were analytic ones, however, sufficient semiosis sanctions no such transfer. Instead, it emphasizes the cultural horizontality of natural language and its non-linguistic relations. [...] In truth-oriented semantics 'this politician is corrupt' is intelligible because we can judge whether it is true or false. From the perspective of sufficient semiosis all that is required is that we are able to imagine a sufficiently coherent 'world' with the help of quasi-perceptual acts.[16]

In a similar vein but taking a more radical position, Deleuze and Guattari wholly appropriate Peirce's interlocking typology of the sign for their own purposes, importantly refusing its grounding in empirical-scientific observation. A telling footnote in their cowritten book *A Thousand Plateaus* argues, for example, that " ... we can borrow [Peirce's] terms, even while changing their connotations. First, indexes, icons, and symbols seem to us to be distinguished by territoriality-deterritorialization relations, not signifier-signified relations."[17] There will be more to say about their translation of Peirce in the next chapter, but in changing the meaning of these terms, Deleuze and Guattari want to emphasize the material processes in life that always involve decontextualizing some existing local sets of relations and reorganizing them so that they can be acted upon in a relation of power. Like Ruthrof, Deleuze and Guattari are less interested in logical formalization as the semiotic ground for thinking than with the immanent interrelations of material and linguistic signs in particular milieus. These must be understood as irreducibly and already social, having important non-linguistic and embodied components, and asymmetries at work around the power to define and to be defined.

From Russell to Codd

Given their field-defining status, there were unsurprisingly many important debates in twentieth-century philosophy that centered on Frege's and Peirce's ideas, especially among people like Russell and Wittgenstein who had sought to extend Frege's logical idealization of meaning. As Richard Rorty explains, Wittgenstein wondered, for example, how Frege and Russell's arguments for logic as the condition of possibility for meaning could themselves somehow remain *exceptions* to the argument they were making: "The propositions of logic were not truth-functional combinations of elementary statements about the objects which make up the world. Yet 'logic' seemed to tell us that only such combinations had meaning."[18] Without getting too far into this style of early twentieth-century analytic philosophy, we can say just a few more basic things about the connection between databases and early logical theories of meaning.

Judgments observing states of affairs in the world follow the form of elementary, atomic facts in Russell's work, for example, and subsequently, as we saw in the chapter's epigraph, the work of Rudolf Carnap. For these thinkers, facts hang together in particular distributions of properties and relations in ways that largely mirror our contemporary thinking about data. Complexity of meaning is reduced to the purely propositional contents of single sentences via 'protocol sentences' that break apart that complexity to establish clearly differentiated descriptions that uniquely specify each and every entity or relation involved in the assertion. Database practitioners still think this way when specifying the primitive-objects of a system in its planning phase. Wittgenstein gives a similar account in his *Tractatus Logico-Philosophicus* writing that to avoid the fundamental confusions of everyday reference in language,

> ... we must employ a symbolism which excludes them, by not applying the same sign in different symbols and by not applying signs in the same way which signify in different ways. A symbolism, that is to say, which obeys the rules of logical grammar—of logical syntax.[19]

As Wittgenstein struggled mightily to unearth the exact nature of this isomorphic relationship between linguistic reference and logical symbolism in his picture theory of meaning, Russell's work on definite descriptions proposed a workable solution by individualizing the elements of a proposition so that there could exist only one, some, or all of x, whatever x might be. This move to precision through formalization is a key feature of how databases organize meaning. When someone asserts that "the present King of France is bald," as Russell famously claimed in an example, they were implicitly making three separate logical assertions:

1   There is an x such that x is a present King of France.
2   For every x that is a present King of France and every y that is a present King of France, x is y (i.e., there is at most one present King of France).
3   For every x that is a present King of France, x is bald.

Taken together, the atomic propositions give conditions for deducing whether the present King of France is bald in a way that sidesteps the indeterminacy of ordinary reference in an everyday sentence. The problem of ambiguity around possible falsity—false because the present King of France has a beautiful head of hair, or because there is actually no present King of France?—gets resolved by decomposing the assertion into logical sub-assertions. With every element in the sentence made over into an atomic, definite meaning, one can categorically determine that the statement is false because nothing fulfills the existential clause that "there is some x such that..." (i.e., There is no King of France!) Any sentence can be broken down into its atomic statements in this way; to be analyzed as true or false, in a conceptual innovation has since been called an 'Archimedean point' in the philosophy of language.

How do these individualizing procedures around language and meaning connect up to theories of numbers and the subject? The answer lies somewhere in the disputes of the neo-Kantians of Russell's time. Mathematics had historically served as a point of translation in Immanuel Kant's transcendental idealism, mediating between the pure *a priori* form of sensory inputs and the pure *a priori* form of the logical categories, which together produce the transcendental subject, or the 'I'. Describing the conditions of thought in his *Critique of Pure Reason*, ordinary sensory inputs were supported by the pure structures of space and time, the province of mathematics and geometry. Ordinary concepts were supported by the structures of pure understanding: forms of logic applied to the objects of experience. The two interleaved in mathematics where categories yielded *synthetic* a priori principles for appearances. It was in this way that mathematical structures underwrote necessary principles like causation, for example, and the transcendental subject's "pure intuition of space as a three-dimensional Euclidean 'container'..."[20]

If for Kant mathematical-objects were secured by the transcendental subject in pure intuition, the logical empiricists would later argue that knowledge should instead be grounded in the transcendental-objective justification of *number*, according greater epistemological primacy to logical sets, and arguing for logic to define the subject in a new way. Through a series of complex formalizations, described by mathematicians like David Hilbert, Gödel, and Albert Einstein, and logical empiricists like Moritz Schlick and Rudolph Carnap, philosophy's appropriation of modern mathematical physics and the general theory of relativity eventually came to replace Kant's Newtonian worldview. Through to the mid-twentieth century, these ideas were part of an intellectual ferment around the birth of computing, and eventually came to influence database theory through the early, seminal work of the computer scientist Edgar Codd.

Trained as a doctoral student by the Peircean scholar Arthur W. Burks, Codd wrote in the 1970s that representing data structures from a logical-empirical perspective could introduce sorely needed rigor into the discipline of data management.[21] More durable and flexible relationships between software programs and data records could be maintained by following Fregean-style rules of sense and reference. Through their application, actors and roles with differing levels of access to stored information could come and go over time without substantially disturbing the underlying records themselves, forming an ideal basis for long-term organizational clarity. Codd argued for the superiority of theories of sense and reference over more idiosyncratically 'networked' relations that were popular at the time. Ironically, through the newer knowledge graphs described below, it is more networked approaches to database management systems that have since resurged.

Codd was focused on a split or 'immunity' between model and implementation; between how data-objects flowed in an abstract, logical-conceptual sense in a given domain of knowledge and the various ways that these flows might get stored and indexed as implementations of the model in a physical system. His goal was to address a common difficulty with the burgeoning expansion of information technology: idiosyncrasies introduced into non-standard designs were causing particular physical hardware and software configurations to become conceptually entangled with the records themselves, making their expansion or reformatting into new technologies or paradigms a frustrating affair. It was on this basis that Codd advocated for a clarification and regimentation of databases by way of propositional and predicate logic; according to a senior practitioner, Codd "saw the potential of using the ideas of predicate logic as a foundation for database management, and defined both a relational algebra and a relational calculus as a basis for dealing with data in relational form."[22] Through designs based in interconnected, analytically true propositions about domain of knowledge, today's databases continue to materially instantiate logicist ideas about meaning.

Statements like "The sun is further away than the moon," "Justin Trudeau is the prime minister of Canada," and "The population density of Brazil is 23.1 people/km^2" are atomic facts that, as they come to be interleaved into an overall world of facts, allow for compound, analytically valid statements to emerge. Like the capacity to compose novel sentences once one has learned a basic set of grammatical rules, individual propositions yield through design to more variable, truth valued functions inside a database system: "j is further away than k." "x is the current prime minister of y." "a has a population density of b." Multi-predicate statements emerge as the system achieves still greater complexity too, producing propositions of the type "a is the current prime minister of b, which has a population density of c, which is further away from d than e."

In other words, as they accumulate these variable predicates, database relations generate a logical space for meaning against which *new* atomic facts can be constructed and compared within a domain of knowledge. Construction is (in theory) complete when the full schema achieves the status of a closed, functional world of analytically true statements; any relation relevant to the domain that has not yet been described can be safely assumed to be irrelevant, rendered invisible, or meaningless. The upshot is that Peircean, Fregean, logical-empiricist and early-Wittgensteinian ideas put logic on a transcendental footing as the technical condition for meaning, deeply materialized into computers through both their origins and their subsequent implementations of data- and knowledge-management techniques. As their philosophical interlocutor William van Orman Quine coined the slogan, for logicians and database designers alike, "To be is to be the value of a bound variable."

The Turn to Linked Data

What changes in the turn from Codd's traditional relational theory to newer graph databases? In the late 1990s context of developing core data standards for the World Wide Web, Berners-Lee and James Hendler began to speak of how the entire web could be understood as one massively interlinked database. As more people and institutions were moving online, their increasing real time interconnection was prompting new ways of thinking about knowledge representation and data management. Their 2001 *Scientific American* article gives an early popularizing take of the possibilities of social machines; note, here, their explicit emphasis on interconnected entities or units of fact in the following passage, to be manipulated automatically by software agents:

> At the doctor's office, Lucy instructed her Semantic Web agent through her handheld Web browser. The agent promptly retrieved

information about Mom's **prescribed treatment** from the doctor's agent, looked up several lists of **providers**, and checked for the ones **in-plan** for Mom's insurance within a **20-mile radius** of her **home** and with a **rating** of **excellent** or **very good** on trusted rating services. It then began trying to find a match between available **appointment times** (supplied by the agents of individual providers through their Web sites) and Pete's and Lucy's busy schedules. (The emphasized keywords indicate terms whose semantics, or meaning, were defined for the agent through the Semantic Web.)

In a few minutes the agent presented them with a plan. Pete didn't like it. University Hospital was all the way across town from Mom's place, and he'd be driving back in the middle of rush hour. He set his own agent to redo the search with stricter preferences about **location** and **time**. Lucy's agent, having **complete trust** in Pete's agent in the context of the present task, automatically assisted by supplying access certificates and shortcuts to the data it had already sorted through.[23]

The relations requiring orchestration here might feasibly be maintained by a single database, but it certainly would be an unwieldy one. The problem at the time was that relational databases were very efficient at maintaining the aforementioned well-planned, unified domains of knowledge, typically for one or a handful of closely connected institutions. But in this example, there are multiple, overlapping contexts in which the data relationships are embedded; many 'conversations of fact' to be had simultaneously, using knowledge maintained by a variety of actors and institutions. Insurance companies, private clinics, government patient-record databases, smartphone calendaring apps, and other actors all appear to be interacting seamlessly with one another in real time. To move from science fiction to reality in making such complex automated exchanges possible, Hendler and Berners-Lee were arguing for a shift in technical scope for the web itself: away from a paradigm of static documents and the planned, unified structures of traditional relational databases and toward more dynamic network data structures that could model relations of fact in more object-oriented terms; for our purposes, more 'flush' with the social complexities of rational discourse around things, as it was taking place on a daily basis.

Database practitioners can again offer some pragmatic insight into the resulting shift; creators of the pioneering *neo4J* graph database system came to the realization that their 1999 Internet startup software was, for example,

> managing not just a lot of individual, isolate and *discrete* data items, but also the *connections* between them. And while we could easily fit the discrete data in relational tables, the connected data was more challenging to store and tremendously slow to query.[24]

Slow queries were a side effect of relational database designs, which, as we've seen, build up units of meaning through complex multi-term predicate relations across stored data tables (*"a* was the Prime Minister of country *b* from the years *c* to *d*...*"*). Graph approaches *simulate* these multi-argument relations by simply taking them one at a time, serially decomposed into binary predicates. Reducing the number of arguments that a predicate involves—in computing lingo, reducing its arity—is a trade-off of formal efficiency for sake of expressive simplicity, harmonizing the pairwise relationality of graphs with our need to express complex social interconnections of fact.

Isolating subjects and objects into binary relations using graph data techniques makes it much easier for either entity to be appropriated as a referential node of knowledge by some software process across the web. It also makes queries to databases less computationally intense and, therefore, quicker to execute. Finally, it makes data records more amenable to statistical analysis, the conceptual power behind mathematical graph theory and network science. Knowledge graphs become much easier to compose, in what amounts to a hypertext-style stringing together of atomic facts among different actors into knowledge networks. The resulting so-called 'linked data' still organizes entities analytically into sets and classes, of the type that Boole conceived, e.g.

A isPartOf B
B hasType C
C isMemberOf D

But because of their more modular, network structure, knowledge graphs allow for a much more nuanced automated reasoning to occur among different actors. Siri's functionality using Wolfram Alpha from the opening of the chapter is a good example.

Turning back to the intellectual lineage of these practices, the shift to graph databases has connections to the longer-term trajectory of the linguistic turn in twentieth-century philosophy. One way to understand the shifting practices between relational and graph databases is by analogy to changes in Wittgenstein's thinking about logic, meaning, and language. Whereas the early Wittgenstein of the *Tractatus Logico-Philosophicus* argued, along with Frege and Russell, that precise meaning could only be achieved through the transcendental imposition of logic upon language, the later Wittgenstein came to understand that meaning was always embedded in some particular set of background practices and embodied dispositions in what he called a 'form of life'. Though they continue to follow the representational model of logical atomism, graph databases represent an analogously reflexive moment in thinking about data. It is definitely a bit of Whig history to say so, but generally speaking, shifting philosophical ideas about the nature of meaning made their way into new paradigms for information technology, especially in attempts to make computer tools more pragmatically flexible and responsive to actually-existing forms of life. Rejecting the position that language has its foundations in logic, as the computer scientist David Blair writes, the later Wittgenstein saw that

> Language can be as determinate as necessary. To see the indeterminacy as a defect is to look at ordinary language as if it were a kind of formal calculus, which it is not. We can make language very precise if we want, not by bringing out some kind of hidden logical underpinning, but by looking at the context, circumstances and practices in which language is used.[25]

The tension can be seen in a slightly different light by again noting the differences between Frege's approach to logic and Peirce as a semiotician. Where Frege took the view that logic should be transcendentally imposed upon language, Peirce—whose work in so-called 'existential graphs' was the most important philosophical precursor to both relational and graph databases—took a more practical, model-theoretic view. The details are complicated, but the upshot is that Frege's way of thinking starts from the primacy of universal sets in order to determine how a domain of knowledge hangs together. For Peirce, a domain of knowledge is a kind of diagram of the world, like a flowchart, from which iconic relations emerge and change based on a shifting context but which may nevertheless be modeled in logic. To venture a more speculative analogy, traditional relational databases seem to start from a Fregean perspective, organizing entities and their attributes by way of interconnected tables, which ultimately lay claim to a kind of universal scientific objectivity for a given context.

Foregoing tables in favor of treating data-objects as self-contained units, graphs shift the pragmatics of meaning from units secured through table relations to relations secured *through the units themselves* in a way that more faithfully reflects the ongoing and shifting indexicality of everyday social practice. A related way to characterize the wider effects of this shift to graph databases is to say that the organizational "spacing" of knowledge becomes less architectural and more contiguous or topological. Manuel DeLanda's work on assemblages suggests that this was not just a new approach in computing or logic; it also has intellectual roots in macro-level accounts of social science. In the case of relations of *interiority*, which traditionally defined relational databases,

> [...] the component parts are constituted by the very relations they have to other parts in the whole. A part detached from such a whole ceases to be what it is, since being this particular part is one of its constitutive properties.[26]

Contrast this account of parts and wholes with a more modern one, which argues that parts *themselves* have intrinsic capacities on a level separate from how their parthood is defined in relation to some overall unity:

> Allowing the possibility of complex interactions between component parts is crucial to define mechanisms of emergence, but this possibility disappears if the parts are fused together into a seamless web... We can distinguish, for example, the properties defining a given entity from its capacities to interact with other entities.[27]

With its resulting altered focus on the *exteriorized* relations of parts, structured data graphs allow for just this more autonomous style of definition. From an approach concerned with the totalizing counter-position of facts, there has been a move toward their more ad-hoc, modal combination for shifting purposes over time. Redefined as freestanding-objects, assertions of fact can be more loosely connected together across the network in different ways, opening up the possibilities of so-called 'big data'. Prior to the advent of computing, Peirce called these looser networks of relation existential graphs, a term later re-conceptualized by the ontologist and artificial intelligence researcher John Sowa as *conceptual graphs.*[28]

   Using them to represent networks of meaning inside a computer, relations become paths with a head and tail, which nevertheless continue to mirror Fregean-style propositional slots: a subject [head] predicates an object [tail], as in the example "Justin Trudeau" is_a Prime_Minister. Looser head-to-tail dynamics effectively marry the power of predicate calculus to the more open referentiality of hypertext. To quote extensively from an online introduction to Resource Description Framework (RDF)—an especially straightforward knowledge graph language, akin to Hypertext Markup Language—these so-called 'triples' (Table 2.1)

> [e]xpress information as a list of statements in the form SUBJECT PREDICATE OBJECT. The subject and object are names for two things in the world, and the predicate is the name of a relation between the two. You can think of predicates as verbs. Here's how I would break down information about my apartment into RDF statements:

Table 2.1 A simple knowledge graph structure

Subject	Predicate	Object
I	Own	my_apartment
My_apartment	Has	my_computer
My_apartment	Has	my_bed
My_apartment	is_in	Philadelphia

These four lines express four facts. Each line is called a statement or triple. The subjects, predicates, and objects in RDF are always simple names for things: concrete things, like my_apartment, or abstract concepts, like has. These names don't have internal structure or significance of their own. They're like proper names or variables. It doesn't matter what name you choose for anything, as long as you use it consistently throughout.[29]

At the level of social ordering, the turn to data structured in this way reflects an increased concern for flexible communication *between* actors on the web. Structured graph data schemes enable a more fluid exchange of fact, whether through public-facing access to commercial knowledge graphs like IBM's Watson or Wolfram Alpha or through more collaborative knowledge modeling projects like the World Wide Web Consortium's Open Annotation Data Model, Wikidata, or the now-defunct Freebase. Before its acquisition by Google in 2010, the latter was a major open repository for graph knowledge, storing some 1.9 billion triples produced entirely by crowd-sourced labor. Describing everything from skiing to heraldry in terms of their predicate relations, the whole point of projects like Wikidata and Freebase is to represent the world's knowledge not by way of documents but by representing and orchestrating different domains of fact directly in concert with one another as *formal ontologies*, thus providing a powerful basis for the future of computer-automated reasoning.

Criticisms of Linked Data

Whether commercial or public in scope, projects devoted to the construction of grand universes of fact using knowledge graphs have not been without their detractors. As it was originally proposed by Hendler and Berners-Lee, for example, representation by global graph was to take the form of a Semantic Web, which came in for criticism on two levels: (1) at the level of professional practice, with some arguing that collaborative effort toward building such massive graphs was a pointless, utopian project without end and (2) at the level of commercialization, in the sense that their maintenance by big companies like Microsoft and Google could eventually represent a troubling economic rationalization of discourse itself. I want to address each of these criticisms in more detail, but will continue to do so in the register of philosophy.

To reiterate, conceptual structures established by relational databases focus by design on relations of interiority, while newer knowledge graph protocols in social computing are better structured for communicative exteriority. Facts are more individualized in knowledge graphs so that they may fluidly interact with other data structures from other actors and institutions. This means that greater emphasis is placed on the networked performativity of meaning, in a shift of functionality that might be shorthanded as moving from an objectivist account of knowing to a more pragmatic one. Where Frege and Russell had originally argued that logic formed an underlying basis for socially achieved meaning, Wittgenstein later came to conclude that what really mattered was the systematic usage of linguistic reference in *shared practices*, principally through habits and learning.

Others like Austin, Searle, and Habermas developed this way of thinking further, in proposing systematic approaches to rational meaning that begin from the side of social context rather than logic, while still leaving conceptual room for the latter in their perspectives. Placing greater emphasis on the performance of language between speaker and hearer, their accounts of speech acts and formal pragmatics have since been especially influential in the field of computer-supported cooperative work, underwriting a *language-action* approach in computer science that gained prominence through the 1980s. Because they have been so influential in the development of social computing, I leave discussion of Austin and Searle to the next chapter and will instead say a bit more about Habermas' ideas concerning the role of maintaining truth in communication; these are more immediately relevant to a discussion of knowledge graphs.

Like Frege, Habermas believes that understanding is based in the exchange of criticizable validity claims that follow a propositional form. But there are aspects beyond logic for him that also contribute to meaning and reference: normative rightness and interpersonal truthfulness are factors in a broader context of situated collective action; to simplify, semantic consensus matters, but so too do the lived possibilities of *dissensus*—and it's here that Habermas' theory of communicative rationality brings out a technical limitation of knowledge graphs for some—alerting us to potentially negative consequences that come along with their widespread application to everyday discourse.

For Habermas, when an objective horizon of meaning has been thoroughly established, *media-steered strategic interaction* becomes a viable alternative to the negotiations of truthfulness and normative rightness through linguistic exchange. This happens to be an excellent way to characterize what Hendler and Berners-Lee had in mind in proposing structured knowledge graphs in support of a Semantic Web. Like negotiating Lucy's doctor's appointment, the idea is that steering media provide efficient symbolic substitution for the energy and time that would otherwise be expended in reaching consensus through discourse, whether in argumentation or the simple back-and-forth of conversation. Traditional examples of steering media that substitute for discourse include money, power, and law: each represent conditions under which intersubjective meaning can be replaced by stereotyped utterances or symbols, substituting the efficient performance of meaning for its potentially more fraught and time-consuming constitution through mutual understanding; 'taking over' from the conscious intentions of subjects.

If money works as a medium by orchestrating utility and exchange value, power does so by focusing on the purposive effectiveness achieved through binding decisions. According to Habermas, both are effective through backing by guarantees; national wealth in the case of the former and the means of enforcement in the case of the latter. For our purposes though, the question is whether knowledge graphs have analogous features. Via his instrumentalization theory, the philosopher of technology Andrew Feenberg argues that in fact, all technology does, and that its significant intertwinement with other steering media justifies its inclusion in Habermas' account.[30] Like other media, formatting strategies like knowledge graphs orient actors toward success by taking certain settled validity claims for granted as a basis for purposive behavior; in this case, the facts stored as structured data.

Interestingly, in his original writings on communicative rationality, Habermas did not find it credible that the social could have such intrinsic influence upon the technological. For him, technology was not a medium unto itself capable of being affected by social forces; it was rather an extrinsically rational mediator for *other* media, like law. Feenberg later countered by demonstrating that technology offers a set of precise parallels to law. Through instrumentalizations embedded into encoding techniques like knowledge triples, technology guides purposive action *juridically*: just as Habermas conceives of law as a coordinating media, technology (1) operates as both idealized institution and form of mediation, (2) mediates between system and life-world, in ways that are sometimes pathological, (3) makes nominal claims on our actions through prescriptions embedded into its design, and (4) has a reserve backing just like the other media:

> Power requires means of enforcement; in the case of technology, the natural consequences of error have a similar function, often mediated by organizational sanctions of some sort. If you refuse the technical norms, say, by driving on the wrong side of the street, you risk your life.[31]

The point in highlighting all of this in relation to knowledge graphs is that the technology has now come to coordinate communication *itself* in ways similar to money and power. In the now-global context of social computing, whether you are seeking a job, starting a small business, or providing a government service, to refuse the embedded norms of meaning constructed by their attendant data strategies and interfaces is to risk invisibility and ineffectiveness.

But knowledge graphs are a peculiar kind of steering medium in that their shift to a more flexible logic comes partly as an effect of technologically formalizing the very elements of linguistically and communicatively structured validity norms that Habermas worked so hard to *distinguish from* his early conceptualization of steering media. Systems designers have relied on his criticisms of overly disembedded Fregean semantics in order to better conceptualize communication and performativity at the level of interface; yet, social computing nevertheless holds on to logical effectivity at the level of protocol to engineer communication. As a result, the process of 'semantifying' the web has arguably transformed it into one big steering medium, with a transactional conception of communication at its core. We can temper such a stark reading by saying that knowledge graphs are an emerging feature of social computing that gives quantifiable, calculable form to interpretive aspects of meaning that Habermas held could not, or should not, receive *empirical* definition—like influence and value commitment. He originally remarks emphatically that " ... media of this kind cannot technicize the lifeworld."[32] And yet, because they achieve a formalistic but still basically *dyadic* rationality in their propositional structure and reliance on pairwise computation by directed graph, knowledge graphs are building new levels of formally steered procedurality into everyday communication.

Whether traced back in origin to Aristotle, Frege, Peirce, or Wittgenstein, it is clear that a great deal of conceptual power has always been invested into the propositional assertion as a liminal philosophical and technical tool for grasping the relationship between language and the countable. We inhabit these theories as media through social computing, where the relationship between constative propositions and their more socially situated, norm-constrained dimensions of meaning circulate in novel and complex ways. As someone who was deeply invested in the idea of a fundamentally intersubjective, *communicative* rationality, Habermas took pains to clarify the exact points of contact between the truth-bearing proposition and social normativity, so understanding his different levels of analysis can help to draw out certain concerns around the role of knowledge graphs.

Building on the Fregean tradition, Habermas sought to generate a more complete account of social rationality by including teleological and communicative dimensions alongside the logical structure of the assertion; he was simultaneously concerned with knowing, acting, and speaking. Knowledge graphs fit mostly into the first and second categories: although ostensibly derived from intersubjective consensus, they represent a depersonalized basis upon which everyone involved can act in agreement, based on the assumption that logic combined with empirical evidence is the right ground for knowing a given entity. Knowledge here is an explicit knowing-what, "[...] built up from propositions or judgments—those elementary units that can be true or false."[33] But as they are formatted to act as a backdrop for knowing-what, knowledge graphs inevitably come to condition the social context of meaning too. Habermas' idealized model involves two people in discourse who may 'agree to disagree' in different ways over precise meaning; reflecting tacit motives, changing one's mind, or being convinced of something, also including wider relations of power that these might involve.

The potential problem is that knowledge graphs now mediate social life by adapting this dyadic, dialogical relation to be *monological*: meaning it becomes an object that can be handed off between two agents—whether human or non-human—transacted as units in a logical-symbolic system. An analogy is to the classic Marxist distinction between use-value and exchange value, in this case applied to the circulation of signs and meaning. Meaning-as-use—phenomenal reference and the achievement of consensus through the social, dialogical possibilities of dissensus— gets formatted into meaning-as-exchange, where signs have power by empirical reference and logic alone.

Habermas' ideal of a steering medium is one where formal schemas achieve this action only after having undergone collective justification through argumentation, connecting their knowing-what up to a knowing-why. The co-implicated space between knowing, acting, and speaking leaves open the important possibility for assertions to be socially challenged, revised, improved, and expanded; he writes that a cluster of propositions, like a knowledge graph, remains

> [...] dependent on its embodiment in speech and action: it is not a *self-supporting* structure. It is the linguistic representation of what is known, and the confrontation of knowledge with a reality against which a justified expectation can shatter, that first make it possible to deal with knowledge in a rational way.[34]

In other words, the factual units put into play by knowledge graphs are supposed to function well because they have survived discursive 'trials of strength', which test their potential falsity. Exactly how do these trials occur?

Feminist standpoint epistemologist Helen Longino offers the useful heuristic that "Objectivity, [as] the maximal minimization of subjective (whether individual or collective) preference, is secured through assuring the inclusion of all socially relevant perspectives in the community engaged in the critical construction of knowledge."[35] Certainly, there are many moments where this occurs in the production of knowledge representations for social computing. When building a resource like Freebase, developers spend endless hours deliberating over the relevant entities and their mereological, hierarchical interconnections, all in an effort to minimize the subjective.[36] Any information system design will have its own biases as to how such schemas should be structured; some will put expert biases to work in helpful ways, insisting on logical-empiricist principles as a guide to success. Others will involve stakeholders and end users in a more participatory, ethnomethodological mode, trying to generate a knowledge schema that genuinely reflects a given domain or set of cultural practices.

Add to these possibilities that startup companies are competing with one another to try to become the knowledge platform for all kinds of practices. And of course, individuals interfacing with knowledge platforms in the course of their everyday activities—information workers, academics, salespeople, scientists—will inevitably discover missing, incorrectly structured, or incomplete information. Different actors may agitate for simple corrections or total overhauls, with bureaucracies and system designers responding through adjustments to the propositional structures of their data. In other words, the gap between knowing-what and knowing-why is where disembedded, formal knowledge schemes meet up with acting subjects, and here, politics inevitably enters the picture. As one computer scientist puts it,

> In the lifeworld, whilst engaged in action, we presume and do not question the truths of the propositions we operate under. Only when these break down do we move from action to discourse and offer our beliefs up for debate and justification. Once we have become convinced of the truth of a proposition through the process of rational discourse we can then move back and adopt it within the sphere of engaged action.[37]

But are these punctuated arguments among actors, concerning initial designs or the occasional quirk or mistake, really the only political dynamic when it comes to the representation of knowledge? How might we better characterize the relationship between stable meaning and its breakdown in today's constant, networked circulation of propositional units via knowledge graph? What is the conceptual middle ground between stable empirical facts like the planes above me right now and the pitched battles around semantics that increasingly mark our 'hashtag politics' on Twitter? Is one knowledge and the other mere opinion? Here it may help to consider the perspective of those who've argued that large-scale global graph approaches are far too naïve to the politics of knowledge.

Berners-Lee's early Semantic Web was supposed to usher in an era of personalization and rapid retrieval; but early critics focused on its overly universalizing aspirations, calling out large-scale knowledge graph projects as utopian and impractical. The technology pundit Clay Shirky was an early naysayer, offering the following example of how graphs were simply not useful:

> Because meta-data describes a worldview, incompatibility is an inevitable by-product of vigorous argument. It would be relatively easy, for

example, to encode a description of genes in XML, but it would be impossible to get a universal standard for such a description, because biologists are still arguing about what a gene actually is. There are several competing standards for describing genetic information, and the semantic divergence is an artifact of a real conversation among biologists. You can't get a standard until you have an agreement, and you can't force an agreement to exist where none actually does.[38]

Hendler and Berners-Lee's vision of the Semantic Web also came in for later criticism in a 2007 lecture by the media scholar Florian Cramer. Arguing that the formalized nomenclature of web-wide knowledge graphs were "[...] doomed to fail by any critical standard of cultural reflection," Cramer went on to claim that the Semantic Web was

> [...] nothing else but technocratic neo-scholasticism based on a naïve if not dangerous belief that the world can be described according to a single and universally valid viewpoint; in other words, a blatant example of cybernetic control ideology and engineering blindness to ambiguity and cultural issues.[39]

Cramer is somewhat inattentive here of the move to exteriorized performativity that comes along with graph data, overstating the case that knowledge graphs are somehow necessarily wedded to a total 'cosmology' for the web. Just as in the past with relational databases, even a small group of people engaged in knowledge representation can benefit from developing a knowledge graph, and the ability to interlink it with others, in the manner that Berners-Lee had in mind. Collaboration over semantic networks can take place within a single institution just as easily as it can through some monolithic global project. That said, both Shirky and Cramer's critiques have a certain ring of truth in that the engineering approach taken by knowledge graphs focuses on the propositional sentence in such a way as to largely disembed it from the social conditions that support it. While nominally a formal pragmatics, the resulting models do little to faithfully account for the social conditions and political investments around validity in knowledge production, as these were brought to the fore in philosophy and critical social theory by people like Habermas and Michel Foucault in the later twentieth century.

The protocols do usefully instrumentalize assertions in a way that subjects them to conditions of possibly being false. But in this process, other elements that go along with discursive rationality, as Habermas more holistically understands it—including the disciplinary power structures that accompany *saying* in speech acts and the ways one may intersubjectively *intend* communicative action, based on differing roles—get stripped out of technical mediation, for all but those expert system designers who debate and design a graph in its initial construction.

Propositional statements interconnected into semantic networks are premised on the constative speech act, but from a critical perspective, they do not preserve in technique one of its central features: communicative breakdown, or the potential for *disagreement* over meaning. These dimensions are left to be recuperated in the creative construction of interface designs, and by no means do I want to diminish their power. Computer interfaces are an important space for enacting a politics of knowledge; but they often remain materially wedded to the formal-analytic approaches to meaning that are in operation 'under the hood'.

For Habermas, knowledge is not just about semantic precision; it is also about sincere and insincere orientations toward others and legitimate and illegitimate motivations in a context. In the case of knowledge graphs, dissensus essentially becomes invisible, or is rather transformed into a private signal of formal differentiation, because social computing technique is simply not oriented toward carrying such dynamics into the representable unit of computing. Beyond analytic falsity, the technology is not well structured to service discursive breakdown around a given meaningful entity. Breakdown becomes a case of syntax error, where the user or agent has failed to retrieve the meaning they were looking for. The overall effect is to reinforce administrative or traffic-controlling attitudes that reify discourse itself as retrieval, and the exchange of information as content-objects.

I am by no means the first to make such critiques, which tend to be leveled at related scientific and bureaucratic practices. But I have been trying to suggest that the problem lies at the level of technical mediation too, where the intersubjective reciprocity of utterances is too quickly assimilated to the dyadic steering of graphs. The epistemically formatted subject that 'comes out the other side' is inclined to understand their cultural norms and epistemic dispositions through knowledge graphs as a kind of linguistified steering medium, rendering the subject as a mono-logical rational agent in search of formal-objects, labeled according to their particular interests. The effect is to bring decisionistic qualities of communication to the fore and to condition discourse in ways that lead to a kind of self-objectification.

It's important not to overstate the case. Immense flexibility has been gained in the realignment of digital information to suit a more pragmatically focused networked environment. People can now easily coordinate knowledge, goals, and relationships with one another through the subjectively styled manipulation of topics and areas of interest that concerns them. Through tools like neo4J, NoSQL, and RDF, semantic interfaces are being built in ways that are far more fluidly responsive to situated reference and much more attentive to people's embedded interactions in a social context. Users can align themselves with their globally like-minded ilk far more quickly and multi-modally than ever before with a variety of social benefits that accrue to those who in turn represent *themselves* through knowledge graphs, a matter to be discussed in terms of social graphs in the next chapter. Self-objectification of one's personal identity as a clustered set of facts helps to make coordinating commitments with others more efficient, particularly in some of the emerging very large-scale conversations that take place on platforms like Twitter.

Following the ideas of writers like Yochai Benkler, this surely has enormously positive political and cultural effects, helping groups and organizations to vault past the limitations of twentieth-century mass media.[40] But another important result has been the more intimate penetration of the formalized proposition into everyday discourse. As mediation through knowledge graphs comes to affect many-to-many communication on a global scale through our devices, the question is whether intersubjective norms achieved through social influence, and the cultural expression of value commitments in discourse, risk anything in their greater objectification. Habermas thought the possibility unlikely, writing that

> ... it is not particularly plausible to place influence and value commitment on a par with money and power, for they cannot be calculated like the latter. It is possible to wield influence and value commitment strategically only when they are treated like deposits of money or power, that is, only when we make manipulative use of non-manipulable goods. Influence and value commitments can, naturally, be *interpreted* as media.[41]

The issue is that social computing via knowledge graphs seems to be setting the conditions for us to do just that, to actual material consequence, where the intersubjective constitution of expression is fast becoming inter-*objective* instead.

More than was ever possible in smaller, standalone computer-mediated communication systems, on the one hand, users can now amplify the subjective sense of their utterances by delegating them to this efficient new form of reference coordination. What they gain in exchange on its terms is greater global visibility: more followers, or other kinds of quantifiable influence, which increasingly may translate into institutional trust, mediated prestige, or financial gain. What they potentially sacrifice is a critical element of discursive validity claims in substituting the 'yes/no' responses of claims to sense between people for a more procedural unit exchange that stimulates network communication in the formal terms of 'yes/*not*', or 'sense/nonsense'. In short, datafication by knowledge graph socially rationalizes the performative force of speech in the name of communicatively rational participation, with those who control knowledge graphs coming to act as powerful new brokers for significance.

Feenberg's work on social rationalization offers a helpful analogy here, once again to Marx's distinction between exchange value and use value. Exchange value introduces formally equal relations between commodities, which replaces domination and subordination as a force in production. From there,

> The price under which things are exchanged governs their movement, often independent of use, rather than the immediate connection between the producer and an individual consumer as in former times. Similarly, functions float free from the wider context of the lifeworld and appear as the essence of artifacts that may in fact have many other relations to the human beings who live them. The fetishism of function obscures the relations much as the fetishism of commodities masks the human reality of the economy.[42]

Mimicking the exchange of commodities, social computing rationalizes an epistemic relationship of exchange between domains of knowledge that have been formally equalized through the propositional fact to 'float free', with public discourse constantly feeding and refining the empirical interrelationship of facts in a given graph.

It is the pliable status of the proposition that makes this possible: when properly embedded in discourse, a proposition bears the subjective force of intention, the manifestation of a singularly existing person, and a normative context for its status as a speech act, *along with* its constative, or factual, status. These are the features that make it eventually assimilable to epistemic logic in the first place. But in the name of preserving truth conditions at global level, graph data structures separate out these features and wind up *inverting* the relationship: as propositions are extracted or derived from discourse so as to contribute to knowledge graphs, their singular, manifestational features retreat from view, so as to make assertions amenable to information processing, re-expressed in the neutralizing terms of the predicate calculus.

Social Computing's Mixed Semiotic

The takeaway of all of this discussion is to mark an important tension in philosophy, extending via design into social computing theory: between appeals to the experiential, subjective dimensions of thinking as a basis for shared meaning, and more objectivist ones. Frege, Russell, and the early Wittgenstein took an inter-objective, analytic approach to meaning, elaborating models of rational thought that were based in the special capacities of logic to idealize and individualize entities and their attributes in language. Embedding this power in information technology, knowledge graphs are the latest tool for us to represent, organize, and intervene into the world on scientific terms. Meanwhile, the later

Wittgenstein, Searle, Habermas, and others in the Continental tradition like Husserl and Heidegger placed much greater emphasis on shared experience and the reproduction of language as a living horizon of meaning. Successful linguistic performance here is more focused on grasping consensus meaning in a particular context or form of life.

Pragmatically speaking, one can be entirely satisfied by knowledge graphs on either terms, and I have tried to emphasize their real power in efficiently coordinating life in networked societies. But as was briefly outlined in the introductory chapter, I want to conclude by starting to lay out a third way of thinking, involving Deleuze and Guattari's mixed semiotic. Diagnosing the tension between these two ways of thinking about meaning and reference in terms of a failure to theorize the sub-representative dimensions of language and bodies, Deleuze and Guattari sought to sidestep *both* inter-objective and intersubjective positions—to ground our relationship to signs in the permanent flux of transcendental, qualitative change instead. From their perspective, both formal-analytic and socio-analytic approaches to meaning remain overly committed to a linguistified model of the sign.

Rejecting the usual intersubjective appeals observed in this chapter, they argue that defining the world as entirely conditioned by thought—whether by logic or communication—makes it impossible for the subject to ever be ontogenetically *self-effective* in its reference. In allowing signification to entirely define the world's sense, we trap ourselves in opinion and orthodoxy; and Deleuze and Guattari propose instead that sense is simply not at all in the domain of the subject, signification, or objective reference. Through the work of Danish linguist Louis Hjelmslev, they argue that signification is in fact a product of the dynamic processes of an *abstract machine*, a concept they use to describe the actualization of reality from a virtual sense that sits outside of, but nevertheless produces the conditions of denotation, manifestation and signification. In their altered understanding, sense is not psychological or subjective as in Frege, but is rather an abstract *impersonal field*, to which non-formalized propositions respond as potential solutions to problems, essentially producing a form of questioning that we experience as a 'form of the I', in terms of how some concrete assemblage patterns the virtual, stratifying order from out of hetero-semiotic milieus, to explicate subjects and objects in different ways, and to different effects.

To be a bit more concrete, Frege and Russell's views actually come in for explicit criticism in Deleuze and Guattari's final book, *What Is Philosophy?* They write that

> In its desire to supplant philosophy, logic detaches the proposition from all its psychological dimensions, but clings all the more to the set of postulates that limited and subjected thought to the constraints of a recognition of truth in the proposition.[43]

In other words, Frege's strident disavowal of psychology kept him tacitly captured by its assumptions. Deleuze expresses the problem in similar terms elsewhere when he writes that in relying on the structure of the proposition for meaning,

> One is perpetually referred from the conditioned to the condition, and also from the condition to the conditioned. It ought to have *something unconditioned* capable of assuring a real genesis of denotation and of the other dimensions of the proposition.[44]

One should recognize the Peirce-Frege slot-structure for propositional meaning here as the target of Deleuze's complaint; knowledge graphs represent a technical embedding of precisely the problem he is diagnosing.

But what does he mean by the 'other dimensions' of the proposition? In their radical rethinking of sense, Deleuze and Guattari acknowledge the power of the formalizing isomorphisms between propositions, bodies, and meaning that Peirce, Frege, and Russell established in symbolic logic and mathematics. But they also insist upon bringing back the hetero- and inter-semiotic diversity of the world that their tradition sought to bracket; especially the manifestational singularities of reference and our affective, pre-conscious investments into collectivizing institutions and systems. In an admittedly estranging account, to do so, they push the human being who exchanges logical or socio-communicative meaning from center stage, to no longer be the philosophical main event. Bodies human and otherwise interacting in the world are better understood as dynamic material-semiotic conglomerations that participate and connect with other dynamic material-semiotic conglomerations in intersecting planes of becoming. Linguistic meaning secured by the proposition is but one stabilized element in these dynamic formations, a stratified product of interacting bodies in pragmatic assemblages.

The benefit of such a perspective is to leave off from the dominant subject-object orthodoxies of Western philosophy, which have lately telescoped more deeply into our lives via social computing technology, especially via design approaches committed to the DIKW pyramid laid out in Chapter 1. In the context of social computing, their mixed semiotic approach offers us a vocabulary for 'moving back up' the pyramid in a critical way; to conceive of technologies like knowledge graphs as involving more than just the efficient intersubjective representation of factuality. These representations are dependent upon underlying pragmatic processes by which both people and technology together mark, stratify, and direct signs from out of flows in the world; conjunctions and disjunctions of affect between people, interrelated things, and processes. All too quickly and generically, we call this *data*; Deleuze and Guattari opt instead to describe such processes of stratification and ordering as the capture of part-signs in the production of a content-substance, which acts in reciprocal presupposition to an expression-substance.

I will give a more systematic account of their conceptual apparatus in the next chapter. For now, we can say that, following Frege and Russell, the produced expression-substance of knowledge graphs involves a semiological focus on empirical objects and logical concepts, organized through the slots, or triple structure, described earlier. Socially, this corresponds to a content-substance of bodies in terms of the widespread social application of a universalizing, communicatively rational correctness. The problem is that by remaining satisfied at this level of productive oscillation between semantic condition and socio-rationally conditioned, knowledge graphs fail to account for other relations of power that make this content-expression relation so persistent and effective in the first place. Habermas' criticisms of Frege and his concerns around steering media get us part of the way there, but to get further, we must adopt Deleuze and Guattari's lingo in a more full-throated way.

In their terms, when we take a knowledge graph platform like Google Knowledge Graph or Wolfram Alpha up into our practices, we accede to the technology as a concrete assemblage of enunciation, allowing its machinic action to set up a natural and cultural correspondence between signifiers and signifieds that orients both bodies and language into a semiotic relation, in this case defined as a functive of the predicate calculus. At stake for Deleuze and Guattari in this unthinking move is the status of collective conceptuality itself. Let me rely in conclusion on Bryan Behrenshausen's excellent recent work on informatic assemblages to offer a bit more detail.[45]

Moving backward from the notion of content-substance and expression-substance, content and expression are themselves two intersecting assemblages: groupings of multiplicities, or singular things—in philosophical jargon, *haecceities*—which have been distinguished from the irruptive flows of virtual sense and channeled toward a first-order consistency. Content is the production of an assemblage that channels singular *bodies* into a pragmatic system, interrelating them into existential coherency. Expression is the production of a second assemblage, called a collective assemblage of enunciation—our main point of focus. The latter gives singular *acts and statements about* bodies consistency, determining the discursive rules for their incorporeal transformation—how they may become different as bodies through utterances. Complicating the layers of the DIKW pyramid in IS, which assume data to be an already well-formed semiotic substance given proper form through its divisions into syntax, semantics, and pragmatics, for Deleuze and Guattari, what results instead is a set of substance/form *doublings*.

From the traditional perspective of semantics, the world is made up of rational-objects, and we are stable egos who refer to them together in factual terms, through public assertions submitted to the possibility of their falsity. Such conceptual commitments form a global basis for our social rationality in communication: in science, at work, in bureaucracy, and, of course, over networked media. Yet according to Deleuze and Guattari, this relationality needs to be analyzed still more holistically, as the production of assemblages stages it through the positing of a non-corresponding isomorphism between bodies and statements. Effectively producing, yet only modally grounding identity, the power of a collective assemblage is to harness and produce *variational change,* in the double articulation of a form and substance of content, and a form and substance of expression.

I will have more to say about how this works in the next chapter. For now, it suffices to indicate that form of content and form of expression are multiplicities, produced in the ordering of signs into either determinable or determining materials. Reading the Peirce-Frege-Russell complex around logic as operating as an enunciative assemblage amounts to the determination of subjective sense as content by the determinability of objective reference as expression, made possible via the symbologies of set theory, mathematics, and modus ponens/modus tollens in logic, and secured materially in computing through its asignifying properties across layers of hardware and software infrastructure, all the way to the logic gates at the heart of computers. As we shall see in the next chapter, a more directly social account of this ordering entails a similar substance/form doubling, but this time according to illocutionary speech acts that operate smoothly alongside the knowledge graph paradigm.

Notes

1 See, for example, Davis, *Engines of Logic*; Ceruzzi, *A History of Modern Computing*; Campbell-Kelly et al., *Computer.*
2 O'Regan, *A Brief History of Computing*, 195.
3 Manovich, *The Language of New Media (Leonardo Books) [Paperback] [2002] Lev Manovich*, 223.
4 Date, *Logic and Databases*, 119.
5 Roberts, *The Logic of Reflection*, 64.
6 Carl, *Frege's Theory of Sense and Reference*, 145.
7 Frege, "Sense and Reference," 217.
8 Ibid., 214–15.
9 Russell, "On Denoting."
10 Vellodi, "Diagrammatic Thought: Two Forms Of Constructivism In C.S. Peirce And Gilles Deleuze," 81.
11 Atkin, *Peirce*, 145.
12 Atkin, *Peirce.*
13 Ibid., 146.
14 Peirce, *Collected Papers of Charles Sanders Peirce*, 229.
15 Liszka, *A General Introduction to the Semeiotic of Charles Sanders Peirce.*, 42.
16 Ruthrof, *Semantics and the Body*, 49.
17 Deleuze and Guattari, *A Thousand Plateaus*, 531.

18 Rorty, *Essays on Heidegger and Others*, 341.
19 Wittgenstein et al., *Tractatus Logico-Philosophicus*, 41.
20 Friedman, Michael, "Coordination, Constitution and Convention: The Evolution of the A Priori in Logical Empiricism," 94.
21 Codd, "A Relational Model of Data for Large Shared Data Banks."
22 Date, "The Birth of the Relational Model, Part 1."
23 Berners-Lee, Hendler, and Lassila, Ora, "The Semantic Web."
24 Robinson, Webber, and Eifrem, *Graph Databases*, 8.
25 Blair, *Wittgenstein, Language and Information*, 17.
26 DeLanda, *A New Philosophy of Society*, 10.
27 Ibid.
28 See Sowa, *Knowledge Representation*.
29 Tauberer, "JoshData/Rdfabout."
30 Feenberg, *Questioning Technology*, 175.
31 Ibid., 170.
32 Habermas, *The Theory of Communicative Action*, 277.
33 Habermas, *On the Pragmatics of Communication*, 311.
34 Ibid., 313.
35 Longino, *The Fate of Knowledge*, 203.
36 See, for example, Iliadis, "A Black Art."
37 Mingers, *Realising Systems Thinking*, 144.
38 Shirky, "Shirky: Ontology Is Overrated—Categories, Links, and Tags."
39 Cramer, "Failing Universal Classification Schemes from Aristotle to the Semantic Web."
40 Benkler, *The Wealth of Networks*.
41 Habermas, *The Theory of Communicative Action*, 275.
42 Feenberg, "From Critical Theory of Technology to the Rational Critique of Rationality," 18.
43 Deleuze and Guattari, *What Is Philosophy?*, 139.
44 Deleuze, *The Logic of Sense*, 19.
45 Behrenshausen, "Information in Formation: Power and Agency in Contemporary Informatic Assemblages."

3 The Performatively Formatted Subject

What can people do in your app? People can TASTE an object.
—Creating Custom Open Graph Stories,
Facebook for Developers documentation

In the last chapter, I suggested that in its reconfiguration into a more sentence-like format, knowledge graph technology is bringing automated reasoning more intimately into our lives. Companies like Google, IBM, Apple, and Microsoft are especially keen to facilitate our everyday communicative activities through their vast webs of factuality, promoting their graph services across our devices as a new type of artificial intelligence. On the one hand, the turn to this technology is helping to resolve complicated new dynamics of meaning coordination across diverse and overlapping contexts. But on the other, it is changing how we think together through its automatisms, potentially leading to the increased rationalization and commodification of discourse itself. Early critics of knowledge graphs expressed concerns over their universalist aspirations. When we ground social interaction around knowledge on a mapping of reality that is so heavily based in the disembedded assertion, we fail to technically register the more practical and contextual features of collective thinking—things like disagreement and dissensus, obligation and status, delineated roles, and group dynamics.

In other words, there are *performative* dimensions of knowledge use and communication that travel alongside our reliance on logic, which are necessary for connecting disembedded facts to the social norms that secure their effectivity in utterance. Some will recognize in this gap between assertion and utterance certain conceptual debates that followed the twentieth-century linguistic turn, and over time led to some basic divergences in perspective between the analytic and Continental traditions in philosophy. Today, the battle lines between them are less sharply drawn, but generally, we can say that where thinkers in the analytic tradition have tended to ground meaning in empirical factuality and logical form, those in the Continental have done so through appeals to phenomenal experience, interpretation, and dialogue; especially as these pertain to cultural embeddedness, or what Martin Heidegger called 'being-in-the-world'.

Both traditions have been influential in information systems (IS) design. Having focused on knowledge graphs and their principal basis in the analytic tradition in the last chapter, in this one, I turn to phenomenologically informed sociology, as it has been taken up in social computing, to influence thinking around today's *social graph*-based platforms. Developing an account of what I will call a performatively formatted subject, I lay out some of the ways that practitioners in the field have reconciled philosophies of social embedding and situated language-use to the formal requirements of software code.

Theoretical connections between Continental philosophy and contemporary platforms like Facebook and Twitter are mostly latent, but significant, having evolved out of 1980s research in computer-supported cooperative work (CSCW) to influence latter-day Web 2.0-style tools and their latest iterations in today's social media. In contrast to a more objectivist emphasis on logical idealization, phenomenological approaches to social computing reflect what some experts in the field call a *subjectivist* paradigm for data modeling. Labeled neo-humanist in the field of critical IS theory, it is a paradigm based in the idea that

> The solidarity of our friends and associates comforts us all and in return we are willing to make adjustments to our own opinions until a common basis of agreement is reached. If the primary interest is one of achieving consensual mutual understanding and agreement, then one must acknowledge the other person as a partner for human interaction rather than an object of manipulation.[1]

To make sense of how neo-humanist approaches inform social graphs, I lay out three core intellectual influences upon their development. The first is the philosopher John Searle's ideas about illocutionary point and force, elaborated in his performative classification of speech acts. The second involves the formal pragmatics of conversation, as laid out in ethnomethodology by Harold Garfinkel, Erving Goffman, and Harvey Sacks. The third, and probably most direct, influence upon the capacities of social graph platforms is social network analysis, developed over the twentieth century in analytic sociology by people like JL Moreno, Dorwin Cartwright, Clyde Mitchell, and Harrison White. The important takeaway for the chapter will be to show that social graph platforms appropriate these various conceptualizations of sociality in order to establish calculable formalizations of mutual accountability, alliance, influence, and esteem. To mark the connections between social theory and IS design, I pair each of the three influences to some key people responsible for their implementation in social computing: Terry Winograd and Fernando Flores in the case of Searle; Lucy Suchman in the case of ethnomethodology, and, most briefly, in the case of social network analysis, the computer scientist Alex "Sandy" Pentland.

Along the way, it will be important to keep in mind that today's social media represent a vast expansion of the subjectivist paradigm. Recalling Jürgen Habermas' concept of steering media in the last chapter, neo-humanist-style social graph platforms like Facebook and Twitter have reached such a scale and intensity of global influence that we are over-due to unpack their technicity, while not taking on faith their original basis in the collegiality and mutual understanding of small-group office work. At the same time, it will be important to temper overly-simplistic criticisms of social media; that their coordination effects are somehow intrinsically distorting simply because they involve a quantification of the 'lifeworld'. Phenomenological and social-constructionist approaches to meaning and context that lie at the heart of the subjectivist paradigm have been a watershed for creative global communication over the past few decades. But we now find this same paradigm, nominally rooted in the basic solidarity of friendship, to be increasingly co-implicated with much wider economic, political, and population-governing systems of control; so it may be time to theorize limits to the paradigm.

The upshot then will be to think through a performatively formatted subject by reexamining a rather traditional concern, lately framed in a more thoroughly sociotechnical way: the relationship between self and society. Social computing develops rich theoretical relays between, on the one hand, a phenomenological perspective toward the social at the level of user interfaces that have been built according to a design focus on shared meaning in embodied, situated contexts; and on the other, a social-scientific perspective at the level of information processing, which produces a more positivist lawfulness of *social facts* about abstract pop-ulations. From Adolphe Quetelet and Auguste Comte to Max Weber and Émile Durkheim, social science has always understood sociality in quantified and statistical terms. The difference is that its commitments now come embedded more intimately into the discursive fabric of soci-eties through social computing in ways that foster the ongoing modeling of social order in real time, as a kind of social physics—modern graph theory developed alongside Richard Feynmann's perturbation theory in quantum mechanics, for example.

To ground discussion around this tension between analytical social science and more phenomenological perspectives, I begin with a thumb-nail history of one of social computing's more popular affordances: collaborative filtering (CF). Initial designs for CF developed out of a mix-ture of web, email, and Usenet services in the early 1990s as a strategy for coordinating people together around information, music, and mov-ies. Managing information in terms of friendships, social connections, and tacit preference, CF systems establish forms of datafication that, in addition to assertions of fact, involve what Searle called illocutionary acts—like the expression of attitude, the declaration of friendship, or the marking of taste and preference. Early systems achieved this fit between computation and social performativity using algorithms like *k*-nearest neighbor, which are still in use today and so helpful for foreshadowing later discussions of machine learning in the next chapter. Most will recognize CF systems as helping us to find novel entities of interest on the basis of expressing what we already prefer—whether the entity in question is a consumer product, a new friend, a band, or a potential mate.

The chapter concludes by once again centering on the relationship between graph technology, philosophy, semiosis, and collective behavior. Pulling together various strands—social physics modeled according to directed graphs, Searle's social ontology of performatives, and points where phenomenology has influenced social computing design—I eventually turn to a further elaboration of Gilles Deleuze and Félix Guattari's mixed semiotic. As with the chapter on knowledge graphs, social graphs presuppose a linguistic, signifier/signified relation to the technology, with stable subjects and objects. But as was suggested in the conclusion of the last chapter, this relation can be more holistically understood as semiotically constructed from out of the reciprocal presupposition of a plane of content and a place of expression. This time, social-constructionist insights about what it means to think and act together subjectively at the level of interface design fit together with functionalist and calculative accounts of social network analysis at the level of information processing through the mediating figure of the graph, thereby setting the two planes into operational modulation.

The Rise of CF

Since Douglas Engelbart's first experimental hypertext-style systems and the early days of the Internet, collaborative approaches to information have been an intrinsic part of computing environments. Even Vannevar Bush's 1945 *Atlantic* article on futuristic information devices describes a conversation between two friends who use his hypothetical Memex machine to print off electronic 'trails' of information that they can share.[2] Researchers working with modern CF systems typically reference their conception much later though, often pointing to an experimental groupware email program called Tapestry.[3] Produced at Xerox's famed Palo Alto Research Center, Tapestry's original design evoked a now well-worn motif: the crisis of information overload, which better software tools were designed to address.

Working in the early 1990s, Tapestry's architects were looking for a way to cope with increasing volumes of personal electronic mail and began to work out a pre-filtration architecture for incoming streams of private messages, listserv posts, and news clipping services. The idea was that to mitigate the flow of information, people should be able to establish sorting criteria that pegged incoming messages at different levels of salience or importance. Today's standard email applications take such features for granted, offering sophisticated filtering rules for when messages arrive. In its time though, Tapestry was novel for 'banking attention' by allowing users to set up more personalized foci for their incoming emails. Filters threw certain messages to the top of a daily pile, while letting others of less immediate concern sit to one side, rolling the affordances of a relational database, a search engine, and a communications archive into a single system.

Tapestry's important innovation was to store separate sets of *annotations* about items as they arrived on the email server. Members could filter items collaboratively according to various contextually marked prioritizations, enabling a metadata structure for workgroups to emerge. If I believed that when a colleague marked an item as important that I too would find it important, a filter could be set up to express this relation, subsequently flagging her prioritized items in my own inbox automatically. Similarly, if a colleague annotated an incoming document as related to a topic of interest while also giving it a measure of endorsement of 'four out of five', then a filter based on our shared interest would bring this item more quickly to my attention. By treating typical data fields in emails—date sent, subject, and recipient—as collaborative rather than private, Tapestry helped to coordinate flows of information more effectively. With users, keywords, endorsement ratings, and time horizons all receiving objective definition in socially shared metadata, the system was pioneering for establishing shared affinities, interests, and tastes as governing principles for organization.

Tapestry had its limitations. For one, the system required too much user effort to function effectively. Between elaborate query construction and the need to manually 'seed' Tapestry with many endorsements in order for it to be at all useful, the system was seen by some to withdraw attention rather than bank it. This initial seeding of opinion would remain an issue for subsequent CF systems like Netflix or Amazon's Recommended for You; people won't use a system unless it can give them aggregated pointers to novel information, but a system can't do that until enough users get involved. This challenge of initial data sparsity, dubbed the 'cold start' problem by developers, has made it much more likely that systems will observe user activity passively, inferring relationships of taste and preference from behavior rather than requiring that they be actively input by users. Deployed at a global scale, this turn to passive observation continues to provoke deep concerns around corporate and state surveillance via social graph.

A second limitation was that Tapestry focused by design on 'user-to-user' similarity relationships. Deriving these relationships is computationally intense, requiring constant recalculation as a system scales up, with users befriending new users all the time—an issue to which Facebook's engineers would certainly attest, with its now more than 1.86 billion active users. An earlier large-scale example was again

Amazon's recommendation engine, which scaled much more effectively to the online environment once its developers switched focus away from user-to-user similarity and on to item-to-item similarity—discovering generalized patterns of taste around the books and movies themselves, irrespective of any relationships marked between friends on the system, in a further turn to passive observation. The Tapestry system was groundbreaking work in spite of these limitations, and was later influential upon enterprise-level collaborative systems, like Lotus Notes.

There are three other projects that bear brief mention alongside Tapestry as formative of today's social graph-based environments. All of them implement in software the basic conditions of a social-scientific interval scale to define and measure attitude (think 'strongly agree' to 'strongly disagree') toward some data entity. Paul Resnick et al. created a more distributed CF system called GroupLens, which focused on the interval scale rating of the quality of news articles on Usenet.[4] The platform used ratings from good to bad to collaboratively mark worthy items floating amid the dreck of advertising and bickering that 1990s Netnews had become. GroupLens took the novel step of having an open and distributed architecture of rating servers called Better Bit Bureaus, to which any news reader could connect across the Internet. Ratings were made and received by whoever was reading news with a compatible client, and while there was still an affordance for linking up to friends, like the other systems, it was ultimately indifferent to who was rating what. Aggregating all of this activity, GroupLens made statistical predictions as to what a user might also find relevant by comparing previous reading-and-rating activity to anyone who'd read and rated similar items.

Focused on films rather than news, the videos@bellcore rating community was constructed with similar motivations. Participants in Will Hill et al.'s video recommender system emailed the service to get back an automated message, consisting of a list of five hundred movies for them to rate.[5] By putting 1–10 ratings next to films they'd seen, along with categorizations like 'must-see' and 'not interested' for those they hadn't, users automatically generated a pool for computing recommendations. From there, the system correlated new users into a subset of existing users with similar tastes, with users also able to specify friends and colleagues to whom they would like to be compared. An early example of functionality now taken for granted on streaming media services like Netflix, people could express a 1–10 scale interest in overall genres of films too. Like Netflix, rating films on the Bellcore system sometimes generated spot-on recommendations; other times, choices seemed absurdly mismatched.

Finally, work on the popular Ringo system by Upendra Shardanand and Pattie Maes followed a similar strategy for rating music, the first in a long line of CF-driven services recognizable today in Spotify, last. fm, and Google Play.[6] The MIT developers of Ringo went on to found

Firefly Inc., one of the first major web-based CF systems to attract substantial financing from major corporations. Companies sought both to license the technology and to advertise on the Firefly website; Madison Avenue advertising firms were keen to mine the emerging, more personalized demographics that it had begun to catalog.

The kNN Algorithm

Before moving on to a more philosophically framed discussion of social graphs, it's worth describing how algorithms used in these early systems calculated social affinity and the similarity of taste. The very latest CF systems combine layers of statistical regression analysis into multi-staged strategies called ensemble or deep learning. For sake of simplicity, it can be easier to focus on just one of these techniques, illustrative of the basic process. The k-nearest-neighbor (kNN) algorithm is memory-based as opposed to model-based, meaning that rather than trying to extract a formal model of that activity that can be applied to all users, the algorithm repeatedly traverses an entire database of user activity, comparing and calculating taste, social connection, and preference in an ongoing fashion. Memory-based CF platforms like videos@bellcore and Ringo underwent constant recalibration through the application of algorithmic technique to existing user-item relations.

Data entries read much like knowledge graph triples, but rather than model relations of constative fact (e.g. "Justin Trudeau is the Prime Minister of Canada"), CF systems are designed more with an eye toward modeling performative relations that predicatively express *attitude toward* some content, of the type "Celia S. watched the *The Lion King* and rated it 3/5." The underlying materiality remains the same, but conceptual emphasis subtly shifts from epistemic assertion to performative agency, as CF systems store and circulate what people have done, what they prefer, and with whom they associate, modeling these ongoing actions as edges between nodes in a directed graph. Whether the units in question are books, public events, consumer goods, websites, or other people, there are three basic stages for calculating recommendations: neighborhood formation, opinion aggregation, and finally, recommendation.[7]

Though the term neighborhood has the mathematical sense of a topological feature space, we can see the whole set of people recorded on a given system as like a town or city, with each neighborhood consisting of a unique sub-community of those who share at least a few similar attitudes or attributes. Each user must have at least some items that have been co-rated between them to occupy a neighborhood; absent overlap, there is no way to score similarity. For every pair of users the system asks, of the entire set of items rated by either user A or B, what proportion of those items have been rated by both? Like a Venn diagram of two people who have overlapping zones of 'friends with', 'liked', or 'have watched', what is the union of their intersection? Graph theory facilitates the efficient and exhaustive pairwise comparison of all relations in the system, where, initially, the actual strength of ratings given by individuals is of less concern than the simple fact that they have rated similar things.

To control for analytic weakness, statistical tactics get introduced alongside the initial calculation of similarity. Two users may have a high similarity coefficient as a result of each having rated just a few items in the system; were they to go on rating a more representative total number of items, similarity might rapidly drop off. To address this potential unreliability, researchers introduce the idea of a threshold: if two compared users don't have enough co-rated items between them, then their similarity score will be statistically dampened until they do. Another weighting focuses on variance within a CF system: greater weight is given to those items that provoke strong responses in the overall system, whether good or bad. The reasoning goes that if there is a high level of disagreement around an item, then it represents an especially dramatic exemplar of taste in action. Controversy around fake news items circulating on social media during the 2016 US election can be seen as at least partly a reflection of this basic feature of CF systems; items can surface into significance precisely *because* they provoke such a calculable flurry of taste discrimination. Statistical strategies like these are necessary though to tune a CF system so that it can eventually provide useful results.

In a second step, CF systems select already-rated items as useful variables for regression analysis to predictively focus attention on a nearby neighborhood of other items or users that have not yet been encountered. The rank of what one might be interested in, in the neighborhood of what one is currently observing, is based on the weighted average of ratings performed by similar users in the past. In some cases, rank is passively derived from activity around an item: users around me bought this book, or put it on their wish list, so the system infers endorsement. Other times it is actively derived: some user in my neighborhood fed the system by giving an item a 'thumbs up', or by using the same keyword as I did, to find it. Statistical tactics vary in this step, too; in some cases, only the user's most similar neighbors contribute to the average rating, while in others, *any* nearby neighbor that has previously rated the item will contribute to its significance. The latter guarantees that all predictions will be made, even though they will be made up of ratings provided by only modestly similar users.[8] The whole mathematical process by which this average-weighted influence is derived gives the kNN algorithm its prefix: *k* is an open variable standing for however many neighbors beyond one are being consulted as independent variables, in order to derive a coefficient of similarity.

In the final step where a user acts upon some recommendation—putting something in a shopping cart, applying a hashtag they've seen before, or following a link—the system shifts from the transmission of prior taste to the reception of future taste. The user has been presented with a list of information-objects that they may find useful, based on the average weighted response of people like them. Selecting an item from that list—voting up a comment deemed salient, messaging a potential mate to say hi, or agreeing to attend a concert—causes the system to register that selection as *itself* a useful unit of performativity. In other words, preferential selection of entities by people moving through the system constantly feeds back into its overall structure, conjoining map and territory.

In the computer science literature, the kNN algorithm as I have just described it is a bit of a mouthful: it is a non-parametric, lazy learning algorithm. Non-parametric means that its processing makes no advance assumptions as to how the information contained within a corpus of data should be ranked or distributed. CF systems are auto-conditioning in this respect; they allow the ongoing, internal dynamics of participation to train and guide subsequent effectiveness. The designation 'lazy learning' is connected to this idea: memory-based means that the kNN algorithm avoids making overarching causal inferences about what's 'really going on'. Newer machine-learning algorithms are model-based, or trained to make choice more efficient as they go along according to certain designed criteria.

In the case of kNN, training and testing data never really disconnect. Through our continuous collective participation, information-objects circulating among individuals in a social graph are never definitively analyzed, only resynthesized; persisting as a field to be traversed endomorphically over and over. This requires designers at companies like Facebook to think in sophisticated ways about scale and temporality; for just how long should prior choices influence future ones? If for too long, then the system becomes overly static and biased against new items. But if prior choice fails to affect future choice for a sufficiently long period of time, then important historical patterns, upon which useful collective judgments are based, will too quickly disappear from view. As new users join and rate items, everyone's prior choice needs to slide around in just the right way, hitting a sweet spot that accommodates conservative-but-useful change of perspective brought on by new inputs.

Discretizing Performativity

CF systems like videos@bellcore and Ringo illustrate some of the ways that early social computing designs sought to adapt statistical strategies from social science to the emerging communicative context of the Internet and web, by harnessing the dynamics of what Durkheim called our *collective consciousness*, into prototypical social graphs. Durkheim understood the latter in terms of what he called mechanical and organic solidarity: what makes us all the same according to the (sometimes repressive) regulatory powers of society, and what makes us different under those conditions of sameness, which can often lead to more flexible, creative, and cooperative interaction. He wrote that each one of us carries these two consciousnesses in our selves:

> one that we share in common with our group in its entirety, which is consequently not ourselves, but society living and acting within us; the other that, on the contrary, represents us alone in what is personal and distinctive about us, what makes us an individual.[9]

Effects between the two became more pronounced, he argued, as individuals fell into greater contact with one another through the increasing densification of social ties.

Durkheim saw that societies based in mechanical solidarity, with everyone sharing the same beliefs, were giving way to those defined by organic solidarity, where people become more inclined to think for themselves. His emphasis on these collective ties that bind, yet enable, the individual has since been a cornerstone for an entire structural-functional tradition in sociology, researching the underlying lawfulness of societies. In his early studies of crowd behavior that prefigure what we would today call *virality*, Durkheim's contemporary Gustave Le Bon took things from a slightly different angle, theorizing the relationship between collective ties, flows of information, and the *loss* of individual identity.[10] Later sociologists like Paul Lazarsfeld and Robert Merton sought to theorize the social in similar terms of the relays between the micro and macro-scale, in conversation with Durkheim and other twentieth-century 'grand theorists' of social structure, like Talcott Parsons.

CF systems can be understood as part of this lineage, where modern structural sociology offers a conceptualization of the social as a complex and interconnected system and sees personal behavior as in tension with adaptation to an environment, the pursuit of collective goals, and the integration of groups along lines of solidarity. CF platforms are effectively an instance of computational social science research, possessing an analytic sensitivity to the connections and distinctions between the micro and macro. Combining empirical social network analysis and complexity science as ways of simulating sociality, these practices now travel more generally under the contemporary name of *multi-agent modeling*. CF systems share an affinity with these practices in that they represent a powerful tool for thinking about, as Tiziana Terranova writes, " ... any informational milieu where each point is directly connected to its immediate neighbours (on whom it acts and to whom it reacts); and is indirectly, but no less effectively, affected by the movements of the whole."[11]

Whether one is dealing with populations of real people on a social networking platform or virtual agents in a computational social science model, sociality in multi-agent modeling relies on the exchange of some symbolic token. Like the factual assertion in knowledge graphs, there must be some computable unit of representation that the model can rely upon to activate its underlying population dynamics so as to model change and see emergent social patterns over time. For instance, in the case of biologically themed multi-agent simulations, the unit transferred among individuals is typically styled as a resource, like food or energy— a popular open source 'artificial society' modeler in the 1990s was called *Sugarscape*.[12] In the case of modeling market dynamics, goods or stocks are the modeled unit of exchange; and when simulating crowd panic, units are symbolized as disturbing messages passing from agent to agent, inducing them to patterns of self-interested flight in simulated, built environments. The overall approach reflects long-standing ties between social science and ethology, where nineteenth-century works on the social patterning of ants and bees were later influential upon Moreno's work in sociometry.

What does this have to do with today's social graphs? Today's social science increasingly relies on the continuous data production of social graphs like Facebook, Netflix, and Amazon for actual behavioral data, standing in place of interactions between simulated agents. Social graph platforms deploy the *informational entities we seek online* as their symbolic tokens of exchange while also constructing performative exchange units specific to their needs, such as 'likes', 'emotions', stars, 'thumbs-up', or other forms of 'virtual karma'. If knowledge graphs represent a more rationalist approach to data, expressing unit entities in terms of their inductive and deductive interrelations of fact, then CF systems and social graphs place greater emphasis on intersubjectivity, the performative features of semiosis, and the role that resemblance as *social consensus* plays in a given context.

This in mind, the more detailed differences between knowledge and social graphs can be grasped by once again turning to their underlying basis in philosophy. As suggested in the last chapter, Gottlob Frege was an important representative of the objectivist tradition: like Charles Sanders Peirce, he developed notational strategies for logic and came to similar conclusions about its impersonal role in reason. But as an eventual consequence of how the linguistic turn developed in philosophy, Frege's ideas about language and signs were subsequently opened up to critique and reconfiguration in ways ultimately relevant for understanding social graphs in comparison to knowledge graphs as a structured data technique. Frege's interpreters and critics were especially concerned to retrieve the underlying language *context* or *situation* of meaning, which seemed to disappear in his overly logical idealizations of the sign.

As already mentioned, Ludwig Wittgenstein, JL Austin, and Searle are important figures in this respect; so too were phenomenological thinkers like Edmund Husserl, Heidegger, Habermas, and, specific to computing,

the Heideggerean pragmatist Hubert Dreyfus. Over time, their philosophical critiques of the logical idealization of language came to ground the
neo-humanist paradigm in IS, offering practitioners a set of alternative,
more subjectivist and existential ideas for thinking through the relationship between data, meaning, and social order. To help make sense of the
connections between this paradigm and today's platforms, I turn now to
three major theoretical influences on the development of what we might
shorthand as the *discretization* of performativity online; ways in which
designers and practitioners formalized subjectivity, via markers of preference, social affinity, attitude, role, and belief, so as to make them amenable to computation by directed graph. They are (1) the use of Searle's
speech act pragmatics in the work of Winograd and Flores, (2) Suchman's
reliance upon the formal pragmatics of conversation analysis, developed
in ethnomethodology, and (3) a reliance upon strategies from analytic
sociology to formalize the social 'ties that bind' in calculable ways.

Searle and the Language/Action Perspective

As intimated at the beginning of the chapter, systematic approaches
to collaboration and conversation over computers have been around
for much longer than one might think. Inventor-engineer Engelbart
and his team developed social computing strategies as far back as the
1960s, for example, building early prototype systems for sharing files,
computer-supported meetings, email, and online communities. Their
work stood in marked contrast to the more rationalistic approaches to
computing of the era, helping to catalyze a more design-centered approach
to IS while also laying down certain foundational idioms for personal
computing.

Research by Winograd and Flores in the field of CSCW represents
another important milestone in the articulation of computers as social
tools, as expressed systematically in their 1986 book *Understanding
Computers and Cognition*. Their work is historically significant for first
proposing the incorporation of concepts from phenomenology, neurobiol-
ogy, self-organizing systems theory, and the philosophy of language into
new designs for IS. The work was framed as a way of concretely transforming the communicative and coordinating practices of office workgroups. Against the rationalist tradition in computing that had largely
taken its pragmatics from people like Wittgenstein, Bertrand Russell, and
Peirce, Winograd and Flores conceived of thinking and understanding
as more socially based, arising from an individual's "committed participation in mutually oriented patterns of behavior that are embedded in a
socially shared background of concerns, actions and beliefs."[13] It was on
this basis that they developed an approach to performative social graphs.

Heidegger's approach to ontology strongly influences their view,
a central commitment of his philosophy being that relations between

individuals and things in the world cannot be properly accounted for in terms of separate, dualistic domains of subject and object that come to relate according to the rules of valid reference in language. Rather, our relationship to things always also involves ongoing interpretation and the contours of existence, as these stem from a practical embedding: our being-in-the-world. Phenomenological significance as a ground for the sign is different than logic in that it is an always contextually and historically involved *event* of reference: a singularity marking something-as-itself. Complicating Frege's vision of sense and reference, Josef Simon writes, for example, that,

> A sign is [...] not an 'appearance' (re-presentation) of a thing, but rather a temporal phenomenon. In it there does not appear 'something,' understood as something behind the signs, but rather in it there is neutralized the thought of a something-in-itself in the understanding of the sign.[14]

In other words, signs have a situated, hermeneutic sense and not just a formal, symbolic one, stemming from a life being lived with others in a *world*, which Heidegger took to be a mixture of equipment and place through which meaning is disclosed rather than inferred. Language is still a fundamental component of the phenomenological perspective, but cannot be so readily idealized into factual reference as the exclusive bearer of signs. Automobile turn signals and storm clouds alike indicated for Heidegger not just the phenomena of language patterns observed between subjects referring to objects, but also to the very orientation of our being within an environment. In his own words,

> A sign is not a Thing which stands to another Thing in the relationship of indicating; it is rather an item of equipment which explicitly raises a totality of equipment into our circumspection [...] A sign to mark something indicates what one is 'at' at any time. Signs always indicate primarily 'wherein' one lives, where one's concern dwells, what sort of involvement there is with something.[15]

Winograd and Flores were among the first to encourage system designers to see computers as just such a form of equipment. Through affordances developed in software and interface, computers were, for them, a platform upon which our concern dwells, mediating our prejudices, affective responses to one another, and our discerning judgment through signs in irreducibly social and public ways. "Listening for our possibilities in a world in which we already dwell," they write, "allows us to speak and to elicit the cooperation of others."[16] Their driving concern was to adapt these ideas to the material-semiotic formalizations of software through the figure of the graph, thereby operationalizing a hermeneutic approach to reference.

To do so, Winograd and Flores turned to Searle's philosophy of speech acts. Searle studied under the ordinary language philosopher Austin, who famously argued in his book *How to Do Things With Words* that over and above their idealized propositional content as assertions, sentences also *effect situations* and *do* things in the tumult of practical social affairs. A similar criticism of language philosophy emerged in the later work of Wittgenstein, who, in rejecting his earlier approach, came to believe that one simply could not theorize the meaning of words separately from their use. Trained in the Fregean tradition, Austin and, later, his pupil Searle argued that a focus on propositional validity highlighted just one of the socially normative features of language. Alongside correct reference, the things we say to one another are inevitably also inflected by the point and force of *illocutionary acts:* what effect does a speaker intend to produce in making an utterance? Are they posing a question to the hearer, issuing a command, or making a request?[17]

All of these circumstances point to the underlying context of utterances, suggesting that there were important social dimensions latent in sense and reference. Building on Austin's work, Searle laid out a new strategy toward meaning, which assumed that propositional content also involved mutual conditions of satisfaction and sincerity—what he called felicity conditions—as well as the possibility for communicative breakdown and repair in a given language context. Searle went on to develop an entire typology of these performative features of language, and in their work, Winograd and Flores explicitly rely on it to formalize social interactions for computer-supported group environments.

An early implementation of their Language/Action Perspective called *The Coordinator* demonstrated that nodes in a directed graph could indeed be understood as speakers and hearers, making and responding to performative utterances in networks of recurring *conversations for action.* Office work, they argued, consisted largely in regularized speech acts that Searle called *directives* and *commissives:* respectively, utterances that try to get an addressee to perform some action through a request or order and those that involve eliciting, accepting, or rejecting promises to act in the future. Computer-based collaborative systems could efficiently manage these conversations by organizing them into directed graphs, producing a horizon for anticipating possible breakdowns, and heading them off through datafication on illocutionary terms. Such a system would afford office groups better coping strategies for dealing with complex decision making by marking and monitoring the ongoing state of their responsibilities to one another in the system.

The finite categories laid out in Searle's speech act theory offered a fitting means for automating the back-and-forth dynamics of shared tasks, allowing users to leave behind semiotic traces of mutual responsibility in the system itself, focusing the collective actions of an office workgroup into conjunctive flows of accountability. Such a system would be more effective than focusing on propositional content, they wrote, because "A person working within an organization is always concerned with questions such as 'What is missing?', 'What needs to be done?', and 'Where do I stand in terms of my obligations and opportunities?'"[18] Most will recognize some of the ways that thinking about data in this way now come baked into modern email clients, with their integrated to-do, meeting, and read receipt features, as well as in more recent social media platforms designed specifically for work, like Pyrus and Slack.

The Coordinator's original context was collaboration in an office setting, but it's not hard to see how Winograd and Flores' ideas have been influential upon today's social networking platforms. Following Searle's ideas about illocutionary point and force, graph edges in any social graph platform now ostensibly act as presuppositions of attitude and intent. Social networking platforms like Facebook afford the electronic expression between speakers and hearers of Searlesian declarative speech acts, as when we publicly note friendship and kinship ties, use emotional expressives (such as 'likes', stars, and 'thumbs-up'), make intersubjective requests or promises to act, or engage in moments of counter-negotiation, like posing a question or declining requests for friendship or attendance. Analogous to knowledge graphs, where the outcome of their action is new information achieved through factual premises and a drawn conclusion, in the world of *The Coordinator*, entities constructed for social graph calculation are people and their performative *declarations*, which follow Searle's pragmatics in their formatting as calculable units that "bring about the correspondence between the propositional content of the speech act and reality, as illustrated by the example of pronouncing a couple married."[19]

Situated Actions and Ethnomethodology

A second influence upon socially structured data graphs is ethnomethodology, a school of thought developed mainly by the sociologist Garfinkel. Again in response to dominant analytic accounts of language and logic of his era, Garfinkel argued that people already possessed a capacity for practical reasoning as a feature of their phenomenological involvement in everyday conversational activities. Rational accountability need not be articulated to logic because it already happens in an ongoing way between 'members'—a term Garfinkel deployed to cover both individuals and larger social entities, like institutions and organizations—who engage with one another in the formulation of utterances. By formulation, Garfinkel meant that any conversation directed toward collective action in a social context involves taking up the situated features *of* that conversation; characterizing, correcting, summarizing, and explicating them as they unfold. Members perform, observe, and report on formulations in an ongoing and contingent fashion according to the in situ particulars of occasions of discourse as they accomplish shared understanding together, practically.

The upshot was to render the role of formal logic in language somewhat superfluous; in its place, ethnomethodology laid out what Jeff Coulter calls an endogenous logic.[20] Because correctness was completely immanent to the creation and reproduction of social facts in the conversational process itself, Garfinkel argued, performativity could not admit of stable categories in the manner that Searle had proposed. The situated, performative features of language resist such classifications because they always occur according to the permanent and necessary ambiguity of indexical expressions and shifters—words like I, this, she, here, and now. Steering through formulations in this way is nevertheless rational, Garfinkel argued, because doing so remedies for a given group of members the problem of distinguishing between objective and indexical expressions, always with an eye to substituting the objective for the indexical.[21]

In other words, social intercourse is about objectively specifying the people and things around us to generate social facts not through sharing the apparatus of the predicate calculus, but by trying to get to the bottom of each other's social groupings conversationally: figuring out what people *mean* exactly when they gesture indexically to things. The point is to figure out what a group will accept as a transformation of that indexical reference into an objective one, to realize a worldview through the ongoing categorization of the things that are in it. Similar to Searle's speech act theory, ethnomethodology has played an important and unorthodox role in shaping how we think about social computing. It is in part thanks to the challenges that ethnomethodology posed to conventional social science that human-computer interaction (HCI) now places much greater emphasis on cultural specificity and notions of participatory design, for example. Garfinkel's ideas were systematically articulated to HCI by Suchman in her 1987 text *Plans and Situated Actions.*

Like Winograd and Flores, Suchman proposed a conceptual turn to ethnomethodology as a critical response to a then-dominant objectivist paradigm. But she also later relied on the approach as a foil for a long journal debate prosecuted in the mid-1990s where Suchman actually took Winograd and Flores to task over their Language/Action Perspective and its reliance on Searlesian speech acts. Formatting 'conversations for action' according to the classifications of illocutionary force, she argued, was not just socially rational; it was socially rationalizing. She argued that the approach risked enacting managerial control and the domestication of utterances in organizational life in ways that were potentially disempowering for workers. Her concern was that the use of Searle's classifications wound up conflating "the simplicity of the category with the subtlety and complexity of the phenomenon categorized."[22] Twenty years on, we can still recognize her concerns at play in social media, as when the public laments the circulation of fake news based on our overreliance on the declarative functions of liking and sharing, or when Facebook users complain about the lack of a 'dislike' button, recently addressed by the company's turn to a wider range of performative emojis.

Some working in computer-supported cooperative work later expressed unease around the uptake of ethnomethodology into social computing because of its seeming indifference to social-scientific generalization. With the need to formulate some material-semiotic connection between sociality and a generalized rational unit of exchange, under the terms of ethnomethodology, it is difficult to generate working theories about the overall role that context plays in social interaction. Remarking on the later wave of ethnographic research in CSCW that sought to better understand the role of cultural specificity in social computing design, Victor Kaptelinin and Bonnie Nardi write, for example, that "We cannot merely relate accounts of endless detail with no summarizing, shaping, transforming tools at hand. We need the power to compare, abstract, and generalize."[23] At this point, we are nearly in a position to see how these concerns wind up largely addressed by socio-metric approaches to performatively structured social graphs. Social network theory seems to have stepped in to fill the void, becoming a de facto strategy for dealing with the conceptual difficulties of generalizing across social contexts. Stepping beyond the speech act pragmatics deployed in Winograd and Flores' *The Coordinator*, social network analysis has become a powerful calculative means for showing connections of acquaintance, conversation, and affinity of belief, and now functions as the main strategy for processing computable edge relations in modern social graphs.

But before moving on, it's worth noting a connection between knowledge graphs and social graphs in terms of how ethnomethodology conceived of knowledge production. The power of Garfinkel's original formulation, later expanded by Warren Sacks into an entire method of conversation analysis, was to set up alternative sequential constraints on the *inferential options* of knowledge, no matter the particular context of naturally occurring 'turns-at-talk'. Knowledge graphs and social graphs marshal this sequential constraint in different but overlapping ways. Our social interactions self-organize and shift according to how we make appeals to local knowledge in our everyday talk, and knowledge graphs certainly help to foster this behavior through their focus on the advancement of beliefs into their public airing at the hands of logic, now made automatic through our instantaneous access to facts. But as discussed via Habermas in the last chapter, these interactions around facts must also inevitably involve how we recognize or fail to recognize *one another* as having membership in social groups, on the basis of those epistemic appeals.

On the one hand, we have stable social categorizations available to us as group members, which give us quasi-formal conditions for judging others: as Democrats, surfers, welders, or Buddhists, for example; groups with endogenous criteria for judging the correct usage of their local knowledge. On the other hand, in moments of actual social praxis, and in a manner very similar to Peirce's scheme of unsaturated rhema and saturated dicents, ethnomethodology highlights how we must remain concerned in conversation to observe the distinction between the possibilities of *correct social categorization*—e.g. the private belief that this person belongs to that group and/or is correctly referring to something objectively in conversation on the basis of their local knowledge—and the *advancement* of that categorization into public discourse through signification, in order to secure belonging to a group when appropriate, in the achievement of shared understanding with them.

Like the risk of a belief being false, failure always remains an option. Social media platforms afford us an efficient technological means for negotiating the overall process of social performance along these lines, producing what Goffman called 'tie signs' through the twinned interactions of 'turns-at-talk,' using tools like Facebook walls, fora, and messaging, as well as local knowledge categorization relying on affordances like hashtags. It is these overall conditions in interface that set up the traces we leave behind, making them available for pairwise statistical comparison using social graphs.

Social Network Analysis and Social Physics

Having marked the role of philosophy and social theory in office-ware precursors to social platforms, it's important to finally highlight how the technology owes a major conceptual debt to social network analysis— a discipline with roots in early twentieth-century social psychology and anthropology. As early as 1908, the sociologist Georg Simmel observed that modern individuals find themselves drawn away from the traditional and static groupings of rural life to occupy multiple and intersecting groups in a more urban setting; he called these social circles, but today we would call them social networks. Similar to the ways that we think about social media, Simmel thought that the intensification of social connection was fostering a greater freedom of personality, but also new anxieties around one's psychic and social differentiation from others.[24]

The psycho-sociologist Moreno was among the first to devise graphical maps of these interpersonal connections and differentiations, conceiving of his early socio-grams in a dramaturgical context. Moreno saw his network-style diagrams as a way of recording patterns of affinity between actors, a measure of the therapeutic potential of the theater that derived from how closely actors stood to one another and how much time they spent together on stage.[25] Moreno quickly came to understand his socio-metric strategies as offering novel answers to the problem of relating structure to agency in sociology, usefully combining qualitative and quantitative methods to explain overall group stability in terms of its micro-social dynamics. The way forward, he argued, was to conceive of the individual as a social atom, entering into relationships of attraction and repulsion with other atoms, whose bonds he called *teles*. Like the telephone, teles were two-way lines of potential empathy, which, in larger patterns, generated persistent 'extra-individuals'; scalar structures that linked people together into groups, groups together into communities, and communities into societies.[26]

Using diagrams of points and lines, Moreno analyzed groups like high school football teams and girls-school runaways in terms of their influential relations of friendship; these could be reciprocal (traveling in both directions from person-to-person) or asymmetrically directed, as when a popular person (in his terms, a 'star') received friendship from others but did not extend their friendship back to each and all.[27] Moreno unfortunately later became his own worst enemy, insisting somewhat megalomaniacally that sociometry remain the province of group psychotherapy, policing it from others like Kurt Lewin who sought to take it in the direction of a more systematic social science. Before his untimely death in 1947, Lewin managed to develop an entire research program around what he called topological psychology, mapping the interpersonal fields of force that might impact an individual's behavior. Cartwright and Frank Harary's later application of mathematical graph theory to Lewin's interpersonal strategies was subsequently influential, shifting conceptual emphasis in sociometry away from individual minds seeking equilibrium with one another and toward social groups seeking interpersonal balance.[28]

Secondary research undertaken during William Lloyd Warner's famous Hawthorne productivity studies of the Western Electric company in the 1920s and 1930s led to further socio-grams of workers interacting in its relay assembly test room, diagrammed according to their friendships, antagonisms, and sub-group cliques. The anthropologists Eliot Chapple and Conrad Arensberg began to time interactions between pairs of individuals based on this work, using a device of their own making called the interaction chronograph. Dissatisfied with a lack of rigor in social science, Chapple and Arensberg wanted to model people in their social interactions operationally, like particles in physics. Data produced through their participation in Warner's Yankee City studies in social interaction led them to further develop algebraic models for sociality, with help from the mathematician-logician W.V.O. Quine.[29]

Diagramming social relations using networks developed in several different directions through the 1940s and 1950s before firming up through the 1960s and 1970s into what we would now recognize as modern social network analysis. Individual mapping projects gave way to more universalizing abstractions around egocentric networks, especially through field-defining research by people like Marc Granovetter.[30] Building on Stanley Milgram's work on the small world problem, Granovetter gave empirical support to a now well-worn shibboleth, first coined by the Hungarian author Frigyes Karinthy, that we are all connected together through 'six degrees of separation'. The point here is that social networks emerged as a conceptually global phenomenon, and not just a matter of situated groups. Some in the tradition continued to understand the networks metaphorically, as a way of simply gesturing to an assumed underlying social structure, but others increasingly relied upon directed graph theory to actually *analyze* social relations as networks in empirically measurable ways.

Proliferating mathematical strategies gave impetus and shape to the problem of defining the exact nature of social ties. Should interpersonal relations be analyzed according to the algebraic treatment of kinship structures or conjugal roles, as in the work of Sir Francis Galton or Claude Levi-Strauss? Did ties indicate general relations of homophily, leadership, status, and influence? Or should they rather be analyzed in terms of flows of information and conversation, as in a 1957 study concerning the diffusion of knowledge among physicians about new drugs?[31] Parallel to the issues surrounding early CF designs, was it better to interview actors about their social ties, or to gather interpersonal relationship data passively through the ongoing observation of who actually interacted with whom? As we saw with services like Netflix and Amazon's Recommended for You, structured data used in and generated by social network analysis has since coalesced around passive observation, leading to sociality being modeled as a kind of social physics.

Harvard sociologist Harrison C. White is an important figure in this respect. Trained in theoretical physics, White describes personal identity and social relations as having a molecular character, arising from dynamic and contingent interactions that occur in overlapping *social disciplines*, a term with intriguing parallels to Deleuze and Guattari's notion of the collective assemblage of enunciation; White defines social disciplines as the "self-reproducing formations which sustain identity."[32] Like Durkheim and Simmel, identity for White is a product of persons trying to make sense of the multiple and fractured contexts in which they circulate. Traditional social ties of uniformity, with their fixed roles and obligations, continually give way to more flexible and temporary bonds of identity and personhood. These arise out of the functional interdependencies of densifying societies and, more importantly, the division and specialization of labor.[33]

Under these circumstances, identity simply cannot be presupposed and must rather be derived from the concrete work of establishing White's social disciplines, produced through our collective attempts to invoke and wrest control within them in the ongoing production of order. Akin to the endogenous logic of Garfinkel and Goffman's ethnomethodology, White thereby defines the social individual as a constructive and reticular process where social ties interact and chain together to produce a dynamic equilibrium, maintained in patterned interactions that he calls stories.[34] For our purposes, the important parallel is that topological metaphors and flocking logics, of the type deployed in CF systems, take on a deeper, existential significance in his thinking. White writes, for example, that "The triggering of one identity activates control searches by other identities with their own impetuses toward control of any and all exigencies, including each other's."[35] He is keen to observe social processes in their full complexity and maximum concreteness and develops social network analysis as a formal science in pursuit of these goals.

As a way of drawing discussion back toward today's social graph platforms, consider White's formal use of the term stories alongside Facebook's use of the same term to describe its Open Graph Stories application programming interface (API). The Stories' API is a technical means for third-party developers to connect their apps and web pages into Facebook's social graph, allowing them to observe, aggregate, and thereby monetize user activity on their own services. Following its documentation, Open Graph Stories have three parts: an actor, an action, and an object. The actor is the person who wants to express himself or herself, and the action is whatever activity the actor is performing: sharing a link, reading a book, running a certain distance, or rating a film. The object is whatever sign the actor happens to be interacting with, based on the app's functionality; a reading app might encourage me to post the completion of a book's chapter to my Facebook page, for example, while a music app would do the same for my current playlist.

In other words, we arrive back at the graph data triple structure from the last chapter, but this time styled performatively: *someone-did-something-with-an-object*, rather than subject-predicates-object. Facebook's Stories architecture is a generic way for both users and developers to contribute to its vast social graph, incentivizing and organizing users as speakers and hearers in all manner of contexts to follow its designed logics of conversational and illocutionary conjunction. By indicating, sharing, commenting upon, and generally making public the entities that represent our selves through its frameworks, we position ourselves into White's social disciplines: reproducing and sometimes policing the boundaries of our local context while expressing our hobbies, tastes, political leanings, gender embodiments, and lifestyles, as all of these performatively converge with and diverge from other formatted subjects continually doing the same. As Taina Bucher writes, it is through such social organization that Facebook "seeks to induce and simulate the emotional and intimate connections seen as a defining feature of friendship."[36]

At the level of actually *computing* the sign-relation though, Facebook parses the objects and people in its graph in a dizzying number of statistical ways, the process having less to do with communicative signs as performatively exchanged in stories or social disciplines and much more to do with signs as ordered, asemantic signals that fuel the calculative metabolism of the platform as a software service. The graph is again a middle figure between giving us pleasurable interpersonal tools for forging social ties with one another along illocutionary lines of force at the level of interface, while simultaneously putting those same illocutionary lines of force to work as a social physics at the level of algorithm, relying on modeling techniques that essentially treat that force as if it were one of intermolecular attraction and repulsion, to be modeled as a stochastic process.

Summing up, like knowledge graphs in the last chapter, social graphs operate according to a mixture of linguistically styled and material-semiotic precepts. On one level, they solicit the registration of significant performative events in everyday experience, as users produce shared meaning in communication; these are read in phenomenological terms. On another level, social graph platforms technically *encode* those performative moments to act as molecules in a more probabilistic modeling process, having semiotic dimensions but little actual basis in shared meaning. The resulting dynamics between semiological content and semiotic expression operate in the service of a third level, in which the platform is able to extract value from their ongoing flux: hiving off and storing valuable locutionary knowledge derived from ongoing illocutionary dynamics, in generating a fixed social graph that has the economic potential of a knowledge graph, but styled to be *about people*, with a performatively styled assertoric structure at its core.

To get a sense of how these levels of social performativity, statistical organization, and structured data may operate in the broader future of social science research, it can be instructive to complete this section with brief mention of work in social physics by the MIT computer scientist Pentland. Pentland sees a revolution underway in ubiquitous social computing, with its ever-increasing generation of social graph-style performative signals. Whether discussing shopping, interpersonal communication with friends and family, or the ways we interface with bureaucracies, when mediated by digital devices, all produce the performative conditions for social scientists to observe the flows and intensities of social networks *as they occur*, at a fine-grained level of detail. On his telling, Chapple and Arensberg's interaction chronometer now runs continuously on our phones, with a potential to sense our social interactions throughout the day. Pentland advocates for instrumenting phones and other devices, like socio-metric badges, to capture all of this social networking data, arguing that it will open up whole new venues for doing research into the sociology of work and organizational change.

Given the basic premise of the neo-humanist paradigm—that we act in the world according to our solidarity with others—Pentland wants to analyze how organizations can best leverage and optimize social relations for the sake of increased productivity. His approach is to rely on social graphs, as we have been discussing them, to study the modulation of what he calls *idea flow*: a collective intelligence that constantly shapes our preferences and habits over time as we talk to, learn from, and mimic others in our social networks. Advocating for a kind of sociocognitive Taylorism, Pentland believes that greater egalitarianism around conversational turn-taking, combined with targeted support for influential people on the basis of empirically observed social networks, will make future organizations vastly more efficient. Structural incentives like financial bonuses or managerial discipline will be nowhere near as effective as changing someone's behavior via social pressure applied through their networks.[37] It's here that concerns over the rationalization of discourse laid out in the last chapter return.

As in Moreno's star system, charismatic and popular individuals remain the connectors for Pentland, facilitating idea flow through their influence, and so well positioned to set convivial conditions for turn-taking in the overall promotion of a collective intelligence.[38] His account of social physics is fascinating, and from a certain angle deeply troubling, in its arguing for the extension of these logics out from organizations to encompass entire cities, and even whole societies. I want to pick up on this element of charisma in his work as a way of pivoting to talk about the relationship between signification and desire in social graphs. Desire is an important component in Deleuze and Guattari's mixed semiotic theory, so this is perhaps the right moment to further develop their framework over the remainder of the chapter.

Fleshing Out the Mixed Semiotic

Deleuze and Guattari are quick to criticize any approach to the sign that would presume it to be based in what they call a 'well-formed substance'. By this, they mean accounts given of the sign's form (its signifier) that presuppose a semiotic substance (its signified) in such a way as to condition in advance the latter as communicated *content*. A classic target in this regard would be Saussurean linguistics, a standard bearer for what they call semiological approaches to signs, which Deleuze and Guattari want to distinguish from semiotic approaches, their preferred term for insisting on the systematic inclusion of an overall material complex in which the sign manifests, and not just its role in discourse. Over the last century, semiological approaches to the sign have tended to cement a binaristic and psychologistic view of signs, they argue, by idealizing language as a self-sufficient substance and structure.

Lacanian psychoanalysis is another target for them in this regard, given its tendency to define the familial Oedipal triangle in relation to unconscious *desire* as a semiotically well-formed substance. Their cowritten work *Anti-Oedipus* rails against the field for trapping desire and its socio-semiotic functions in the analytic circuits of the family, thereby depoliticizing the sign's potential in wider political formations. As we have been discussing social computing platforms in this chapter, the criticism of semiotically well-formed substances can be equally extended to contemporary theorizations of social *information;* a simple example would be when we fail to pay heed to the specific material-semiotic modalities of online practices by flattening all cultural production to 'content'. When we focus on interpersonal communication to the point of obscuring material-semiotic strata, they argue, our relationship to the sign boils down to what they call the "atmospherization or mundanization of contents." The approach leads Deleuze and Guattari to criticize semiotics as a field overall, for under-theorizing the signifier/signified relation as being only a matter of linguistified semiology.[39]

Socially motivated approaches to data as we have been discussing them similarly fall prey to the criticism, the problem being that they fail to account for the fact that, as Guattari writes,

> Every power formation organizes its own system of verbal packaging for what it has to say. The expression machine, which extends over all these formations, is there only to normalize local formalizations, to centralize and render translatable the unchanging signification recognized by the dominant order, to demonstrate a consensus...[40]

In the case of knowledge graphs, it was the predicative slots of sense and reference that, in their production of an epistemically well-formed substance made up of logical entities, open up the technology to Deleuze and Guattari's charge of "semiotic despotism." Pentland's appeal to charisma as a force worth operationalizing via social graph is another simple instance where desire gets organized to matter only as it can be productively channeled into the binaristic communications of self and other through a *socially* well-formed substance, in the maintenance of a dominant order.

In fact, it would seem that all platforms based in social network analysis do this by establishing sociality as a separated domain or substance, whether according to the semiotic formalizations of illocutionary force, the emergent back-and-forth dynamics of conversation analysis, or the well-established social science categories of affinity and connection. While it may be true that all of these strategies enable us to communicate and socialize in efficient ways, for Deleuze and Guattari, that efficiency comes at a cost. Whenever such a process is in evidence, they argue, the intensities of desire undergo a micro-political violence at the hands of some authority, blunting the sign's potential. To be clear, their goal is not to be done entirely with the semio-logically well-formed substance, but only to diminish its pride of place in favor of seeing how it functions in wider assemblages; it is a late phase of well-ordered redundancy in what Guattari would call an assemblage's more immanent, machinic intensities.

To construct a theoretical alternative that can account for these intensities, and thus potentially escape dominant encodings, Deleuze and Guattari turn to work by the Danish semiotician Louis Hjelmslev. Hjelmslev's system of glossematics is memorable for taking a step beyond de Saussure's binaristic, linguistically focused conceptualization of the sign to discover a still-more decomposable dimension of the signifier-signified relationship that he called *figurae*. Figurae involve some material plane of non-signifying expression whose sole purpose is to distinguish meaningful elements from one another, without the plane itself being meaningful. Directed graphs as a purely mathematical abstraction are an excellent example here. Thanks to their simple functionality of chaining along in a syntagmatic dimension, while framing direction or choice in a paradigmatic one, graphs are an ideal figure for producing what Hjelmslev called matter-purport, or unformed matter: articulating a plane of expression to a plane of content, in a double articulation of communicative meaningfulness, that is organized on a strata of material meaning*less*ness.

Ever attentive to the micro-politics of desire, Deleuze and Guattari understand figurae as always involving power; so they reconfigure Hjelmslev's ideas about language into a wider ontological vocabulary, useful for relativizing the functions and effects of communicative meaning making beyond language, to the particular collective assemblages of enunciation upon which they are being constituted. It's worth saying straight away that an enunciative assemblage involves but does not reduce to what we normally would understand as a media technology. The term is rather meant to describe field-like, dynamical open systems that intervene in and combine with bodies and their actions and passions, organizing them through the aforementioned reciprocal planes of content and expression.

We have been examining the figure of the graph as a contemporary site where this content/expression relation occurs, thanks to its very flexible capacity for semiotizing unformed matter as data in so many different ways. When it comes to social graphs, one way to describe their success is in generating a global plane of data-as-content that presupposes a plane of expression based in performatively rational communication. But at this point, we can no longer talk about the technology in isolation, nor the social in isolation; what's important are the ways in which sociality is produced through a particular pragmatics of the sign, effectively relating language, meaning, and bodies on the one hand to the machinic redundancies of logic, network science, and computability theory on the other. The role of language in an enunciative assemblage is not to represent or to refer—although it does have this effect at the semiological level, as a matter of redundant operations—it is simply to *do things*.

Here, it can admittedly be difficult to see the difference from 'doing things with language' in the performative sense that Austin and Searle conceived of illocutionary force. One way to think about it is to say that in Deleuze and Guattari's understanding, something like an illocutionary force is in all things, and not just keyed to some role in a social context. To see the world in their terms is to accept that, as Jennifer Slack and J. Macgregor Wise write,

> the agency active in any assemblage isn't necessarily human agency, and that human subjectivity itself is an assemblage. [...] To think of something as an assemblage is to see it as an emergence, but we must be cautious not to immediately attribute a human, political, ideological, cultural, or social logic to that emergence.[41]

It is true that, given the highly stratified practices and phases of design, coding, user testing, real time practice, and even academic study, both humanistic and engineering approaches have increasingly begun to account for this mixed nature of social computing assemblages. That said, the politically potent element of assemblage theory too often falls by the wayside: Deleuze and Guattari consistently declined to isolate desire to individual egos or minds, or to some discrete set of social roles. On their more Spinozist understanding, *everything* is transversally productive of desire, as it expresses itself and has effects across layers of ecology, biology, language, and technology. By extension, grasping the effectuating dimensions of language cannot be isolated to the conventions of those who obviously possess the power to effect material change in a given situation, like a judge or a doctor, nor to discursive subcategories in language, as in both Habermas' theory of communicative rationality and Searle's illocutionary typology.

It may be true that performative power is often *vested* in roles, but this vesting happens according to the distributional logic of the wider enunciative assemblage in which it is produced and not simply according to specifiable pragmatics of speakers and hearers. In this respect, Deleuze and Guattari prefer to describe the effective force of signs in terms of the particular "incorporeal transformations" that an assemblage realizes, on the basis of what they call its *order-words*; and as they write, "Order-words do not concern commands only, but every act that is linked to statements by a 'social obligation'."[42]

From all of this, we can gather that our semiotic relation to the world is only secondarily defined in terms of human beings communicating with one another in cultural solidarity. It is primarily defined by the on-going indexation of combined material, desiring fluxes in the production of an enunciative assemblage's *machinic sense*, made socially productive according to the principles of its semiotic organization. Holding on to this core inversion in their work is about maintaining desire's transversal, or multi-form status, and insisting on the sign's always-latent potential for reconfiguration toward greater and more radical openness. Guattari seems especially convinced of this when he writes in *The Three Ecologies* that "The resingularization of subjectivity, the liberation of singularities that are repressed by a dominant and dominating mass-media subjectivity, has nothing to do with individuals."[43]

How then might we re-describe the social subject? Against formulations of the sign that see it as always-already a matter of performed consensus and shared meaning, our social-semiotic orientation to assemblages and their capacity for effectuating incorporeal transformations comes down to the shifting habit of saying I, as this habit gets produced as a *refrain* through what Guattari calls machinic redundancies. Again, the term machinic should not be understood as mechanical, or as referring only to technology. Instead, it refers to a mixture of operational redundancies produced by an assemblage, between groups, cultural symbolizations, and the desiring production of the unconscious, harmonized semiotically to technology. The social subject, in sum, is a product of the mode of subjectivation produced by the assemblage. I will circle back to Facebook Stories in a moment to make this more concrete; but first, I need to describe two additional types of signs that Deleuze and Guattari deploy in their mixed semiotic to relativize linguistic semiologies in the manner that we have been discussing: what they call *part-signs* and *asignifying* signs.

Part-signs do not represent anything, but, like Hjelmslev's matter-purport, serve as a "hypothetic or simply minute" basis for an affective relation to the world, setting up desiring investments between human and non-human patternings and processes.[44] Like a river flowing over rocks, part-sign flows may or may not contribute to the organizational dynamics of an enunciative assemblage, as when a river is dammed so that it can be managed for productive purposes. But part-signs may also remain latent in the background as simply unacknowledged corporeal intensities, as when Gary Genosko describes them in terms of a "[...] seething, dynamic stew of largely unformed but not completely amorphous matter out of which emerge part-objects (including part-signs)."[45] On more than one occasion, Deleuze and Guattari explain part-signs through the example of babies, as in the following passage:

> From his very earliest infancy, the child has a wide-ranging life of desire—a whole set of nonfamilial relations with the objects and the machines of desire—that is not related to the parents from the point

of view of immediate production, but that is ascribed to them (with either love or hatred) from the point of view of the recording of the process...[46]

So, for example, a baby orients itself via part-signs as it forms a conjunctive relationship to the mother's breast; first affected by it through an inchoate hunger to connect, and then, in the moment of being full, spitting up. The latter amounts to a recording-back on the baby-mother-assemblage, of its connective relationship to part-signs, which, through repetition, would eventually lead to the habituated modulation, or conjunction, of regular feedings.[47] Later on in life, parents support the child in terms of its connections, disjunctions, and conjunctions to the cultural order, an overlapping set of assemblages to which they must orient them by selecting and reinforcing certain moments and behaviors of the child's part-sign relationalities of free play. It is in this manner that the child will become semiotically invested in the family assemblage and its cultural codes, once again steering inchoate habits toward the ordered regularities of proper behavior.

At the end of the day though, it is not just babies and children who are steered by part-signs; the entire socius constantly invests in and emits them in different ways, as they are decoded into collective assemblages of enunciation. The decoding process is where Guattari's second term comes in—asignifying signs. The latter form the basis for *producing* a well-formed substance of social and linguistic communication. Asignifying signs are in the position to take up part-signs and put them to work as semiotic components because they operate below fields of linguistic meaning. They 'skip over' the form/substance relation and align directly to the fluxes and resonances of part-signs, causing them to modulate on some stratified material flux in the production of planes of content and expression that ground meaning. Asignifying signs sit outside the field of discursive statements in collective assemblages of enunciation, bypassing interpretive processes altogether to operate "flush with the real," as Guattari puts it, at the intersection of human and non-human processes.

Guattari sometimes uses credit cards as an example. The magnetic polarity of the iron oxide particles on the strip of the card have a direct material-semiotic relationship to the binary digits they represent, and once swiped, the indexical chain leading from reading the account number, to querying the current balance, to approving the sale occurs principally at the level of asignification. Its semiotic involvements are diagrammatic in nature, having to do with the special formalizations of logic, mathematics, and statistics, and not meaning as we traditionally consider it. Swiping our card is unreservedly a highly social and cultural moment where we are meaningfully interpellated as consumers; but materially speaking, it is also a series of *triggering relations* that are more signaletic than semiological, involving computers talking to one another through software codes. Like part-signs, asignifying signs have a poly-vocal status, a fact that will become especially relevant for us in the next chapter when discussing predictive-analytic graphs.

The important, and I hope productive, point to draw from all of this ex-position is that social meaning changes in status for Deleuze and Guattari: from being a presumed ground to being a kind of operational effect of the material alignments of part-signs to asignifying ones, in a given con-crete machinic assemblage. Noted in Chapter 1, the DIKW pyramid in computing treats these operational effects and material alignments in the conventional terms of semiotically engineering efficient communication between humans and machines. The crucial difference between such a stance and the mixed semiotic is to see the process of datafication in terms of a micro-political order: as a neutralization of the semiotic power of part-signs, through the justifications of signification that predominate in philosophies of logic, language, and information. The combination, Deleuze and Guattari argue, acts to biunivocalize the sign, rendering so-ciality in the diminished terms of a universally transposable population. Like dissensus in the case of knowledge graphs, what's lost in translation are those crucial details concerning the pathic apprehension of actual social life amidst overlapping enunciative assemblages.

When we organize meaning to follow the Peircean-style, tiered ax-iological relations of designation through syntax, appraisal through semantics, and normative prescription through pragmatics, we fail to account for the ways that signs in their full and immanent material in-tensities get decanted and filtered through such orderings; the resulting distortion being to frame the sign's effects according to some "univo-cal reference point, a transcendent invariable, not itself significative, whereby to explain the sum of the significative arrangements."[48]

With Deleuze and Guattari's apparatus now fully to hand, we can briefly conclude by returning to Facebook's Stories and its social graph. Nominally, the platform is about the recognition of self and other through social performance, status, and identity construction at the level of meaning making. But these performances are in turn technically articulated to some set of enunciative triggering relations, which model meaning making in terms of the asignifying repetitions and calculative decisions made by machines, on the basis of the significational diagrams of mathematics and logic. As in the case of users 'tasting' objects at the top of the chapter, our declarations of friendship, promises to attend, likes, and replies are pleasurable and performatively meaningful to us, but in Facebook, they are put to work semiotically in the same manner as our IP addresses, device identifiers, clicks, and taps: all are asignifying signs, which, through the machinic consistencies of datafication, feed com-putational practices in operation both *beyond* and *below* hermeneutic communication, producing regulative fields for meaning that are not in themselves meaningful.

To conclude with an emphasis on the micro-political stakes of technical assemblages, the whole point is to be thinking about ways of recovering the sign's freestanding status as emerging out of the fields of intensity and constellations of part-signs that we may encounter together but do not necessarily *find consensus around in communication*. Non-verbal semiotizations, the start and stop commands of technical machines, and our unconscious, felt investments of desire toward cultural symbols are all in play, in ongoing processes of semiotic conjunction, as the individual meaning making, or as I have been calling it, formatted subject, is constituted as adjacent to them in different ways. The level of asignification becomes especially important here because of its considerable political potential as a middle ground for staging meaningful representation. Asignifying signs organize the 'well-formed substance' of the social in one direction by fitting the stabilized agencies of performative meaning making together with our ongoing unconscious habits and desires, while in the other direction, through analytic social science practices, it reconciles those habits to the material necessities of asignifying informational processes that rely on quantification and calculation.

So far, we have been exploring social computing and structured data in terms of two intellectual reference points by which this successfully occurs—logico-semantic validity and performative intersubjectivity—both of which Deleuze and Guattari would diagnose as univocal, signifying semiologies. In contrast to being an assumed starting point for semiosis itself, their mixed semiotic understands these as a final *result* of prior semiotic processes in operation below and alongside consciousness. On this view, the accounts of the sign from philosophy and social theory that I have been describing are less intellectual theories than they are components or diagrams for sign machines, built to produce subject-object relations and a capacity for meaning-exchange. Alongside signifying semiologies, the *semiotic* operates according to a different set of assumptions, involving asignifying signs: mathematical and statistical strategies like those found in protocols and algorithms, which have nothing to do with human beings meaningfully addressing one another.

Deleuze and Guattari are polemical about retrieving this underlying moment of machinic and diagrammatic configuration as a way to challenge our assumptions about language and signs. We can understand the criticism more concretely in terms of the CF platforms and multi-agent models described earlier. Although each is socially productive in terms of modeling intersubjective engagement according to some quantum of taste or energy, it is only through a certain indifference to meaning at the level of algorithm and calculation that the platforms actually produce strategies for steering us together and apart. The propositionally styled performative slots of taste in social graphs 'solve' the problem of sociality in a similar way by organizing it behaviorally along syntactical and strategic lines. In Deleuze and Guattari's telling, what results is an impoverished pragmatics that flattens our collective semiotic creativity by *over-coding* it as individualized preference.

As a matter of fully understanding the performatively formatted subject, it is only from a mixed semiotic perspective that we can see the stakes of these arrangements and, further, see a potential mistake in believing that universalizing or univocal semiologies are the source of our social pragmatics when in fact the reverse is true. Deleuze and Guattari write that

> It is language that is based on regimes of signs, and regimes of signs on abstract machines, diagrammatic functions, and machinic assemblages that go beyond any system of semiology, linguistics, or logic. There is no universal propositional logic, nor is there grammaticality in itself, any more than there is signifier for itself.[49]

These issues come to a head in the next chapter, as both transcendental accounts of logic and sociality wind up entirely reconfigured into yet another style of graph, this time styled under the auspices of Humean empiricism, and with near-total asignification at its core.

Notes

1 Hirschheim, Klein, and Lyytinen, *Information Systems Development and Data Modeling [Electronic Resource]*, 82.
2 Bush, "As We May Think."
3 Goldberg et al., "Using Collaborative Filtering to Weave an Information Tapestry."
4 Resnick et al., "GroupLens."
5 Hill et al., "Recommending and Evaluating Choices in a Virtual Community of Use."
6 Shardanand and Maes, "Social Information Filtering."
7 Lathia, Hailes, and Capra, "kNN CF."
8 Lathia, "Computing Recommendations with Collaborative Filtering."
9 Durkheim, *The Division of Labor in Society*, 101.
10 See Sampson, *Virality*.
11 Terranova, *Network Culture*, 100.
12 See Epstein and Axtell, *Growing Artificial Societies*.
13 Winograd and Flores, *Understanding Computers and Cognition*, 78.
14 Simon, *Philosophy of the Sign*, 81.
15 Heidegger, *Being and Time*, 110–11.
16 Winograd and Flores, *Understanding Computers and Cognition*, 58.
17 See Searle, *Speech Acts*.
18 Winograd and Flores, *Understanding Computers and Cognition*, 158.
19 Ibid., 59.
20 Coulter, "Logic: Ethnomethodology and the Logic of Language," 39.
21 Garfinkel and Sacks, "On Formal Structures of Practical Action," 353.
22 Suchman, "Do Categories Have Politics?" 185.
23 Kaptelinin and Nardi, *Acting with Technology*, 22.
24 Chayko, "The First Web Theorist?" 1420.

25 Freeman, *The Development of Social Network Analysis*, 34.
26 Moreno and Jennings, *Who Shall Survive?* 25.
27 Freeman, *The Development of Social Network Analysis*, 37–38; Scott, *Social Network Analysis*, 14.
28 Scott, *Social Network Analysis*, 16.
29 Freeman, *The Development of Social Network Analysis*, 61.
30 Granovetter, "The Strength of Weak Ties."
31 Mitchell, *Social Networks in Urban Situations*, 4.
32 Azarian, *The General Sociology of Harrison C. White*, 22.
33 Ibid., 44–47.
34 White, *Identity and Control*, 186.
35 Ibid., 6.
36 Bucher, "The Friendship Assemblage," 487.
37 Pentland, *Social Physics*, 66.
38 Ibid., 117.
39 Deleuze and Guattari, *A Thousand Plateaus*, 112.
40 Guattari and Cooper, *Molecular Revolution*, 83.
41 Slack and Wise, *Culture and Technology*, 159.
42 Deleuze and Guattari, *A Thousand Plateaus*, 79.
43 Guattari, *The Three Ecologies*, 9.
44 Genosko and Bouissac, *Critical Semiotics*, 23.
45 Genosko, *Félix Guattari*, 91.
46 Deleuze and Guattari, *Anti-Oedipus*, 47.
47 I am grateful to Steve Wiley for pointing this example out to me on more than one occasion.
48 Guattari and Cooper, *Molecular Revolution*, 89.
49 Deleuze and Guattari, *A Thousand Plateaus*, 148.

4 The Signaletically Formatted Subject

The essence and destiny of empiricism are not tied to the atom but rather to the essence of association; therefore, empiricism does not raise the problem of the origin of the mind but rather the problem of the constitution of the subject. Moreover, it envisages this constitution in the mind as the effect of transcending principles and not as the product of a genesis.

—Gilles Deleuze, Empiricism and Subjectivity

So far, we've seen that knowledge graphs coordinate sociality through semantic networks of fact, affording the efficient communication of validity through a semiotics of inductive and deductive reasoning. Social graphs, meanwhile, mix statistical techniques with theories of conversational turn taking, speaker/hearer intentionality, and recognitional flows of affinity to produce a semiotics of performativity. It remains to describe one last style of graph, which I will gather under the umbrella term of predictive-analytic (PA) graphs. PA graphs are the basis for artificial intelligence (AI) and machine learning and involve the construction of second-order models of purposive behavior over top of existing structured data practices. If big data is indeed the new oil, then PA graphs are cracking towers, built to fractionate and refine stored data into novel correlations that are useful in the discovery of new knowledge, increasing efficiency, or producing new value. While often framed in the fateful language of outpacing human intelligence, in more prosaic terms, PA graphs are about deriving patterns from structured and unstructured data to enable the automatic classification of, or decision toward, as-yet unseen entities and future circumstances.

It's worth saying one last time just how tricky it can be to draw clear lines of demarcation between the three styles of graphs; their distinctions will become even blurrier in this chapter. We saw how the k-nearest neighbor algorithm functioned predictively when deployed on early collaborative filtering platforms; for example, orchestrating people and things together as significant based on the traces of past preferences for movies, music, and one another. This is a basic type of predictive analysis performed on social graph data. Similarly, machine learning platforms like Node and IBM's Watson rely on knowledge graph data as it was characterized in Chapter 2, but do so by combining that data with sophisticated PA methods, like reinforcement learning. Both examples speak to a broader distinction in computing between data structures and algorithms.

Social platforms are powerful in their capacity to incentivize the regular input of large amounts of data from users and, yet, successfully aggregate and reflect back that data to users algorithmically in a meaningful and ongoing way. Knowledge and social graphs lie on the one side, while PA graphs fall on the other, in that they are about processing data in search of useful patterns. But as we will see, PA graphs are themselves also a kind of data structure, with entitative nodes and lines of relation between them. If knowledge graphs are like a dictionary, and social graphs are like a who's who directory, then PA graphs are like an instruction manual, representing *steps for action*.

The difference between them follows broader philosophical lines of contrast that are also important for our purposes. Knowledge and social graphs are based in formalized philosophical accounts of people thinking and acting together, the former modeling a social pragmatics of arguing and reasoning over the fact of the matter and the latter our interpersonal affinities and disaffinities as we come to belong to one grouping rather than another. PA graphs reflect a quite different philosophical position in that they are about transforming these collective activities into experimental patterns for a system conceived as an individual learning mind, receiving impressions and making habitual associations through the pairwise comparison of dependent and explanatory variables. It may come as little surprise to learn then that machine-learning practitioners tend to eschew linguistically or socially framed representations of subjectivity altogether in favor of manipulating large datasets as cognitive signals that optimize the performance of an AI.

In his discussion of models of communication, Gary Genosko borrows a distinction from Rom Harré that can help further highlight the difference. Knowledge and social graphs are a kind of homeomorphic modeling, meaning that their source (what is known) and subject (what is unknown) are the same. Their creative, idealizing role corresponds to their representative role, based in a minimum of what Harré called dramaturgical simulation, or individuals thinking and acting together in a context.[1] In contrast, PA graphs are *paramorphic*; source and subject of the model are different, insofar as social activity traced in gigabytes of data gets reconfigured to act like the physiological interactions of a brain, loosely modeled in the terms of neurons being nodes in a graph with edges like axons transmitting impulses between them. In effect, PA graphs transcode structured data from a substance-based paradigm into a more cognitively or perceptually based one.

Along these lines, if Charles Sanders Peirce and Gottlob Frege's ideas represent an important touchstone for the objectivist tradition of knowledge graphs, and phenomenological social science and speech act theory give impetus to social graphs in a more subjectivist vein, then the ideas of British empiricist David Hume perhaps best capture the intellectual and semiotic commitments of PA graphs. Hume famously argued that reason was 'slave to the passions'; that complex ideas in the mind were built upon simpler affects and impressions, brought into atomic relation according to our capacities to imagine and associate. Relating impressions together according to their resemblance, contiguity, and cause and effect laid the conjunctive grounds for reason, Hume believed; but he also argued that these grounds were ultimately illusory. Hume is renowned for casting pernicious doubt on the notion that we could ever really know anything (including ourselves) with any certainty, because for him, reason and subjectivity were simply a product of our associative *habits*, brought to bear on atomic perceptions. As Kim Atkins summarizes, quoting Hume,

> The seamless transition of perception to perception leads us to mistake the (synthetic) identity of the object in consciousness for the identity of a substance, when in reality consciousness is more like 'a kind of theatre, where several perceptions successively make their appearance; pass, repass, glide away, and mingle in an infinite variety of postures and situations'.[2]

The above passage is helpful to begin to characterize PA graphs as a medium, the goal being to once again draw out their semiotic assumptions. PA graphs represent a more experimental attitude toward the sociosemiological nodes of the graphs that we have been examining in that they treat these nodes as asignifying training data for a machine-learning platform that is learning to see the world according to its contextual cues. Stored data comes to act in the manner of Hume's transitional perceptions, as practitioners supervise and tune, but sometimes simply observe, a PA graph as an algorithmic process. As first developed by physicists like James Clerk Maxwell and Ludwig Boltzmann, probability and statistics continue to be the general frame of reference here, applied to induce classification from out of variable distributions of data, treated as atomic particles interacting in stochastic processes.

Addressing the social under these circumstances becomes a more strictly informational or engineering problem—like troubleshooting a machine with many moving parts, or studying and manipulating a complex adaptive system. On this front, Google stands out among platform giants for its embrace of PA graph methods, having recently adapted its machine-learning software libraries to work locally on mobile devices and even using its DeepMind neural network to cut down on the use of electricity at its data centers.[3] So, after describing some basic historical connections between knowledge graphs and what's known as the symbolist paradigm in AI, I turn to Google's original algorithm to offer yet another brief historical vignette. Its PageRank approach to web search, which took the web by storm at the turn of the twentieth century, illustrates in fairly accessible terms a ubiquitous PA method called Monte Carlo Markov chains. The algorithm and overall approach were innovative at the time in search, for representing web pages as nodes in a directed graph, with hyperlinks acting as edges, indicating the likelihood of where a simulated user might move next as they jumped around Google's cache of the web.

PageRank is a Bayesian strategy in this regard; a way of treating graph edges as a probabilistic measure of decision, against which the chapter briefly contrasts more connectionist approaches. The latter have roots in early work on neural networks by Warren McCulloch and Walter Pitts, logicians who set out to model propositional logic in terms of signaling relations between artificial neurons. The chapter concludes by once again gathering these methods together to consider them in the mixed semiotic terms of an enunciative assemblage. Fuller explanation of the mixed semiotic given in the last chapter puts us in a better position to think through some of the consequences of the rise of PA graphs, which flatten out the diverse social activity of a platform into an empirical field of signals—as we shall see, relying more fully on asignification. This has consequences for our understanding of the social and its role in producing difference in the service of formatted subjectivity.

In all of this discussion, the challenge of course will be to summarize the strategies of a complex and shifting field of practice while still managing a reasonable level of technical accuracy. Leading AI researcher Pedro Domingos describes his work as a black art, for example, and it is probably no coincidence that he named his research group's open-source machine-learning platform Alchemy.[4]

Knowledge Engineering and Decision Tree AI

Traditional symbolic AI shares important roots with the rationalist paradigm laid out in Chapter 2. There, I focused more generally on how relational databases and knowledge graph structures extend into our social lives as media; but it's important to recognize that a further goal of knowledge representation is the emulation of expert decision-making. If one affordance of our devices is to store personal information as a communicable mixture of knowledge and social graph data to be retrieved, then another is for them to be able to *act* autonomously on that data on our behalf. In his discussion of symbolic AI and expert systems, Harry Collins understands the difference as involving any circumstance where we want to substitute concerted *action*—our individual, intentional negotiations of the world, where each of us may have different goals and outcomes in mind—with concerted *behavior;* relying on precise rules for decision-making that obviate the need for meaning negotiation.[5] I used Habermas' term 'steering media' to gesture to this distinction when it comes to the communicative circumstances of knowledge graphs; bringing AI into the picture means a further streamlining of language, so that machines become autonomous agents in their own right.

In symbolist AI, this entails a more holistic embracing of logicist thinking, not just descriptively applied to relations but prescriptively to entire actionable situations, in the production of predigested chains of if-then rule sets for decision-making. In the early days of trying to build a general problem-solving AI, devising these rule sets involved characterizing some well-circumscribed context in terms of its problem-state so that rules could be devised for moving the computer toward an eventual solution-state. As Alison Adam relates, initial attempts to get at these steps by computer scientists Allen Newell and Herbert Simon involved psychological experiments with actual human subjects, asked to think aloud as they undertook a logical means-ends analysis of some problem. The hope was that human subjects would "[...] select the most appropriate means to satisfy a given end, gradually reducing the difference between the start and the solution to a given problem, until the correct path is found from the starting position to the answer."[6] This path could then be encoded into a series of conditional statements for the computer, translating their embodied reasoning into a repeatable data structure.

Problems with this more classical style of AI are at this point well-told history. Newell and Simon's approach was pioneering but limited in the same manner that rationalist approaches to computing of the era were in general; overly mentalistic in its depiction of how we reason and insufficiently situational in orientation. As we saw in Chapter 3, Lucy Suchman would later influentially demonstrate that human beings simply do not march stepwise through planned algorithms in their thinking. We bring past experiences, emergent intuitions, and improvisation to our goal seeking in ways that complicated attempts by the symbolists to encode general intelligence into computers. In the subsequent move from general problem solving to so-called 'micro-world' AI, researchers began to include the representation of past experiences and learning in their models as ways to help computers better cope with stereotypical situations. Designing an AI to draw upon an *a priori* bank of example states that represent a situation, against which it could compare and evaluate novel circumstances, the idea was to reason by analogy, using what symbolist AI researchers Marvin Minsky and Roger Schank, respectively, called frames and scripts.

This is another moment where we can see overlap between the symbolist project and knowledge graphs; the distinction once again being that in AI, representational emphasis falls less on the pragmatic communication of pre-described facts between agents than it does on an individual mind coping in a scenario. As Minsky illustrates, under these circumstances, graph structures come to involve events, problems, and questions requiring decisions:

> A frame is a data structure for representing a stereotyped situation, like being in a certain kind of living room, or going to a child's birthday party... We can think of a frame as a network of nodes and relations. The 'top levels' of a frame are fixed, and represent things that are always true about the supposed situation. The lower levels have many terminals—'slots' that must be filled by specific instances or data.[7]

In the case of the conceptual 'slots' of a birthday party, Minsky imagined a directed graph of nodes and edges that would process relations of the type "will X like P?" (as a present?), "Should Y wear C?" (to the party?), and so on in attempting to define the party's overall context. Schank conceived of his scripts in a similar manner, as idealized games based on the primitive rules and steps of a situation, like visiting a restaurant. Problems arose again though in trying to extend this approach into general intelligence, captured in essence by the so-called 'frame problem'. Whenever an AI got something wrong in micro-world designs, the issue lay in knowing where exactly to draw the line in supplying additional mundane contextual references, and updates to the states of those references, in order help the computer negotiate the problem.

Criticizing Schank's script research on Heideggerean grounds, Hubert L. Dreyfus references the frame problem, for example, when arguing that

> What 'normally' happens when one goes to a restaurant can be pre-selected and formalized by the programmer as default assignments; but the background has been left out, so that a program using such a script cannot be said to understand going to a restaurant at all [...] When we understand going to a restaurant we understand how to cope with even these abnormal possibilities because going to a restaurant is part of our everyday activities of going into buildings, getting things we want, interacting with people, and so on.[8]

With important exceptions, like Douglas Lenat's Cyc project—a still-ongoing attempt, begun in 1984, to hand-code general intelligence in the manner of frames and knowledge graphs—research moved on through the 1970s and 1980s from the pursuit of general problem-solving AI to the exploration of more carefully situated types of expert systems.

An early example here was MYCIN, a medical knowledge system for diagnosing infectious disease and recommending antibiotics at the level of a consulting physician, produced by the Stanford Heuristic

Programming Project. Focusing on a relatively narrow domain of knowledge, the project involved a series of analytic mapping conversations between field experts and knowledge engineers, taking place over years, which sought to specify diagnoses solely through symbols and formal decision rules. MYCIN is an example of a PA graph approach called a *decision tree*. Implied in the name, the node-and-edge relationality of a decision tree is less rhizomatic (as in the case of knowledge and social graphs) than it is aborescent, designed for the computer to be able to rapidly sort some entity into the class where it belongs by putting it through a series of high-speed, comparative 'yes/no' and 'either/or' questions. As Domingos (2015) helpfully illustrates,

> A decision tree is like playing a game of twenty questions with an instance. Starting at the root, each node asks about the value of one attribute, and depending on the answer, we follow one or another branch. When we arrive at a leaf, we read off the predicted concept. Each path from the root to a leaf corresponds to a rule. If this reminds you of those annoying phone menus you have to get through when you call customer service, it's not an accident: a phone menu is a decision tree.[9]

In their transformation of intersubjective action into steered behavior, it would again be more accurate to characterize decision trees as automating a series of 'yes/not', rather than 'yes/no' questions, meaning that the same criticisms leveled at knowledge graphs in Chapter 2 return. Hetero-semiotic, embodied, and experiential dimensions of contestation over validity further give way to formal strategies that, in the name of automation, strip out the potential for dissensus. The resulting formatting of subjectivity in our uptake of expert systems and related AI takes a step beyond social communication with the computer as an agent.

When we rely on Siri as an interlocutor to answer a question, the interaction may be styled in terms of an internally modeled representation of self: I am a semiologized ego who, in being thrown back upon myself over some unresolved meaning, requires an answer from another semiologized ego. But as knowledge is reframed by AI to focus on decision—that is, less on an intersubjective quandary of understanding and more on the effectiveness and consequence of action between agents—inevitably, sociality becomes more about externally modeled behavior. As a result, at the level of technique, the semiotic representation of behavior tends to shift from a semiological mode to an asignifying one, with signs more likely to be styled in an imperative mode. The upshot is for subjectivity to be redefined away from intersubjective communication and toward decisionistic flows of habit and activity as a result, further demoting the conceptual 'circuit breaker' that shared reflexivity is supposed to afford.

I will have more to say about it below, but the shift can be further understood in terms of the uptake of Hume's ideas into AI theory, where the tendency is to rely on an analytic reading of his theories of mental perception. Hume made an important distinction between impressions of sensation, such as feeling hot or cold, and impressions of reflection, like feeling hope or fear. Impressions of reflection were the locus for reason's embedding in a social context for Hume, but because machine learning relies on epistemological readings of Hume that focus on individualized cognition, the tendency is for PA graphs to treat all available data as impressions of sensation.

Before we get to Hume, let me also take a brief moment to reintroduce Gilles Deleuze and Félix Guattari's perspective. Following their mixed semiotic approach, it may be true that the reflexive, recognitional sense of self and other that presumed to obtain knowledge and social graphs suffers a kind of fatal blow with PA graphs. Their more formalizing dimensions of fact-exchange and co-presence are being transformed into AI strategies by powerful institutions in order to ensure a greater degree of efficiency in discourse. But in the depreciation, we also find ourselves in a franker position to understand our collective relationality to social computing technologies, as such.

As an example, Jodi Dean diagnoses the issue in terms of a neoliberal context for networked technologies, where we mistake our relationship to social platforms in believing that our individual contributions matter; that what we communicate "[...] means something to and within a context broader than oneself."[10] As we participate in and come to rely on them as a basis for our relationality, the actual impact that our individual contributions have is effectively determined by a moment of formalization where, in Dean's terms, a "subjective registration effect detached from any actual impact or efficacy" takes hold. Critiques on this front often proceed along political-economic lines; but Dean's criticism can be usefully extended into the semio-technical register, too. To understand the more automatic, decisionistic designs of a PA graph is to see, at both a high level of abstraction and a low level of design implementation, how an enunciative assemblage constructed in the name of improving consensual communication can actually wind up acting instead as a collective apparatus for semiotic *subjugation*.

We diagnose the problem clearly enough when talking about the consequences for discourse that come along with consolidation of ownership around the major social computing platforms. Jonathan Taplin writes, for example, that

> The Web has become critical to all our lives as well as the world economy, and yet the decisions on how it is designed have never been voted upon by anyone. Those decisions were made by engineers and executives at Google, Facebook, and Amazon (plus a few others) and imposed upon the public with no regulatory scrutiny.[11]

But consistent with the perspective I have been advancing, what also matters are the underlying semiotic strategies that allow for this capture and accumulation of knowledge-power in the first place, on the basis of a platform's capacity to formalize subjectivity and the social. The increasing application of machine learning and PA graphs to so many aspects of public life represents a strange new horizon for this capture and accumulation, and any cogent political response to effects will need to account for how a PA graph's machinic layers fit together with a platform's interface to produce a communicative context in the first place.

In the introduction, I gestured to these underlying stakes in Foucauldian terms, as a difference between modes of subjectivation and subjectification; Guattari puts the tension in similar terms when he writes that "the equation 'signified + signifier = signification' arises from the *individuation* of phantasies and from *subjugated* groups, whereas the equation 'collective force of utterance = machinic sense/nonsense' arises from *group* phantasy, and the group as *subject*."[12] On Guattari's terms, platforms like Facebook, Microsoft, and Google provide the free technical means for global social signification over knowledge and social graphs; but the arrangement subjectivates us in such a way as to establish a collective force of utterance in favor of the platforms; one that feeds the machinic side of PA graphs in a rather one-sided subject-group equation.

Thinkers have variously criticized the resulting sociality in terms of placing us in filter bubbles,[13] entrenching the dominance of charismatic thought-leaders on social media at the expense of collectivity,[14] and as a means for manipulating sentiment and emotion in coercive ways.[15] I take the view that we also need to be theorizing these problems in the semiotic terms of a platform's representational combinations of data and algorithm, read as different strategies and phases of sense making. It's on these terms that companies are in such a powerful position to cut up our collective imagination in particular ways, potentially at the expense of wider imaginaries that we might globally share, even if conflictingly.

As it stands, imagination and phantasy are being extracted and reserved as fixed capital, to act as an empirical force of calculative differentiation that continuously refines the predictive models of PA graphs. An early example of this was Google's PageRank algorithm, a feature of its search engine that revolutionized the field by way of an approach called Monte Carlo Markov chains. Aside from the technique being invented by Russian mathematician Andrei Markov, the approach is so-named because, like the casino, it is based in the vagaries of chance and, like decision trees, is often used to treat processes in the world as calculable chains of decisions.[16] The difference is that decisions in a Markov chain are not planned as a series of 'either/or', 'yes/no' questions, but rather *emerge* from the observation of choices already taken. Google was innovative at the time for treating the web's global hyperlinking structure in this way.

PageRank and the Monte Carlo Method

Douglas Engelbart, who produced the first working hyperlinks on his experimental computer system called Online System (NLS), and Theodore 'Ted' Nelson, who coined the term hypertext, both credit Vannevar Bush's vision of the Memex as deeply influential. All three shared the view that information systems should have a symbiotic relationship with their users, augmenting their natural capacity for thinking through *associative* techniques applied to information. Of the NLS, Engelbart recalls, for example,

> I had long thought that you would want to link to a document someone else had written. But I also realized that you might want to link directly to something deep in a particular file. Maybe you would want to go straight to a single word inside a paragraph or someday link from one email to another. That led to our making every element in the NLS addressable, so it could be linked to.[17]

While Engelbart's research soberly laid down some key conceptual and creative paradigms for human-computer interaction, Nelson's views on associative thinking over computers were more speculative and agitprop. His vision was one of computers holding revolutionary potential for human emancipation and creativity, especially when it came to hypertext. In his cult-classic book *Computer Lib/Dream Machines*, Nelson suggests that we have been "speaking it all our lives" and not realized it:

> ... the structures of ideas are not sequential. They tie together every which-way. And when we write, we are always trying to tie things together in non-sequential ways [...] the point is, writers do better if they don't have to write in sequence (but may create multiple structures, branches and alternatives), and readers do better if they don't have to read in sequence, but may establish impressions, jump around, and try different pathways until they find the ones they want to study most closely...[18]

The trajectory of hypertext from obscure software technique to daily mediator of Western life has seen many milestones since the time in which Nelson was writing. Notable are Brown University's *Intermedia* system (1986–1990), Apple Computer's *Hypercard* application (1986), work by artists and writers using early multimedia CD-ROM technology, and a long detour through post-structuralist literary theory via works produced with applications like Eastgate Systems' *Storyspace* (1984). At a societal level though, unarguably the biggest impact of hypertext has been the global uptake of the World Wide Web. Its inventor Sir Tim Berners-Lee's ideas concerning the association of documents and text have for nearly three decades now given every connected computer the ability to both host and retrieve hyperlinked documents.

In the face of exponential growth, strategies for the web's rationalization became necessary along the way so that people could find information and have their information be found. Initially following the time-honored strategies of word-of-mouth and expert advice, users also turned to burgeoning search portals like Yahoo! and Lycos, offering directories of subject areas in order to find their way around. As the web grew, these human-sorted schemes gave way to statistical methods with search spiders crawling vast regions of the web to aggregate the occurrence of terms on pages, matching their relevance to users' search queries. Problems connected to word polysemy ('car' can also be found using the term 'automobile') and synonymy ('address' can mean a city location or a scheduled speech) were resolved over time, as more and more sophisticated approaches developed in the field of information retrieval.

It was in this milieu that link analysis came on the scene, exploiting the information inherent in the hyperlinking structures of the web itself to improve the quality of search results. Two algorithms emerged from research labs around the same time in 1998; one at IBM Almaden in Silicon Valley and the other at Stanford University. Both relied on directed graph theory to interpret vast regions of the web's interlinking as recommendations or votes accorded between pages. Adapting a technique from bibliometrics known as citation analysis, both IBM's Jon Kleinberg (author of the Hypertext Induced Topic Search, or HITS algorithm) and Stanford Ph.D. students Larry Page and Sergey Brin (authors of the PageRank algorithm, originally called BackRub) created systems that ranked popularity scores for each of millions of web pages. Kleinberg's HITS algorithm developed to become the Ask.com search engine, while Page and Brin's PageRank algorithm was the seed of their conquest of the Internet.

Page and Brin's novel insight was to use the web as a means for determining a measure of its own authoritativeness. Where in the case of knowledge graphs each node represents an entity about which one wants to predicate a fact, in the case of PageRank, web pages are the nodes. And instead of expressing facts about or between them, the directed arrows or edges in the graph represent forward links (outedges) from a web page, and backlinks (inedges) into a web page. Crawling and storing the web's hyperlinks in a gigantic, cached repository allowed Google to repeatedly parse their connections statistically as inter-endorsements, or votes, as a way to determine global popularity. Based in the citation analysis of scientific papers, their operating premise was that "a page has high rank if the sum of the ranks of its backlinks is high. This covers both the case when a page has many backlinks and when a page has a few highly ranked backlinks."[19] Amy N. Langville and Carl D. Meyer offer a more accessible explanation, which since publication more than a decade ago has taken on a certain unexpected significance:

> ... one personal endorsement from Donald Trump probably does more to strengthen a job application than 20 endorsements from 20 unknown teachers and colleagues. On the other hand, if the job interviewer learns that Donald Trump is very free and generous with his praises of employees, and he (or his secretary) has written over 40,000 recommendations in his life, then his recommendation suddenly drops in weight. Thus, weights signifying the status of a recommender must be lowered for recommenders with little discrimination.[20]

This strategy of flattening the associative flows of hyperlinks between pages into a field of empirical signals denoting recommendation worked extremely well. As a mathematical baseline, every page in Google's early cache of the web began with an equal and finite quantity of popularity. In the initial step of ranking, a chain of hyperlinks was followed randomly among cached pages, with a determination made of which pages received a greater share of backlink endorsement among all. This is the Markov chain element, what's called a random walk; the idea is that repeated random walks will eventually converge on the general probability of any one page being landed upon, proportional to all pages in the network.

Pages landed on more than once in the first random walk, intuiting a higher number of backlinks, take a numerically greater portion of the finite distribution of popularity, at the expense of pages that did not have as many backlinks. At the end of this first pass, each page was assigned a score, represented in the original PageRank algorithm as a whole number from 0 to 100. Then another random walk among the linked pages took place, as if a theoretical user were clicking around the web a certain distance before either getting stuck in a loop of the same pages co-referencing one another, or getting bored and starting again on some new random page. In each subsequent iteration, the results of these walks had the additional attribute of prior page popularity recursively *boosting* any page randomly landed on via more popular backlinks. In other words, the quantity of backlinks a page received remained important, but now an endorsement from a page popular in the previous iteration counted for more than an endorsement from one with smaller prior popularity.

Feeding prior popularity scores into the application of consecutive random walks during the ranking process, and rerunning this whole process over time—every six to eight weeks in the early going at Google, but eventually constantly—had the overall effect of the 'rich getting richer' in terms of rank. In the network science literature, this is generally

held to confirm the actual distribution of people and organizations linking between one another across the web. Studies of large-scale network
structures suggest that communities naturally coalesce around a few key
sites of reliable repute, linking into them frequently in what is known as
a power-law distribution.

PageRank capitalized on the power-law phenomenon to separate the
wheat from the chaff by evenly distributing endorsement received on a
page via its inedges on to its outedges—the pages it linked to. A page
with a very influential PageRank score of 100, for example, spreads two
scores of 50 out to the two pages it links to on outedges, whereas a
page with a score of 9 will spread three endorsements, each only with
a strength of 3, to the trio of pages it linked to through its outedges.
Recursive calculation of rank was made possible via some complicated
linear algebra, used for mathematically modeling an abstract form un-
dergoing a state change, where the resulting transformation of state
changes the topology of the form endomorphically, or from the inside,
without breaking its overall unity.

Imagine squashing down a cube of modeling clay, stretching out a
rubber band, or spreading a glob of soft butter in one direction across a
piece of bread; in each case, a vector of force (represented by the arrows
in a graph) gets applied, which changes the form (represented by the positions of the nodes) in response to the force as a function of the object's
internal makeup. While its shape may have been stretched or squashed,
the form has not been torn or broken; starting shape and end shape have
only shifted, creating different relationships of adjacency among points
on the surface of its topology. Some points in the shape start out in one
location and wind up in another, while others stay in roughly the same
place. Figuratively speaking, Google stretches and squashes the shape of
the web along a vector force of 'popularity' induced from out of its own
internal dynamics.

To introduce two more important terms, the change in distance that
develops between points on a topology as a result of force applied is a
multiplier called an eigenvalue, scoring the differential relationship between the points before and after a stretch; think of the statement "I am
3.2 times taller than when I was born."[21] The formalized force that defines
the meaningful *orientation* of the eigenvalue, for the sake of observing
change, is an operator called an eigenvector. It describes the mathematical transformation that gives operational definition to 'stretched from' in
the case of a rubber band, 'taller than' in the case of height-from-birth,
and 'more popular' in the case of PageRank. Random walks progres-
sively stabilize an eigenvector of 'change-through-popularity' in Google's
cache of the web, stretching the graph in different ways. Sites scoring
a large eigenvalue were those stable enough to maintain their position
in the direction of the eigenvector. Because other sites so consistently
linked into them, they were less affected positionally by the torsion of

change in the graph's shape, emerging with what's called graph central-ity or, more simply, popularity.

The technical jargon is worth elaborating just a bit more in order to grasp its intellectual connections to physics, mathematics, and cybernet-ics. The German prefix *eigen* means own, inherent, or proper. By adopt-ing this set of mathematical tools, PageRank was staging an immanent relationship between the empirical structure and social function of the web itself, producing a self-conditioning differential that drove the improvement of search results. And as we came to understand the power-law distributions that its networks produced and portrayed, web sites began to adopt such strategies for their *own* goals, orienting their writ-ing and publishing strategies to meet PageRank's machinic logic, such that Google's recursive 'winner-takes-all' structures tended to become a self-reinforcing cultural narrative. By reading the micro-generated sta-bilities of association between pages as aggregated decisions among au-thors, objectively ranked results could be fed back to users, upon which they could base *future* decision.

These ideas have obviously not been limited to search engines in their application. The eigenformal approach has been broadly influential via the physicist-philosopher Heinz von Foerster, a pioneer in the field of second-order cybernetics and systems theory. In a discussion of his famous paper, "Objects: tokens for (eigen)-behaviours," Louis Kauffman summarizes von Foerster's contribution like so:

> In an observing system, what is observed is not distinct from the system itself, nor can one make a separation between the observer and the observed. The observer and the observed stand together in a coalescence of perception. From the stance of the observing system all objects are non-local, depending on the presence of the system as a whole. It is within that paradigm that these models begin to live, act and converse with us. We are the models. Map and territory and conjoined.[22]

Through its ever-expanding capacity to observe the web as a PA-style graph, Google leverages just such a 'coalescence of perception' with its users in a circular causality that at this point feels commonplace in our everyday relationship to social computing. Sometimes at an unnerving level of detail, its services are about studying us as populations making decisions in order to be constantly transforming these into an improved map of our wants and needs, conjoined with the territories of signifi-cance that we have traversed in the past.

Joseph Turow describes Google's early efforts on this front as an "in-dustrialization" of the hyperlink, an idea that Anne Helmond develops in her historical characterization of these efforts as just a first phase in the web's broader transformation from a relatively unified, if chaotic, environment into one made up of competing social and search platforms. She writes that "Links passing through various channels become part of the larger link-sharing environment on the web where each device or platform may reconfigure the link in order to fit their medium by making it 'algorithm ready'."[23] In the nearly two decades since PageRank was first implemented, Google's services have retooled on a regular basis to take advantage of new, asignifying markers of behavior that help nuance retrieval results and their related algorithms, further shifting the significance of the web's relationality from its origins in citational association across documents to the real time analysis of *individualized* decision.

Such efforts have lead to effective multilingual search, personalized results based on geographic location and search history, the more constant monitoring and indexing of social networking platforms like Twitter, so-called 'Universal' searches of various media types, like photos and PDFs, and a constantly improving calibration of what constitutes 'authority' in the ranking process. These have all been further refined by Google's acquisition of the Freebase knowledge graph, combining it with all of the other strategies to predict and produce context in still-more powerful ways. PageRank may be ancient history for the company, but its eigenformal strategies based on Markov chains continue to be honed, amplified, and diffused into all levels of Google's social computing services. Taking advantage of its hegemonic status as the world's most visited site, Google is constantly observing decisions made by users working within its various services.

When confronted with a list of results from a search query, for example, users habitually click to proceed to the site that will most likely be what they are looking for. They may once have clicked on a link that would lead them directly to the page in question, but this is no longer the case. Google now inserts a hidden layer in-between the user and their final destination, which momentarily records the click as an input signal on their own servers before sending the user on to their final destination. These accumulating clicks are used to train an artificial neural network, with popular search queries serving as neurons and link selection analogous to the sparks of synaptic activity that adjust the strengths of similarity between the terms, like cell assemblies in a brain. Or to put it instead in the terms of mental generalization, accumulating clicks become particular instances of *reinforcing a concept*. The latter represents somewhat of a departure from the original Markov chain abstractions of PageRank, in a move toward more connectionist approaches to AI.

Connectionist AI

Understanding the semiotics of connectionist-style PA graphs requires that we return one more time to the role played by the assertion in rationalist accounts of the sign. Recall that at the heart of Frege's project was a desire to account for identity objectively by abstracting reference from everyday linguistic expression. Grammatical assertions like "the cat is asleep" more accurately involve a function mapping an argument onto a truth value for Frege, such that an object denoted by a label ('the cat') either does (true) or does not (false) fall under a concept class of "things that are asleep". Ludwig Wittgenstein, Bertrand Russell, and others in the tradition like Rudolf Carnap, refined Frege's views into modern predicate logic, with knowledge engineers like John Sowa continuing the tradition by materializing their ideas into knowledge graphs.

Connectionist AI pioneers McCulloch and Pitts also took up this project, but did so in a physiological idiom, producing a logical calculus that was based in neural events. While they shared a rationalist vision of the sign, even grounding their approach in Carnap's symbolic logic, their work also represents a fascinating extrapolation from its basis in sentential reference. Trained in psychology, McCulloch believed that reason should not be framed in terms of intersubjective engagement around assertions but rather in the psychotic pathologies of a *disordered* mind. As Orit Halpern relates, it was in part on the basis of his and Pitts' work in cybernetics that rationality itself began to be conceptually recast in terms of immanent, signaletic processes, away from its individualization in social subjects. As she writes, theirs was a "[...] radically different concept of perception and mind, one no longer attached to human bodies, and concerned not with limits, disabilities, and pathologies but with capacities, circuits, and channels—in many different types of machines."[24]

Their neural network approach nevertheless represented logical thinking in the sense that the nodes of a graph could represent discrete thresholds of excitation and inhibition in the activities of an electric brain. Correctly combined, these could in turn represent the flows of Boolean algebra that make computing possible—logical conjunction (AND), disjunction (OR), and negation (NOT). Frank Rosenblatt's later work on so-called 'perceptrons' expanded on McCulloch and Pitts' original arrangements by shifting the values of nodes from being discrete (*either* zero or one) to having smoother ranges of probability from zero *to* one, expressed in decimal fractions.

To understand how Rosenblatt's neural nets work, imagine a very simple perceptron as a directed graph made up of two input nodes at the base, connecting up via edges to a single output node at the apex. The edge-relation of each input node to the output node in a perceptron, called a connection weight, can be set to pass an excitation along in a numerical range from 0.0 to 1.0. With this simple arrangement, one is able represent the traditional OR gate in logic (true if *either* or *both* inputs are true, otherwise false) by setting the initial connection strength on each of the two edge-relations to 1.0. If either of the input nodes fire, then the output node will fire. But with the very same perceptron, if one were to adjust the edge-relations on each input node to a connection strength of 0.5, then the output node would act instead like an AND gate—firing the output node only if *both* inputs are true, passing along its excitation into the wider network.[25]

Perceptrons resemble PageRank's Markov chain strategy in this respect; numerical values enter into a node according to certain excitatory or inhibitory weights on its edges, which then get passed along to other nodes in the network, distributed across edges based on how its tenders are organizing and supervising the system. The difference is that in a neural network, nodes are styled to act more as computational units for training the computer to make assertions rather than as a figurative voting population, observed as an empirical phenomenon. The resurgence of today's connectionist AI is a more hybrid case in that the field now mixes the training interventions of programmers with the widespread availability of large datasets.

The idea is to find many useful sources of training data, consisting of either structured or unstructured data, so as to be able to experiment with different discriminatory logics, applied to what one is trying to predict. As we have already seen, structured data comes in the form of relational databases and knowledge and social graphs. The power of machine learning is that *unstructured* data becomes useful here, too: text corpora, audio and video, logs of behavior, casual forms of metadata—anything that exhibits an informational pattern can be put to work as training data, or after sufficient training may itself fall subject to structuration. This is the deep power of PA graphs; to be able to simultaneously induce and impose order recursively, from correlations of data that build up a PA graph's capacity to assert with confidence that some x is a y. Of course, this can occur only after exposing the network to many training examples, steering and correcting its (ir)rational analysis along the way. As Cathy O'Neil writes, a machine-learning model often requires "millions or billions of data points to create its statistical model of cause and effect."[26]

In its original incarnation, Rosenblatt's perceptron had only input nodes and output nodes; this often lead to brittle decision strategies because the entire neural network could be affected by, or 'dragged into', the transactions of a small subset of perceptrons, sending its classifying abilities far wide of the mark. Today's perceptron-style graphs are hooked together in multiple layers with *hidden* layers stacked in-between input and output layers. Hidden layers are so named because they are made up of unlabeled nodes that effect midway transformational functions on unstructured data, pre-processing it to take advantage of its existing visual or conceptual tendencies and sympathies. Hidden layers cluster and polarize data in statistical ways before sending it on either to another hidden layer or, finally, to the output layer. Here's a simpler explanation from a practitioner, for how hidden layers might be used in computer vision:

If you want a computer to tell you if there's a bus in a picture, the computer might have an easier time if it had the right tools. So your bus detector might be made of a wheel detector (to help tell you it's a vehicle) and a box detector (since the bus is shaped like a big box) and a size detector (to tell you it's too big to be a car). These are the three elements of your hidden layer: they're not part of the raw image, they're tools you designed to help you identify busses.[27]

Similar to decision trees, the input nodes in a multilayer perceptron are essentially features taken from existing data, broken down in a binary way as either having (+) or not having (–) some attribute, making them easily comparable using regression analysis to discover causal or correlational dynamics. Take the example of teaching an AI to categorize cats on the basis of a semantic taxonomy. One might begin by making use of the CIFAR-100 image database, containing tens of thousands of tiny pictures of animals, to produce a useful hidden layer for extracting animal features. One might then also include information from Wolfram Alpha's knowledge graph, which has several triple structures involving animals that would help to set up input nodes, like +domesticated, +chordate, +carnivorous, and so on. Programmers might further devise their own semantic features with attributes like +animate, +four-legged, and +furry.[28] These attributes established, the next step would be to train the network by giving it lots of examples of existing data about creatures in the animal kingdom, variously exciting the nodes in the hidden layers, adjusting the connections between them in a process of clustering and combining concepts conjunctively, to determine what something is on the basis of what it is *not*.

As training proceeds, labels like tiger and lion will move eigenformally closer to one another as similar, while terms like dolphin and spider will move away from these, and one another. In terms of output, a very simple multilayer perceptron might predict on just two nodes "is a cat" or "is not a cat". In a more complicated scenario, output nodes might represent different classes of animals, with the strengths passed on by the hidden layer to the output layer resulting in confidence scores that indicate strong or weak prediction, as in 80 percent cat, 15 percent cow, and 5 percent chimpanzee. The *learning* element in multilayer perceptrons comes down to supervising its increasing ability to discriminate cats from other animals by adjusting its outputs to match what the programmers consider to be accurate prediction.

Like PageRank's random walks, the initial forward feed of input to output strengthens certain nodes in the hidden layer at the expense of others. Observing the results on the output layer, programmers can freely adjust the weights of the output nodes in ways that cast back onto the hidden layer, essentially steering the system by telling it what it got right and wrong in a self-coalescing way. Or as Gary Marcus puts it, "[...] using a process of the sort that is sometimes called *blame-assignment*, the algorithm computes the extent to which each hidden node has contributed to the overall error."[29] It's easy to imagine how social graph data would be similarly treated by a neural network, according to socially discriminant attributes like age, income level, cultural tastes, regularity of communication with certain people, past purchases, or other group affiliations.

For our purposes, the important takeaways concerning PA graphs are that (1) satisfying predicate relationality is still the litmus test for knowledge, but this is achieved on perceptual rather than socially assertoric grounds and, relatedly, (2) as a process, PA graphs tacitly rely upon but effectively 'skip over' the linguistic semiological dimension of signs discussed in Chapter 4. As we'll see in the closing section of this chapter, they treat existing data points essentially as *part-signs* affecting a perceiving machine intelligence, using graph theoretical strategies to simulate cognition in ways that, in the terms of Deleuze and Guattari's mixed semiotic, are entirely machinic and asignifying. We may continue to assume and inhabit a semiological relation at the level of interface, especially as the results of PA graphs are styled and redeployed as software 'agents' on social platforms, like Google Now or Facebook's M personal assistant. But at the level of algorithm, relation and rationality lose their one-to-one correspondence with the indexicality of social subjectivity. In its place comes a *distributed* relationality, made up of informational signals of varying influence, which when exhaustively compared as a cascade of minute differences eventually converge on identity. Or as Hume put the matter back in 1772,

> As a great number of views do here concur in one event, they fortify and confirm it to the imagination, beget that sentiment which we call belief, and give its object the preference above the contrary event, which is not supported by an equal number of experiments, and recurs not so frequently to the thought in transferring the past to the future.[30]

Hume and PA Graphs

While it has undergone substantial transformations in modern philosophy of science, Hume's philosophy remains remarkably salient for social computing today. Any platform that treats the past as a set of signals for predicting the future operates on the basis of a problem at the heart of Hume's account of human nature, captured in the following simple question: why do we assume that past experience gives us reason to expect that future experience will be a certain way? What underlies our belief, for example, that just because the earth is rotating, the sun will rise tomorrow just as it rose this morning? We assume a cause and effect relationship, but on what basis do we justify it, aside from its regularity in past observation? Can causality be grounded in past experience alone? On its face it would seem not because this would amount to circular reasoning. Nor can we ground causality strictly in the principles of deductive reasoning, because our generalizations about cause and effect in experience never rise to the level of a priori necessary causation, a fact lately captured in Nassim Taleb's black swan theory, for example.[31]

Reflected in the Markov chain and neural network approaches just described, Hume's response to the quandary has over time led to thinking in very sophisticated ways about the relationship between reason, probability, and causation. Experience produces a uniformity between past and future, which allows us to infer why things happen; but we can only know that uniformity on the basis of that experience. Under these circumstances, it can only be habit, or what Hume called constant conjunction, that could serve as the ground for observing the necessary connections of causation. Scientific and statistical methods have since complicated, and even weakened, Hume's linkage between causality and correlation to see the two as only tendentially or symptomatically linked.[32] For us, it's only important to understand at a basic level how his ideas function as a methodological premise in the construction of PA graphs, given that our concern is to derive a formatted subject from an exploration of their semiotic features. I will, therefore, not spend too much time getting into the details of Hume's theory of causation; but after outlining his original problem of knowledge, with help from Deleuze, I will turn to focus on how his account of knowledge fits together with human nature, subjectivity, and the social.

For Hume, our mental perceptions are atomic and based in the relationship between ideas and impressions, what today we might instead call thoughts and affects. Ideas are produced by memory and the imagination but can always be traced to underlying impressions, which have both external sources—phenomena that impact our senses, like color—and internal ones—like pleasure or pain. Another central feature of Hume's system is that the difference between ideas and impressions is one of degree and not kind; ideas and impressions differ only by the felt impetus of what he called their 'force and vivacity'. This difference of degree means that our ideas are effectively copies of our impressions, as when we experience a shiver of fear from a near-miss traffic incident when recalling it a year on, for example. Generally speaking, ideas are less lively than sensations. In every case where we analyze thoughts, he writes, "we always find that they resolve themselves into such simple ideas as were copied from a precedent feeling of sentiment."[33] Hume's approach is materialist in this regard, meaning, for instance, that blind people cannot imagine color because they have never had the sensation.

This is in no way to downplay the power of ideas though, which compound into complex tableaux of experience through memory and the imagination. The crucial point is that imagination and reason work together, and because ideas are copies or versions of impressions, reason itself is a kind of *feeling*—what he called an impression of reflection. Hume's basic structure for thinking is replicated in the PA graphs that we have been examining, where in each case, some kind of signal from existing atomic data gets organized in such a way as to link stable ideas to impressions. Interestingly though, Hume was critical of rationalist thinkers of his era for the ways that they too readily projected the feeling of reason into logicist representations of causal necessity, the result being a too-strict separation of the passions from reason's reflective power. Reason steers the passions in practice but not by supplanting them; reason is *embedded in* the passions. As Deleuze summarizes the criticism,

> Rationalism has transferred mental determinations to external objects, taking away thereby from philosophy the meaning and intelligibility of practice and of the subject. The fact is, though, that the mind is not reason; reason is an affection of the mind.[34]

Impressions in the senses combine into compounds of ideas in the intellect for Hume, which may proceed along lines of the fancy or the understanding. We can imagine a golden mountain, for instance, only because we have had the simpler impressions of mountains and gold, Hume writes; but the example also illustrates the mind's broad associative capacity to conjure up entire fictional universes out of simple impressions. That said, we can also proceed from the fancy by insisting that ideas *correspond to* reality through reason by having beliefs, and making inferences on the basis of those beliefs, such as that the sun will rise tomorrow because the earth is rotating. The point is that the faculty of the imagination always remains in operation, at work both in conjuring up unicorns and in the formation of general ideas, like categories for things. Again, it's here that we can start to see the underlying theoretical justification for PA graphs, which treat existing data as impressions and combine them through inference to form useful ideas.

Deleuze provides another caution here though, that we should not see the imagination as somehow separate from the rational determination of ideas in the understanding. In fact, the reverse is true; ideas localize the imagination by way of association's constitutive role:

> Association affects the imagination. Rather than finding its origins, association finds in the imagination its term and its object. It is a quality which unifies ideas, not a quality of ideas themselves [...] Association, far from being a product, is a rule of the imagination and a manifestation of its free exercise. It guides the imagination, gives it uniformity, and also constrains it.[35]

What Deleuze is getting at here is that whether we are talking about ideas proceeding according to fancy or the understanding, Hume's principles of association—resemblance, contiguity, and causality—must be foregrounded because they are what produces an initial consistency, even in the imagination's highest delirium of impressions.[36] This is in keeping with Hume's desire (and we should say also McCulloch and Pitts') to see reason not as determinately responsible for relationality, as the rationalists did, but as an organizational affection of the mind.

Resemblance obviously involves perceptions that are like each other, as when an artful drawing of a horse leads us to associate its impression to horses as an idea. Spatio-temporal contiguity involves perceptions that are adjacent rather than far apart, as when we group things alike in size or composition, or blame last night's dinner instead of the previous day's lunch for our indigestion because the dinner is most contiguous to our current suffering in time. It's on the basis of these principles of association that we hone our habitual understanding of the connections of cause and effect, which is how we are able to transcend the given of our impressions. The impression of constant conjunction means that cause and effect are not phenomena to be found in nature but, rather, are an effect of association in the mind—rising through our habits to become a general sense of the necessity and efficacy of the relationships between events and things. As Jon Roffe writes, citing Hume's famous observation of a billiard table, "We associate the white ball's motion and collision with the movement of the red ball, but equally we infer the existence of parents from the fact of our friend's existence."[37]

How do all of these elements combine to give reason reliable traction on our experience in the face of Hume's problem of knowledge? And what does this overall account have to say about PA graphs? To answer the first question, we can say that Hume's subject is motivated by habitual tendencies, as these have been structured by the principles of association: "Custom, then, is the great guide of human life."[38] We project our beliefs into the world as a way of transcending the given, on the assumption that the future will resemble the past. When this regularity comes to pass, our beliefs are reinforced; but when past impressions do not anticipate current circumstances, our beliefs are challenged, and we are provoked to revise them. In other words, the principles of association serve an extensive role in transcending what is given, but they also play a *corrective* role in requiring us to change and update our beliefs.[39] We live probabilistically in the middle; as Hume puts it,

> Though we give the preference to that which has been found most usual, and believe that this effect will exist, we must not overlook the other effects, but must assign to each of them a particular weight and authority, in proportion as we have found it to be more or less frequent.[40]

This gets us toward an answer to the second question. Hume's perspective is a principle for collective thinking materialized in machine learning, applied at the level of technique in ways that mobilize our capacities for social interaction on platforms. Bookended by the input nodes of existing data as impressions, and the output nodes of usefully stabilized classification, PA graphs follow Hume's atomic theory of perception in their design. Existing data traces become sensate, imaginative, and fanciful matter for a neural network's hidden layers, with variation in example serving as fodder for its trained capacities to see resemblance, contiguity, and cause and effect according to the associative strategies of its programmers. As in the case of Google's Deep Dream Generator, designers may allow for the hallucinatory fancy of a PA graph to develop, encouraging it toward open aesthetic association as they train it. More commonplace though is to combine machinic association with the interruptions of empirical *human* association by programmers, supervising the fanciful correlations induced in neural networks through the careful backpropagation of error signals, to train and lead a PA graph toward coherent cause-and-effect relationships in the world, so that it will usefully conform to desirable automatizations in wider practice.

It's worth pausing to note the many connections between Frege, Russell, Peirce, and Hume's ideas here; the differences between their philosophical systems are subtle. Hume was deeply influential on the rest, as each sought to devise a principle for inferential succession on the basis of some objective account of self-same identity that would be compatible with mathematics. More simply, all were looking for a way to give sufficient underlying rationale for the assertion that $a = b$. McCulloch traces a lineage of ideas from Hume to Russell, for example, as responsible for combining perceptions and number in such a way as to establish conventional one-to-one correspondence between signs and things.[41] Based on the ways in which we regularly misconstrue the world linguistically and perceptually in everyday experience, each insisted that achieving this goal required the careful elaboration of logic as an impersonal mediation where thoughts as signs in the mind could stand in for real objects in the world. Contemporary data structures are the medium through which this occurs today.

Frege and Russell's approaches were based in the derivation of sentences into their logically atomic concepts, made socially normative through public assertion and the disambiguation of correct reference. They were trying to give the means for asking, are we logically referring to the same object in our use of different senses for it? Peirce's approach straddles Frege's and Hume's; like Frege's in its concern for linguistic and symbolic convention, but also resembling Hume's at the phenomenal level in connecting linguistic convention to the semiosic habits of sensation and affect. Hume himself was ultimately concerned with the atomic perceptions of an object in terms of mental states—e.g. how can I be sure that I am looking at the same object from one successive moment to the next? In term of an attendant social normativity, at a first pass, we can say that for Hume, abstract ideas become confounding and indistinct from one another as we develop them together. But we can always insist on our own sense impressions as the final arbiter for making them distinct and determinate; perception is what makes it harder for us to collectively fall into error.

But at the same time this would be to focus on the more typical, epistemological reading of Hume, which de-emphasizes social context in its heavy focus on the idea-impression pair.[42] I will have a bit more to say about self-same identity in the next chapter, but what remains to be fleshed out is how the social comes to matter for Hume, and how this might in turn bear on PA graph strategies. Hume drew a parallel between the successive movements of material bodies as we hold them to have causal necessity in our minds, and the successive behavior of human beings as we hold them to have causal necessity of *motive* and *character* in the social order. This would seem to satisfy any concerns that our interactions are sociable through knowledge and social graphs, on the terms already discussed: either through the correct negotiation of reference in language or properly belonging to social groupings. But can we extract something more specific from PA graphs, given their Humean strategy of transmuting social activity and its data traces into impressions and ideas, in a kind of *perceptual* experimentalism?

Hume and the Social

In cognate fields that influence AI research, like epistemology and the philosophy of science, Hume's ideas have tended to be explained and extended along the lines of an already-individualized thinking subject. Saul Traiger writes, for example, that Hume's core account of habitual belief and its correction typically gets interpreted in non-social ways, as concerned with the "private stock of perceptions" of an "epistemic agent."[43] With help from Deleuze and Guattari, I have been trying to think through how such epistemological approaches to the sign similarly construct our relationship to data through PA graphs in the fashion of an epistemic agent, and how we might want to rethink this relationship in a more frankly collectivizing manner. This has basically meant reading traditional epistemology more as a philosophy of media, to see how theories of knowledge get materialized through mathematical and logic procedure, such that they come to function as operational principles for our ongoing sociality. We can likewise extend this approach to Hume's ideas, which, in their application to PA graph representations, also wind up constituting a collective subject formation. In fact, Hume never used the term subjectivity, but did talk about the nature of the self in a punctuated way, in a section of his famous *Treatise* titled "Of Personal Identity."

In the same way that he radically undercut reason as a stable foundation for belief, in this section, Hume deeply undermines the notion that the self could somehow be a constant. He saw no justification for claiming a coherent perception of the self over time because in introspection, we observe only particular impressions—like feeling hot or cold, pain or pleasure, pride or shame. If understanding consists solely in habitual associations of impressions and ideas, but nevertheless produces the illusion of stable objects in the world, then by extension, *self*-identity must be similarly illusory: "The identity, which we ascribe to the mind of man, is only a fictitious one, and of a like kind with that which we ascribe to vegetables and animal bodies."[44] This is his 'bundle' theory of self; somewhat like Harrison White's theory of contingent social interactions, it contends that one is a product of their ever-changing impressions.

Because he takes an empirical approach, Hume is at pains to give definite criteria for how the mind can be a collection of distinct impressions and ideas, and, yet, somehow a subject arises from *out of* this collection, possessing a disposition *toward* it. To be consistent with his views, introspection as an 'impression of reflection' would seem to require treating already-existing mental states as having properties that could associatively resemble other mental states; but this leads to a vicious regress where, as Atkins writes, "*any* mental state would imply another mental state, and so on ad infinitum."[45] Deleuze calls it "[…] a synthesis, which is incomprehensible, since it ties together in its notion, without ever reconciling them, origin and qualification."[46] Deleuze takes a different tack in resolving it, by reading Hume's problem of knowledge more closely alongside the latter's thinking about the governance of one's will according to the general rules of a society. As we saw in the chapter epigraph, Deleuze sees the problem as not involving the origins of a private mind, but rather our constitution as subjects in society.

In the case of the understanding, the combined effects of association and imagination naturally organize our inferential anticipation that the future will resemble the past. In the case of society though, we are obliged to artificially construct the *integrative* means by which we will anticipate one another in moral terms. As Roffe puts it, "Even though their mechanisms differ, both morality and belief involve transcendence: beliefs transcend the given ('the sun will rise tomorrow'), institutions transcend the particularities of my interests."[47] People act in a principled way according to their passions, Hume thought, and, thus, in the collective interest, only relative to the sympathies of association that come from living closely with other beings around them.

Recall also that for Hume, and Deleuze as he interprets him, reason is a kind of feeling. If reason is wrapped up with practicality and the passions in our capacity to imaginatively associate, then, as Deleuze writes, reason's force cannot be self-effectuating; it must be implicated in domains that are *not reason*—that is, in institutions. He writes that

> Reason can always be brought to bear, but it is brought to bear on a preexisting world and presupposes an antecedent ethics and an

order of ends. Thus, it is because practice and morality are in their nature (and not in their circumstances) indifferent to reason that reason seeks its difference.[48]

On this reading, PA graphs represent a kind of techno-institutional solution to the problem. With their self-coalescing strategies, connectionist and Markov-chain-style graphs applied to the social order essentially represent an ongoing management of the paradox. By processing massive volumes of existing data traces as an origin for our perceptions and beliefs, PA graphs are trained to predict and qualify as-yet unseen things and people in the world.

It is easy to read this relationship in a dualistic, means/ends way, to say, for instance, that PA graphs on social platforms 'handle' the reasoning side, while we supply a set of data traces that represent the practical contexts in which we are passionately invested with our beliefs, whose causal relationships we want to rationally manage. But we need to hold on to the priorities of co-articulation between imagination and reason here. In its mobilization of cause-and-effect relations, reason follows our imaginative association as the site or source of purposiveness and not the other way around. Social platform functionality is fascinating in its ambiguity here. By way of interface, the technology incites us to see our capacity to associate as liberated by it; to imagine the world and our role in it according to its framing of cause and effect. As we accede to be socially steered and governed by its principles, we *do* wind up seeing our world in its image, and become further incentivized to continuously refine a platform's associative power, by communicating and relating to one another through it. In the bargain. however, association itself must be formatted to suit the rationalistic version of Humean association that PA graphs mobilize, and we should wonder about the ways that this may ultimately delimit our imagination in general.

Abstracted through formalization into epistemically and socially structured data graphs, the associational power of the passions falls further subject to reason as rationalistic, as platforms translate these passions into their own order of ends, using us to feed their PA graphs. The difference is slippery but amounts to finding something transcendentally rational in the imaginative association to be *extracted* versus privileging imagination itself *as* transcendental. By offering free tools for our social interaction in the form of commercial knowledge and social graphs, platforms guarantee that our passional associations will continue to be framed in ways that reproduce this approach to causality. Although Humean in conceptual structure, except at the moment of the graph's construction and training by practitioners, PA technology possesses no means to represent its cultural situatedness in an antecedent ethics, or order of ends.

If reason is felt and invested in passions, then the underlying practical circumstances that give rise to those passions are supposed to be what determine the conditions under which we feel the necessity of cause and effect, as the mind is affected by "the idea of an object to form the idea of an other object."[49] This feeling gets formatted in pursuit of an instrumental analysis of impressions and ideas on AI-supported social platforms though, which manage their software apparatus as a kind of privatized mind unto itself. Through their social interfaces, platforms stimulate our associative passions as they are embedded in other contexts, but only to format them in ways that ensure their associative power will persist in producing value through their PA graphs, accumulating through delegation of the cause-and-effect relations in our lives. This is in contrast to the individual reasoning that goes on according to the associative feelings of causal necessity generated by particular social groupings; what we might call an individual's embedding in multiple and overlapping collective minds. Ideally it would be the *context* of inference that determines the associative power of the mind's cause-and-effect relation and not the other way around.

Deleuze's more passional reading of Hume helps to bolster the claim. He places an outsized emphasis on Hume's analysis of the moral affections, as these combine with the understanding in the impression of reflection. Human beings for Hume don't just possess beliefs as agents; through the habits of life together they are also naturally sympathetic to one another. In the same way that habitual belief required unpacking, making sense of this habitual sympathy seems crucial. To both good and bad effect, PA graph strategies and the platforms that deploy them increasingly play a cognitive and social role, according to their powerful solutions to the Humean paradox of origin and qualification in thinking. As people like Turow and Helmond suggest, association according to the original, chaotic, but nevertheless more radically open, principle of the hyperlink is being industrially transformed into a particular account of association as a principle of understanding, and a sympathy of connection between people. The continuing problem is that both are designed to serve a commercial social platform's AI strategies.

In line with critiques by people like Taplin and Taylor, but framing the problem in a more explicitly philosophical register, we need to be asking, if cause and effect is the most important associative principle, and if association is ultimately a product of the imagination, then in what sense are we literally ceding our imagination to social platforms and the manner in which they render our impressions and ideas atomically through PA graphs? More speculatively, if we wanted to come up with some new set of protocols, practices, and processes that represent some 'better' social web, but still organized on Humean principles for thinking, then how might we re-conceptualize the atomic unit of data in a way that foregrounds Deleuze's reading of Hume's reason as fundamentally socially imaginative in its associative atomism, and only secondarily associative in the more individualized, cognitive sense that Hume's ideas are currently deployed?

When association is designed to conform to scientifically rational and calculative accounts of what it means for two things to relate, then we shouldn't be surprised that our collective imagination will get channeled in a particular way. This is what happens in the turn to PA graphs, which organize the relationship between association and atomism in the epistemological terms of an already-individualized thinking subject. By returning to Deleuze and Guattari's mixed semiotic, we can see some of the consequences for our understanding of the social.

Asignifying Association

Guattari writes that

> An assemblage of enunciation will be derived sometimes from the side of signification and sometimes from the side of diagrammatism depending on the transformations of its composition. In fact all the assemblages of enunciation involving the human world are mixed.[50]

Picking up on some initial threads of criticism leveled against PA graphs earlier in the chapter, we can say along these lines that although knowledge, social, and PA graphs are mixed, when it comes to PA graphs specifically, the significational as defined by the former two graph styles depreciates as a model for collective thinking in favor of one that is more directly diagrammatic. It is control over the function of the diagrammatic that represents the powerful semiotic dominance of today's commercial social computing platforms. We enter into, or find ourselves captivated by, the principles of association that commercial social computing platforms offer because they speak to certain basic principles of human understanding. Whether framed in terms of epistemic belief or tendential sympathy for one another, they offer us relational logics through which we can imaginatively and usefully transcend our givenness, mobilize our drives and passions, and see ourselves as adhering to the general rules of society through the ordered fixation of these in practical reason. From this broader perspective, we are in a better position to spend some time comparing the various strategies in the next chapter.

Notes

1 Genosko, *Remodelling Communication*, 127.
2 Atkins, *Self and Subjectivity*, 34.
3 Shead, "Google Is Using Its Highly Intelligent Computer Brain to Slash Its Enormous Electricity Bill."
4 Domingos, "A Few Useful Things to Know about Machine Learning."
5 Collins, *Artificial Experts*, 60.
6 Adam, *Artificial Knowing*, 37.
7 As quoted in Dreyfus, "From Micro-Worlds to Knowledge Representation," 162.

8 Ibid., 168.
9 Domingos, *The Master Algorithm*, 86.
10 Dean, *Democracy and Other Neoliberal Fantasies*, 31.
11 Taplin, *Move Fast and Break Things*, 4.
12 Guattari and Cooper, *Molecular Revolution*, 96. Emphasis added.
13 See Pariser, *The Filter Bubble*.
14 See, for example, Tufekci, *Twitter and Tear Gas*; Taylor, *The People's Platform*.
15 See Andrejevic, *Infoglut*.
16 Domingos, *The Master Algorithm*, 164.
17 Wired Staff, "The Click Heard Round The World."
18 Nelson and Brand, *Computer Lib/Dream Machines, Revised Edition.*
19 Page et al., "The PageRank Citation Ranking: Bringing Order to the Web," 27–28.
20 Langville and Meyer, *Google's PageRank and Beyond*, 29.
21 Riordan, "What Are Eigen Values?"
22 Kauffman, "Eigenforms — Objects as Tokens for Eigenbehaviours," 74.
23 Helmond, "The Algorithmization of the Hyperlink."
24 Halpern, *Beautiful Data*, 153.
25 Marcus, *The Algebraic Mind*, 11–13.
26 O'Neil, *Weapons of Math Destruction*, 76.
27 Harris, "Machine Learning - What Does the Hidden Layer in a Neural Network Compute?"
28 Domingos, *The Master Algorithm*, 8.
29 Marcus, *The Algebraic Mind*, 18.
30 Hume, *An Enquiry Concerning Human Understanding*, 39.
31 Taleb, *The Black Swan*.
32 Mumford and Anjum, *Causation*, 119.
33 Hume, *An Enquiry Concerning Human Understanding*, 11.
34 Deleuze, *Empiricism and Subjectivity*, 30.
35 Ibid., 24.
36 Ibid., 83.
37 Roffe, *Gilles Deleuze's Empiricism and Subjectivity*, 24.
38 Hume, *An Enquiry Concerning Human Understanding*, 29.
39 Roffe, *Gilles Deleuze's Empiricism and Subjectivity*, 30.
40 Hume, *An Enquiry Concerning Human Understanding*, 39.
41 McCulloch, *Embodiments of Mind*, 6.
42 Roffe, *Gilles Deleuze's Empiricism and Subjectivity*, 81.
43 Traiger, "Beyond Our Senses: Recasting Book I, Part 3 of Hume's 'Treatise,'" 242.
44 Hume, Norton, and Norton, *A Treatise of Human Nature*, 169.
45 Atkins, *Self and Subjectivity*, 35.
46 Deleuze, *Empiricism and Subjectivity*, 31.
47 Roffe, *Gilles Deleuze's Empiricism and Subjectivity*, 105.
48 Deleuze, *Empiricism and Subjectivity*, 33.
49 Hume, *An Enquiry Concerning Human Understanding*, 36.
50 Guattari, *The Machinic Unconscious*, 54.

5 The Allagmatically Formatted Subject

The pragmatic fields dominated by diagrammatic pragmatic transformations remain haunted by subjects of enunciation that have been
exhausted in the signifying individuation of the enunciation. The representation of a listener-speaker as the fictitious pole of the production of statements becoming increasingly abstract to them and the
fact that 'one continues to speak' through the mouth of individuals
nevertheless takes on an increasingly relative scope.
—Félix Guattari, *The Machinic Unconscious*

We have come an appreciable distance toward understanding the conceptual commitments of global graphs. From their initial abstraction
as labeled nodes that relate together through directed edges, graphs
have since taken on at least three different forms: as networks of predicable fact, performed social connection, and signaletic pattern. When
implemented in support of a social platform, the differences between
them will matter little to the average user. Most of us are content to
manage what's significant in our lives via the convenient affordances
built atop their structures, which operate behind the scenes. By lingering
over their intellectual influences and semiotic commitments though, the
hope is to have made graphs more critically legible; to show that there is
potentially much more at stake in their designs than simple convenience
or conviviality.

Formatting the world by graph now plays a significant role in state
surveillance, for example, and is introducing seismic fault lines into the
division of labor, as predictive-analytic (PA) graphs are being deployed to
automate elements of intellectual labor once thought impossible. In the
more intimate sphere of public and private life, graphs are shifting our
sense of self in relation to other people to become a new site for the performance of identity. We might go so far as to say that our concerns over
big data reflect how graphs are emerging as a kind of scientific blueprint
for the management of complex societies. With four decades of specula-
tion and debate around the information society under our belts though,
it can easy to be nonplussed by such sweeping claims. Aren't global

graphs simply innovation building on innovation, at worst a 'double-edged sword', like so many other technologies?

Three things seem qualitatively different in the deployment of global graphs. The first is the extent to which, through their more flexible structures, graphs enable our friendships, interests, beliefs, public opinions, and private proclivities to become much more transparently individualized. The second is the degree to which statistical modeling of the social order occurs in more sophisticated and nuanced ways as a result, a side effect being for probability theory to take on a new significance in many aspects of life. A third difference is that commercial motivations behind the development of global graphs are driving an intensifying monopolization of the world's information and knowledge on these terms, producing a formatted subject relation that, whatever its technical features may be, is essentially aligned to fit with the needs of a neoliberal order. As Ronald Day puts it, behind surface claims of convenience and efficiency for the end user, "The sociotechnical (self-)modeling of individuals and their (self-)positioning within political economies constitutes much of the state and commercial governance and construction of the subject in modernity."[1]

As with theorizations of the information society in the past, there is a wealth of popular and academic writing that is focused on the potential consequences of this, what Rob Kitchin calls the 'Data Revolution': how people will take advantage of, suffer the effects of, or otherwise realize themselves through the blueprint of global graphs, as societies and individuals turn to their underlying abstractions in the form of big data social platforms. Much of this work is important and timely. But over and above insightful theorizations of citizens or embodied subjects making sense of themselves in this context of creeping datafication, I have been arguing that we must also consider how the representational strategies of graphs—in many ways, datafication itself—produces an individualizing context in the first place, as a matter of formal-semiotic technique.

At this level, platform designs and their underlying graph data structures involve the imposition of pre-individualizing assumptions about our somatic, cognitive, discursive, and social relationship to signs, and these determine, especially at the operational level, what we effectively mean by social relation as a *techno-material* relation. Turning to Gilles Deleuze and Félix Guattari's concept of the enunciative assemblage has, I hope, sensitized us to this aspect of social computing, troubling the notion that the technology is somehow an extension or supplement to communication as we traditionally understand it. It is certainly true that graph technologies help to establish highly engaging and efficient spaces for social interaction, leading to complex practices that we nevertheless can recognize as continuous with past communication technologies. But it is equally true that because real time social computing relies on a particular mixture of statistical practices, protocols, and algorithms to achieve these communicative conditions, we must examine their overall operations for important differences.

To do this, I have been mostly focused on how datafication can be seen in terms of a tension between theorizations of the sign. To return to a bit of the philosopher Horst Ruthrof's vocabulary, we can frame the tension as between an experiential subject who encounters the world *hetero-semiotically*—according to a mixture of discursive and nondiscursive forces, as one negotiates communities of knowers using social computing technology—and theories of the sign that see the world in *homo-semiotic* terms, using formal techniques from logic and mathematics to stipulate and circumscribe meaning operationally, ensuring its causal, imperative, or machinic effectivity. As Mark Hansen writes, this is how mediated experience

> [...] simply is not what it used to be: far more of what goes on in our daily lives is carried out by machines functioning at their own timescales, meaning outside of our direct perceptual grasp but in ways that do significantly affect our activity.[2]

Abstract disciplinary diagrams like the DIKW pyramid, for example, make sense of the tension by stratifying signs in a particular way. According to its layers, selective organization of some lack of uniformity in the world drives an initial empirical pattern, which, when made measurable, comes to act as a homo-semiotic substrate for knowledge, enabling the marking and calculation of significant relationships between phenomena, things, or people. Data gains purpose here as information, as we project principles of inferential decision onto its measurable patterns. Its symbolizing objectivity allows us in turn to mobilize our intentions to one another in a practical context too, resulting in a subject-object relationship that permits efficient communication on social terms, as we circulate valid knowledge. Like traditional relational databases before them, graph data structures have begun to act as a powerful infrastructure for *global* accountability on these terms; whether in scientific practice; between institutions, businesses, and workers; or in the management of interpersonal relations.

Meanwhile, Deleuze and Guattari understand the phenomenon of semiosis, the patterned structures that it organizes, and the underlying teloi its patterns incentivize, in rather different terms. For them, stratifications of the sign implied in models like the DIKW pyramid too often represent a universalizing approach that they seek to criticize for being too beholden to precepts in the philosophy of language and insufficiently attentive to the concrete *effects* of language in its actual conditions of use. At issue for them are the notions of material *constancy* and *variation;* for any enunciative assemblage, on what basis is constancy being produced in bodies and language, and for what purposes is variation being put into play? Models in computer and information science like the DIKW pyramid answer these questions through appeals to *linguistic* constants, like syntax and semantics, which tend to relegate the pragmatics of concrete meaning-use to a kind of socializing 'after effect' of their formal assumptions. We saw this, for example, back in Chapter 3 with John Searle's notion of illocutionary force.

There can be no doubting that treating pragmatics as a byproduct of language, taken as a unified system, can be incredibly powerful. We rely, for example, on search engines that parse words in a strictly syntactical way, and yet derive highly useful metrics of semantic authority in the process, simply by treating language in terms of its empirical-informational variation, divorced from its underlying context. That said, we have also been discussing how pragmatics understood in this way have a kind of sterilizing effect on language. Semiotic formalization can make it difficult for us to capture the more concrete dimensions of language, like dissensus, which should matter to us a great deal when negotiating our collective organization. Overall, the tension between these views is a way of grasping Deleuze and Guattari's underlying position: they are not opposed to using language for communication or understanding; they just always want to put the mixture of bodies, language, and the effected transformations of an enunciative assemblage *ahead* of seeing language itself as somehow the "sufficient basis for explaining the relation of language to events," as James Williams explains.[3]

For them, whenever constancy is secured for the purposes of variable effectivity in speaking and acting, this comes to pass only because power has successfully *vested* itself in bodies, language, and reference, through what they call 'order-words'. Giving the example of a strict schoolteacher who organizes student bodies and their dispositions to speak, they write that "Language is made not to be believed but to be obeyed, and to compel obedience."[4] For the purposes of theorizing the formatted subject in social computing, on this view, we are never simply competent language-users, successful communicators, or knowledge retrievers. As Guattari puts it in *The Three Ecologies*,

> Rather than speak of the 'subject', we should perhaps speak of *components of subjectification*, each working more or less on its own. [...] Vectors of subjectification do not necessarily pass through the individual, which in reality appears to be something like a 'terminal' for processes that involve human groups, socio-economic ensembles, data-processing machines, etc.[5]

Bringing such a perspective to bear on conversations about the future of the Internet and web means complicating the humanistically styled, communicating, empirico-rational subject that is presumed by schemas like the DIKW framework, to insist that any model of communicative sign-relation like it be judged according to its social and political capacities for intervening and *ordering* the world. Let me be clear here that I am in no way agitating against the ordered circulation of knowledge overall, especially as it is framed according to the ethics of fields like library science and information studies. Access to knowledge opens up societies and liberates people from their ignorance.

Nor am I agitating for some kind of romantic refusal of systems of rationality, as we project them into computer technology. Rather, given the current circumstances of global, real time social computing procedures now being a main source of significance for so many people, I am interested in revisiting the underlying semiotic conditions under which the rational and the irrational are separated from one another in today's social platforms, so as to see their effects simultaneously at the level of socio-cognitive and socio-*political* organization. In light of the ways that knowledge gets increasingly captured by information systems (IS) that seek to extract economic value from it, according to semiotic relationalities that seem by design to monopolize these conditions of global expression, I am looking for other approaches to knowledge and other approaches to the sign-relation.

Guattari's concept of the part-sign has been especially helpful in this regard for interrogating what we mean by data. Conceived as affective, hypothetical traits that flow through and alongside our rational communication and knowledge-exchange, part-signs trigger our imaginations as they interlace with order-words to center and motivate associative thinking and acting in rational ways. Obscured by accounts of datafication that privilege already-existing subject-object relationalities on linguistic terms, the idea of the part-sign allows one to see how desire can be channeled by the asignifying imperatives of institutions to promote certain subjectifying effects at the level of collective habit. This is what Guattari means in the chapter's epigraph; we take up institutional frameworks as a way of claiming our signifying individuality but fail to recognize that they are effectively machinic poles of subjects and objects that mostly serve the purposes of that institution. Attention to these features of networked technologies has never mattered so much because, as Bernd Frohmann writes, in our modern context,

> We do not so much use digital writing machines to record and disseminate 'information' as we feed machines that write us in scripts far removed from our knowledge and control. Since in the digitally networked environment writing becomes executable, it takes the form of raw material for cybernetic command and control mechanisms based upon the traces of the movements of persons, data, and machines.[6]

It is a perspective that computer scientists and IS designers must now grapple with, given that social computing environments function as sites not just for the retrieval of knowledge and information, but also for the agonal encounter and expression of knowledge in *political* contention. It can be fascinating to see how commercial platforms harness the energies of political contention as a way to optimize the circulation of knowledge. Strategies like the 'hashtag' continue to serve an intriguing dual role, for example, as both galvanizing force for groups and empirical signal for information retrieval. At the same time, as demonstrated by crude tactics like 'fake news', 'doxxing', and 'web brigading', political conflict is also projecting into social computing environments in strange and deleterious ways. Complicating the picture, political contention plays out on the one hand at the level of the communicating subject, along lines of traditional party and activist politics, as groups seek to promote and realize change with respect to particular issues. But it is also developing in the asignifiying register too, as groups and users seek to challenge oligarchic control over knowledge by the major social computing platforms by engaging in a politics of technology that seeks to break apart and reconfigure our present conditions of global knowledge production, whether through hacking or alternative platform design practices.[7]

Taking all of this in, we might summarize by indicating the pressing need to consider how graph data structures will fit together with the body politic, which John Protevi helpfully describes as an "imbrication of the social and the somatic," as social computing technology continues to develop as an infrastructure of control for both capital and the state.[8] To apply Deleuze and Guattari's core insight here, any sign-function produced by a global graph will be as much about the pre-individual, diagrammatic, and asignifying power operations required to achieve its individualizing sociality than it will be about some capacity for convivial communication or knowledge-exchange between users. Crosscutting debates around the ontological and epistemological status of data, which have begun to converge on common themes in computer and information science, human-computer interaction (HCI) design, philosophy, science and technology studies, and social theory are welcome for putting us in a better position to see in full scope just how important technical formalizations of the sign will be to our collective future.

If only in the more limited sense of how ideas find their way into social computing practice, having these conversations means seeing some of our most convincing accounts of what it means to perceive, act, know, and communicate in more contingent terms. Technical coherence remains the litmus test at the level of operation, of course; but we must continue to interrogate how existing formalizations too quickly assume a 'conduit metaphor' between individuals in their approach; that somehow, the best way to frame the circulation of signs is in terms of their efficient exchange between agents. Questioning this model means complicating the dominant narrative around social computing at the level of technique because it demands that we more carefully account for the affective, cultural, and institutional effects that shape significance in experience.

Putting such concerns to technologists should in no way diminish the fact that, as it stands, knowledge production and social interaction over networked devices occurs with incredible convenience, global reach, and creative power on precisely these 'agentic' terms. Reflected in diagrammatic thinking like the DIKW pyramid, the traditions of analytic philosophy, mathematics, computational social science, and other related fields seem to dovetail with software design and information and systems theory in highly convincing ways to offer a robust account of what knowledge *is*, what purpose it *serves*, and how it might be scientifically separated out from irrelevance and falsehood. As demonstrated by ongoing knowledge and social graph projects like Wikidata or the World Wide Web Consortium (W3C) Social Web Working Group, for example, societies move toward greater openness, and benefit greatly from rigorous approaches to knowledge and information, when we mediatize societies on the basis of empirical factuality and valid reasoning.

Communicating electronically on these terms assures a kind of streamlined social rationality too, with a seemingly desirable mode of subjectification at its core; one framed according to a logic of open decision, and a certain normative structure toward others, that clearly has the potential to modulate social order on a global scale. That said, I have been trying to describe how each graph-style, read as an enunciative assemblage, also brings with it a particular metaphysics of identity and difference upon which this social order and capacity for decision is based. I want to address this aspect in a more comparative way in this chapter, as an exercise in wondering whether the various rationalist, performative, and empiricist frameworks examined so far exhaust our options for thinking through the production of subjects and objects in graph technique.

Given that each style offers such a powerful and efficient coordinating strategy for collective thinking, asking after alternatives may turn out to be a fruitless exercise. Whether we are talking about Peircean or Fregean logical idealization, Habermasian communicative rationality, Searlesian or ethnomethodological performativity, or Humean impression, existing philosophical framings of global graphs seem convincingly well established. Through their semiotic formatting, each offers a way for us to transcend both our private beliefs in relation to the universal objectivity of knowledge and, equally, to at least partially transcend our selfish motives through a communicative relation to members of wider communities and societies. Add to that, each is compatible with the extant material requirements of software design, which represent a hard-won consensus around making technical practices function smoothly across the Internet. Still more generally, each seems to line up with our basic socio-linguistic sense of what it means to be a rational person.

To put it yet another way, we rely on these graph-styles because they function so well as productive *totalizations* of meaning. By selecting features from the semiotic multiplicity of things, people, and processes in which we live and stipulating them as data, global graphs establish a reliable mode of existence; a separated, self-sufficient domain of entities to which we can habitually orient ourselves in language, as we think about and do things in the world together. It's on the basis of such a mode of existence that users, designers, and programmers may compete and cooperate to build upon existing layers in establishing new forms of sociality, too. Perhaps most importantly, each totalization materializes some set of principles for the distribution of identity and difference; not just in terms of how we are made 'self-same' with respect to one another when negotiating our personal identity relative to the difference of others in a social context or system, but also how we, and the things around us, are made 'self-same' in the fuller sense of objectuality and *logical-numerical* identity. It is ultimately according to the latter principles of identity and difference that the world and our selves will get inscribed into computers by becoming different or remaining coherently the same through their semiotic formalizations.

All of this leads me to discuss the graph-styles covered so far in a more comparative way, through appeal to a concept in the chapter's title: the *allagmatic*. I borrow the term from the philosopher Gilbert Simondon to mean *that which can be taken or given in exchange*. The term is useful for generalizing across the graph structures to capture how social computing is ultimately a technology, variously implemented, for our collective becoming-social *through* some theory of change. The formalizing techniques discussed represent a kind of harnessing of the vicissitudes of societies where, as already mentioned, identity and difference are about our personal identities as existential singularities, yet this singularity is keyed to some more universalizing relationality that determines what is the same and what is different through some institutional assemblage that we collectively inhabit. Martin Heidegger gets at the issue in his usual sagacious but enigmatic way when he writes that

> If we think of belonging *together* in the customary way, the meaning of belonging is determined by the word together, that is, by its unity. In that case, 'to belong' means as much as: to be assigned and placed into the order of a 'together,' established in the unity of a manifold, combined into the unity of a system, mediated by the unifying center of an authoritative synthesis. Philosophy represents this belonging together as *nexus* and *connexio*, the necessary connection of the one with the other. However, belonging together can also be thought of as *belonging* together. This means: the 'together' is now determined by the belonging. Of course, we must still ask here what 'belong' means in that case, and how its peculiar 'together' is determined only in its terms.[9]

As Geoffrey C. Bowker and Susan Leigh Star lay out in much more pragmatic terms, classification procedures such as those enabled and supported by global graphs set up certain conditions for belonging together, according to logics of comparability, visibility, and control, as we address one another and think together through them. Practically speaking, they write that at this level, "Blurring categories means that existing differences are covered up, merged, or removed altogether; while distinctions construct new partitions or reinforcement of existing differences."[10] In other words, they take a social-constructionist view toward the politics of classification. Sympathetic to their many resulting insights, I am suggesting a related need to understand the philosophical commitments behind the *selective event* of classification, too; what we might call, following those who debate the matter in philosophy like Gottlob Frege, Charles Sanders Peirce, Heidegger, Deleuze, and Guattari, the semiotic event of *sense*.

Beyond the important insight that our collective prejudices and blind spots in thinking risk material instantiation into information infrastructures, we need to be thinking about potential blind spots in the semiotic regimes that produce and maintain the initial biunivocalizing conditions for classification; those logics that connect representative to represented, signifier to signified, individualized self to other, and so on. Reflexivity around classificatory practice matters, but so too does reflexivity around the underlying metaphysical premises *of* those practices, because it is on those terms that graph platforms will enact their operations, capturing and processing immanent semiotic diversity into subject-object relations and particular social orderings.

At the center of each graph-style lies some transcendent term—logic, performance, cognition—that does this; totalizing our relationship to signs as a way for us to take up a social computing platform as a separable domain that is useful for classifying and retrieving events, things, and people. Where Heidegger saw this locus largely in terms of his existential ontology and the question of being, Deleuze and Guattari see it more as the materialization of a form/substance doubling in an enunciative assemblage. Bodies, things, and language come into being through the reciprocal positing of a plane of content and a plane of expression, leading to the production of a semiotic substance through the imposition onto matter of some transcendental semiotic form.

Insofar as we appreciate a platform's capacity to organize knowledge and discourse in rational ways on the basis of such an assemblage, we will see it as a way of creatively orienting ourselves to things and people, and as a freeing mode of subjectivation, to which we invest what Deleuze and Guattari call our desiring production. At the same time, we have also been considering graph platforms to be 'dividualizing', to use Deleuze's term, or as what Heidegger described as a site for the 'ordering revealing' of the world, via a cybernetic enframing of language itself.

That is to say, not liberating at all, but rather treating semiotic diversity in the world, and language as we rely on it to name that diversity, as matter to be controlled according to some knowledge-power relation. Florian Cramer called it cybernetic control ideology, Guattari called it semiotic subjugation, and, following Guattari, Maurizio Lazzarato most recently describes this ordering relation as *machinic enslavement*.

For our purposes, it may be more productive to say that a kind of loaded, socio-semiotic deal is on offer. In exchange for 'enslavement' to population-governing algorithms and protocols, which follow the form of the proposition in their graph-theoretical processes, we are collectively afforded a powerful and global capacity to observe the world and make statements in it by way of a platform's mixture of techniques, operations, and interface affordances. For this capacity to emerge though, a formal decoding of our affects, beliefs, and dispositions must take place, cross-articulating part-signs into the asignifying possibilities of computers to inflect our behavior at the level of the somatic. I have been remiss in not saying more often that this cross-articulation occurs in endlessly complex and myriad ways, across various and interlocking strata of institution and system. In my defense, I have been so exclusively focused on the decoding of sign-relations into data graphs because I believe this represents a tremendously important locus for the form/substance doubling that Deleuze and Guattari describe.

What I want to accomplish in this chapter, then, is a more general cross-comparison of each graph approach as a product of this doubling moment of content and expression, form and substance. Continuing to rely on Deleuze and Guattari's concepts of part- and asignifying signs, I will suggest some benefits and drawbacks of each system while also including a couple of other styles of graph. The first of these is classical hypertext. As a more contemporary example, I will also make mention of Twitter's graph to show how the strategies that have been pulled apart over the past few chapters for analytical purposes actually come to operate multi-modally on social platforms. Then, as a culmination of the chapter's cross-comparisons, in the concluding chapter, I describe in outline a more speculative approach based directly on the insights of Deleuze and Guattari's collective assemblage of enunciation. The idea here is that after laying out the approaches and limitations of existing graph systems with an eye to cherry-picking their best features, we might begin to imagine some kind of new practice. For want of a catchier name, I will simply call this more speculative example an enunciative graph.

Finally, at the risk of further blunting the radical thrust and nuance of Deleuze and Guattari's philosophy, over the course of this chapter, I will be relying on three much simpler terms of art for the purposes of comparison. They are my own, inspired by the mixed semiotic approach, but simplified to align with social computing practices, in ways that will undoubtedly miss the mark in terms of a careful fidelity to their ideas.

The upside will be some terminology that, again, facilitates the goal of comparison between styles. The three terms I have in mind are *hinting, stating,* and *formatting.*

Hint, State, Format

The term hinting is meant to simplify the relationship between part-signs and asignifying signs, laid out at the end of Chapter 3. The underlying question that it helps us to ask is, what are some of the main, machinic commitments of a particular graph-style? Recall that part-signs are non-representable constellations of intensity and resonance, which operate below meaning at the level of 'start/stop' events, across biological, somatic, and techno-material process. Specific to technology, part-signs are most often conceived as informational signals; but in the turn to a mixed semiotic, we want to hold on to their status as a micro-political site for the organization of asignifying processes, which produce a consistency of meaning as a function of their circulation according to the ordering power of institutions. Not allowing their status to slip too quickly into empirico-rational definition then, part-signs are better understood as captivated by and interfacing with, but not equivalent to, data. It is true that they are like unorganized signals in that they possess an asemantic regularity and a point-like existence. But because precision in our usual understanding of data matters only retroactively according to the linguistic operations of semantics, we want to retain a certain plasticity for part-signs, which, in Guattari's telling, involves their potential for travel or drift from one asignifying system into another.

Hinting short hands the non-verbal potentials of our behavior and disposition, which articulate to, but sit below, the stable, referential units produced by an enunciative assemblage at the level of discourse. Hints are particle-like relations that operate on the level of asignification whose cross-articulation with statements bring about both interpretive and non-interpretive transformations in an assemblage, shifting and altering the contours of intersubjective sociality as they inflect one another over time. A silly example might be the trend toward purposely-misspelled or vowel-free band names in today's music scene. Everyday speech is arguably mixing with the asignifying strategies of search engines here to produce new social formations. This is because glitchy band names travel more efficiently online, in being composed of conspicuous combinations of letters that inhibit polysemous confusion. At the same time, such names also introduce stuttering, asignifying negotiations at the socio-semiological level of speech, and perhaps even provoke new group boundaries between those who are and are not culturally 'in the know' around the name's exact pronunciation.

Again, the simple point here is that signs are never solely linguistic and communicative, but rather come charged with non-verbal and intensive somatic habits at the level of part- and asignifying sign, which may shift and change over time in their articulation to one another into language, illocution, and order, as these are modulated by a concrete assemblage of enunciation. I settle on the term hinting as a somewhat fraught and abridged way to capture the relationship of collectively leading and being led by the vagaries of one's habits and desires in a negotiated way on social platforms, holding onto the notion that part-signs are more than a signaletic, empirical product of the platforms themselves. Clicking on a 'thumbs up' recommendation button, letting our mouse pointer linger over some region of the screen, resetting our search parameters in frustration, or passively registering our GPS coordinates on a social computing platform are all usefully captured data-points, but all happen relative to our position in some wider semiotic field of assembled forces, which modulate our desire to act or to be pre-disposed in certain non-verbal ways. As Gary Genosko puts it more vividly, part-signs operate and combine "in the non-linear ecologies of networked life by diagrams that 'twist' their tendencies and 'blur' their encounters with machine codes."[11]

Finally, hinting obviously aligns with the notion, at this point common to popular and academic writing on social platforms, that life online involves leaving behind data traces. The only difference that I want to underline here is a desire to frame these traces in terms of their potential for ongoing meaning-effects and not simply as 'completed' or left behind for the platform's designers and engineers to use. Platforms do capture these traces as inscribed data points, but the signs we give off and exchange are about more than just inscription. They involve the continuous stabilization and destabilization of a mixture of discursive, technological, and incorporeal processes of collective meaning making.

Continuing along this line of thinking, the term *stating* gathers up those processes of semiotic modulation that are more explicitly framed in terms of communication between an individualized self and other—basically, features styled to be explicitly intersubjective on the basis of language, speakers and hearers, and the propositional form. As compared to non-verbal hints, stating is about subjects participating primarily in the *interpretive* transformations of an enunciative assemblage. In the case of social computing, this generally means a set of stable affordances in a platform's interface that correspond to the propositional slots of a relational or graph-structured database.

When 'linked up' graph data is used to coordinate facts between two government agencies, or when we rely on a social platform like Facebook to declare a new romance or have a conversation with friends, here we are dealing with more clearly-identified referential entities at the level of language, which relate to one another in terms of what Deleuze and Guattari call signifying semiologies. Communicating subjects make statements as they reason together by resemblance, analogy, and consensus. Of course, statements may flow alongside hints, as when we finish off a tweet using a hashtag; or they may themselves become hints, as when we use stored banks of statements (large datasets) to train PA graphs as tools for steering us into new contexts for making statements.

A crucial feature of stating is that it resolves what Deleuze calls the paradox of reference. As he describes it in *The Logic of Sense*, the paradox involves an issue of circularity in the sign relation between what he calls denotation, manifestation, and signification. Denotation involves the propositional form as we have been discussing it so far with respect to data: how we draw upon concepts in common sense, in order to secure the correct intersubjective recognition of entities in good sense. Denotative common sense concerns existing views. Manifestation is focused on personal belief, and the fact that, as we saw in the last chapter with Deleuze's reading of David Hume, any universal or commonsensical conceptuality can ultimately be rooted only in the concrete and ongoing activities of a group or society, as individuals express their beliefs and desires through the sheer habit of saying 'I'. Finally, signification concerns the fact that, as we saw in the case of Frege and Peirce, the necessary *advancement* of our intuitions—testing them as good sense on the basis of denotation in common sense—can occur only relative to whatever dominant semiology is maintaining the logic of denotation.

Each of the phases requires the others, and the point is that each graph-style represents a technological solution for resolving the paradox. The circuit only works if we are willing to subordinate our imaginative capacity to think and associate with one another to some transcendental account that puts the circuit in motion, detailing what it means to refer together in the first place. When it comes to design, the movements of good and common sense are reconciled to operate both at the level of the semiological and the asignifying. In the register of the asignifying, they are reduced to the minimal and highly abstract movements of computational state according to the directed graph, in a strictly denotative mode. But the abstract edges and arrows of graphs also point the way for good sense to be expressed as a conceptual imperative, laid out in the middle range of technique. Through various transformational and asignifying layers of design, common sense eventually articulates to good sense by somehow capturing the manifestational energies of both our non-interpretive habits and our interpretive references to realize good sense in collective signification, as the technology continually reinvests us into the paradox.

As Levi Bryant summarizes it, the problem here for Deleuze is that the whole philosophical arrangement amounts to a *vicious circle*, where "[...] the conditions are supposed to account for the possibility of truth within experience, yet the conditions themselves get their justification insofar as experience is taken to be true."[12] Another way to say this is that with transcendental accounts such as those given by Frege and

Peirce, sense gets defined from *inside* the circle of reference. For Deleuze, it must be located elsewhere, in what he calls the virtual, which Brian Massumi describes as a realm of paradoxical *potential*: "The virtual is a lived paradox where what are normally opposites coexist, coalesce, and connect; where what cannot be experienced cannot but be felt— albeit reduced and contained."[13] For our purposes, the graph-styles can be evaluated as apparatuses for our collective, *technical* resolution of Deleuze's circle of reference, using it as a kind of litmus test for how each truth procedure comes to concretely resolve the paradox of the virtual in ways that organize and structure sociality.

To say this all a bit more colloquially, statements involve the index- ation of change, according to some step or ratio in which the formatted subject is obliged or incentivized to *manifest* themselves as an 'I' in terms of moving from 'where I was', or 'where this entity was' in *denotation*, to 'where I am now', or 'where this entity is, should be, or belongs', in *signification*. Social platforms produce such a process by mobilizing some combination of transcendentally logical, and transcendentally social, accounts of the sign to serialize thinking in a particular way. I continue to conflate their ideas here, but for both Deleuze and Guattari, the problem that emerges from the paradox of reference is that, as mentioned back in Chapter 1, failing proper recourse to the virtual as potential, nothing in the arrangement is left for thinking to condition *it- self* on the basis of one's singularity. Another way to put it is that subjec- tivation continually gives way to subjectification, as thinking gives over its creative, ontogenetic differences so that they may act in the service of the platform's denotative technique.

Finally, consistent with Deleuze and Guattari's move to relativize the sign as only secondarily a communicative phenomenon, I will use the term *formatting* to describe the conditions for co-articulating a plane of content with a plane of expression to produce an enunciative basis for hinting and stating in the first place. The term formatting is meant to ensure that we ultimately compare approaches on the basis of their overall imagined, transcendental appeals to intersubjective relation; it represents a substantial simplification of what Deleuze and Guattari call an *abstract machine*. The latter is where some set of potentiali- ties meets with some other set of potentialities to initialize or set in motion the dynamic planes of an assemblage, generating its capacity to produce existential consistency in the first place. Massumi explains the abstract machine in terms of the moment where material process and patterning first overlap to effect the possibility of meaning in an enunciative assemblage: "Even considered as a diagram enveloping the abstract machine(s), the linguistic expression has no subjective interi- ority, only a redundancy of outsides: the meaning-effect as evaporative double, and the dynamic in-between, or interrelation of relations, that it transformationally duplicates."[14]

In their abstraction, we can see graphs as a technological means for initializing this dynamic; crucial for producing meaning-effects at the material level of computers, and yet their relations ostensibly disappear in the graph-style's transformational duplication into meaning-exchange, as we come to ascribe some quasi-causal force of knowing-that, or knowing-who, according to the purified semiotics of nodes, edges, and arrows of mathematical graph theory. I use the term formatting as a simplifying term for describing one's access to this initializing moment of technical possibility—the power to configure how statements and hints will function on a given platform. Less so than computers, we are talking about the abstracting powers of differential calculus, graph theory, and network science itself to spatialize and temporalize signs in ways that foster their comparison in calculation, upon which meaning-effects will accrue. Mindful of Guattari describing these conditions as micro-political, it is from this vantage point that I will be in a position to offer a, admittedly crude and speculative, sketch of another site for semiotic formatting.

To put matters more simply, formatting involves the power to *design:* to develop, maintain, strengthen, or alter a platform's territorializing effects and redundancies, and the strategies through which it will encounter and deal with the paradox of reference. When a group is in a position to format a graph on their own terms, they have the power to define or alter the asignifying, vectorial conditions of its nodes and edges, the figural forces upon which computers will represent phenomena by quantifying these conditions, *and* the semiological redundancies that will come to be overlaid upon this abstract field through some creative combination of design thinking, philosophy, computability theory, interface, and practice.

Describing each style of graph with these terms in mind—hinting, stating, and formatting—to see how each resolves the paradox of denotation and signification will have the side benefit of putting us in a position to characterize some of the benefits and drawbacks of each style. It may also help us to discriminate certain details around the division of labor between users and designers; between who gets to format and who accedes to be formatted.

Hypertext

Tracing a legacy from Vannevar Bush to today's 'platformization' of the web, George Landow sees hyperlinking as originally grounded in the non-linear association of texts. Set off against the tradition of the printed book, hypertext represents the realization of Roland Barthes' active reader for Landow; one who finds meaning by combining what Barthes called lexia with images and other media to construct meaning on the basis of the user's own idiosyncratic analysis and perspective.

Active reading is the most important frame of reference because, in the broadest terms, the strength of hyperlinking "lies in its capacity of permitting users to find, create, and follow multiple conceptual structures in the same body of information."[15]

Software environments and user practice may have shifted on the basis of forces like technological innovation and market competition, but obviously this associative capacity remains a core feature of our relationship to information and records, not least as we are entreated to share and link together the moods, experiences, and ideas that we have in everyday experience using social media streams. Speaking in more historically situated terms, Landow is quick to point out a myriad of other effects on global writing that hypertext inaugurated, which we lately tend to ignore. For him, linking represents the quintessential poststructural writing technique, with wide-ranging epistemic, political, and cultural effects upon societies that took up the web through the late twentieth century. As it emerged as a democratizing mode of expression, means of publication, and space for pedagogy, hyperlinking, he writes, "reconfigures our experience of both author and authorial property, and this reconception of these ideas promises to affect our conceptions of both the authors (and authority) of texts we study and of ourselves as authors."[16]

The web's subsequent commercializing shift into platforms and practices like social graphs represents a particular evolution of the hyperlink, one that would seem to stretch the boundaries of this reader-writer paradigm. From a technical perspective, it is certainly true that knowledge and social graphs only work thanks to their harmonization with existing layers that make up the Internet's protocol stack, including Tim Berners-Lee's original Hypertext Transfer Protocol. Hyperlinking remains a ubiquitous procedure for precisely locating electronic documents on computer servers, even if technologists are now conceptualizing new forms of association and relation on top of the hyperlink. Issues of technology aside, when it comes to the hyperlinking structures of 'Web 1.0' read as enunciative assemblage, hinting mechanisms were about connecting one document or lexia to another as locations in an information space on the basis of a formatted subject styled as a reader-writer.

At the level of habit, the reader is invested to click on linked words and images as hints, which move them through the web to consume lexia on the basis of associative whim. As a writer, one inscribes their own hints between lexia, marking hyperlinks as edges between web pages as nodes, to indicate how and why 'this' chunk of text connects one to 'that' chunk. The original web's asignifying strategies are largely framed on these terms, of one's train of thought in reading, as driven by the question where am I going *next* in this universe of documents, to continue my narrative of ideas? The elegance and simplicity of hyperlinking in its early form made this free association of blocks of text and media inviting for all, as practices evolved rapidly through the 1990s into both private hobby and cottage industry. Readers became writers by learning HTML, taking up the web's capacities to creatively associate and arrange ideas and narratives into discrete pages, on their own terms.

Hypertext affordances for stating follow this line of thinking. Communication between individuals is about active reading and non-sequential writing, blurring the boundaries of authorship between texts as they increasingly linked together. Early web pages enabled one to think in new ways about how to structure information through one-to-many linking structures, for example, to develop branching narratives and reader choice, or many-to-one linking structures, which fostered the easy reuse of text blocks across different contexts.[17] Hypertext made it easy to cite other people's information and writing from across the web too, affording users novel ways to communicate validity via instantaneous linkage to supporting evidence as one made claims about the world in their writing. It remains easy to style hyperlinks in an illocutionary mode too, to emphasize content in performative ways by linking across the web, as when one writes 'If you don't believe me, *go look at the report for yourself'*.

Hypertext also made it easy to produce branching narratives, leading to stories with alternative unfolding paths and coauthored information spaces that broke down the traditional boundaries between reading and writing of linear books. Whether on rationalistic or imaginative grounds then, hyperlinking allows one to communicate significance through the shared association and serialization of ideas, as these were present in documents. Its power of free association lies in clarifying, complicating, and/or extending the knowledge of those who read according to its logic, as authors chain documents together to communicate the lines of significance that are meaningful to them.

From all of this, we can derive an imagined basis for articulating the machinic and the intersubjective together—a formatting—in terms of what we might call a *transcendental book*. The virtual potential in Deleuze's paradox of reference takes on textual contours, as the (vicious) circle of sense gets framed in terms of an economy of resolution and reinvestment by a subject styled as a reader-writer. Existing denotative locations of a text become a jumping-off point for manifesting one's interest as a reader or author, realized by 'traveling through' a hyperlink into its signification: *this* is related to *that*, based on semiotic conditions that authors are free to alter, and readers are free to ignore. Signifier and signified are construed as spatial locations, with hyperlinking largely operationalizing the sign according to movement through a universal library.

Day's work on the discursive formations that produced our modern notion of information is again helpful here to see how universalizing visions proposed by people like Bush, Ted Nelson, and Berners-Lee connect up with those working still earlier in the scientific foundations of libraries. Paul Otlet was a central figure in the European documentation tradition, for example, who tirelessly promoted the benefits of a scientific and positivistic approach to the organization of books according to the facts they contained. Otlet's vision was of an entire city devoted to containing the world's knowledge cross-indexed on cards, prefiguring hypertext in crucial ways. Day writes, for example, that

> Far from being an antiquated vision, the metaphorical and metonymical power of the book in architecture's construction of social space continues to our own day, even with institutions whose claim is to have entered the 'digital age.' Nor is Otlet's notion of the book antiquated by today's hypertext: it was that of a whole with multiple, interconnected parts, a forerunner of hypertextual linking following what Otlet termed the 'monographic principle' (that is, 'atomic' chunks of text).[18]

Compared with other 'atomic' approaches that have since been mobilized on the model of the directed graph—like social graphs or Markov chain approaches to search like PageRank—we can see in hindsight how the latest scientific approaches have succeeded in ways that Otlet could only imagine. Compared to the other graph-styles that have since transformed the World Wide Web, hypertext was originally an often frustrating and chaotic experience, possessing few guiding principles of rationality besides the insistence that pages observe precise codes for their layout and location.

Knowledge Graphs

A telling passage in Berners-Lee's early writing on global graphs gives one a sense of how technical conversations around the explosion of these hypertextual practices were leading the W3C to rethink meaning on more machine-readable grounds, as metadata:

> The thing which you get when you follow a link, when you dereference a URI, has a lot of names. Formally we call it a resource. Sometimes it is referred to as a document because many of the things currently on the Web are human readable documents. Sometimes it is referred to as an object when the object is something which is more machine readable in nature or has hidden state. I will use the words document and resource interchangeably in what follows and sometimes may slip into using 'object'.[19]

His words are now twenty years old but remain relevant in the sense that as the web continues to undergo sedimentary shifts in practice and technology, relation as linking has been shifting from a basis in the association of documents to a basis in the association of objects according to their factual attributes. Via the triplestore assertion, knowledge graphs reorient the formatted subject away from a basis in hyperlinked active reading and writing to one centered in the social-epistemological judgment of things as correct knowledge entities—a turn to what we might call, following Frege, hyper-*sense*.

Networks of semantic type and interrelated fact form the basis for this transition, as the hinting affordances of knowledge graphs come to focus less on atomic chunks of text than on queries that follow the atomic elements of the Five Ws: who, what, where, when, and why. As we saw in the last chapter, the question of why increasingly is being answered by the Bayesian and connectionist approaches in PA graphs, which take up the other four Ws in knowledge and social graphs as their raw material to impose models of probabilistic causality upon them. And if hyperlinks made the free association of documents possible on the basis of precisely referencing their location, then knowledge graphs make the free association of facts possible through their precise classification in formal ontologies.

As John Sowa writes, when it comes to formatting the affective and semiotic investments of subjects on the terms of knowledge graphs, "The two sources of ontological categories are observation and reasoning. Observation provides knowledge of the physical world, and reasoning makes sense of observation by generating a framework of abstractions called *metaphysics*."[20] As we saw back in Chapter 2, this is a metaphysics based in forward and backward-chaining reasoning, as described in formal logic and semiotic theory by people like Peirce and Frege, but also restyled over time to include elements that contextualize and socialize its empirical assumptions by people like Searle and Jürgen Habermas. Fundamentally, the desires and compulsions of the formatted subject devolve to a hinting strategy that is based in the asignification of deduction and conclusion—the imperative of the ' … therefore…'—as it may act in support of the correction of error.

In terms of the conditions for *stating*, emphasis falls similarly on speaker and hearer conceived as knowledge agents. Shared validity allows for their negotiation around the fact of the matter, and social normativity can be made automatic on this basis. Semantically rigorous association allows us to test beliefs through denotative appeals to common sense in order to secure correct reference in signification on the basis of conceptual class. In a turn away from the more tabular-relational strategies of traditional databases, the flexible structures of knowledge graphs can bring many more elements of speech interactions into the mode of *strategic* action, as the technology styles the achievement of intersubjective understanding as behavior, transforming it along the lines of what Habermas famously called communicative action.

Joseph Heath's work on the differences between linguistic and non-linguistic accounts of rationality is helpful here. He explains that

Habermas' communicative action "[...] explicitly draws upon the public commitments underlying linguistic interactions in order to secure coordination," and goes on to write that when we engage in strategic action, "Language is still in the background, providing agents with the information against which they determine maximizing strategies, for example, common knowledge of preferences, action alternatives, a common prior on probability distributions over states of nature, and so on."[21] It is according to this division that the stating conditions of knowledge graphs function to produce a formatted subject; one that is enabled to do more in strategic terms thanks to the underlying shared epistemic norms that hold in any speech, writing, or behavioral context in which the technology is deployed.

Marking the benefit of distributed access to consensus knowledge, which enables rapid backward- and forward-chaining reasoning by both users and software agents, we must also remember the main drawback of knowledge graphs. As it stands, there seems to be no real affordance in their conceptualization for the inscribed persistence and circulation of shared *dissensus*. As discussed back in Chapter 2, this is because the approach requires a disembedding of knowledge from its hetero-semiotic context in order to make it homo-semiotic on the model of the propositional assertion. Relative to Deleuze's paradox of reference, we might say that this 'formatting-out' of dissensus represents another moment where virtual potential gets actualized in a dissatisfying way. A second drawback is that, unlike hypertext, groups and individuals may be less likely to themselves become formatters of knowledge graphs. We seem increasingly content to rely on networks of fact provided to us by the major commercial social platforms, like Apple, Google, and Microsoft, and so become staters on their terms. That said, knowledge graphs do function according to standardized protocols; their main features are maintained by public consortia like the W3C; and importantly, open-source knowledge graphs like Wikidata remain an ongoing concern.

In the more abstract, Deleuze's concerns over the circularity of reference in philosophy seem squarely aimed at the underlying metaphysics of knowledge graphs, with their emphasis on the proposition as the main lynchpin for conceptuality. Writing with Guattari in *What Is Philosophy?*, Deleuze acknowledges that the role ascribed to sentential logic in the analytic tradition does achieve a kind of transcendental self-consistency of subject and object on the basis of the proposition; one where "an exoreference of the proposition (the action that is linked to it by convention and accomplished by stating the proposition)" meets with an endoreference to the "status or state of affairs that entitles one to formulate the statement..." On the other hand, they continue, "if we ascribe self-consistency to the sentence, this can only reside in the formal noncontradiction of the proposition or between propositions. But this means that propositions do not materially enjoy any endoconsistency or exoconsistency."[22]

When it comes to knowledge graphs, this is how we should be thinking about the interrelation between the machinic and the intersubjective. Being in the world as an epistemically formatted subject means having one's affects, habits, and creative ideas serialized according to a transcendental logic that mines virtual potential for naming the world, and the immanent possibilities for exo and endoconsistency, in a way where naming comes to matter only in terms of being one more assertoric signal of possibility among many. As a matter of assisting the circulation of scientific ideas among those who accept these epistemic conditions, the power of knowledge graphs is enormous. The Open Tree of Life is a dynamic knowledge graph representing 2.3 million species, for example, giving an exhaustive synthesis of phylogenetic trees and their taxonomic data in a project that aspires to be the Wikipedia of evolutionary history.[23] When applied to the social order wholesale, however, knowledge graphs can also be understood as possessing a power to perpetually abstract the subject away from their singularity and toward their reproduction as an epistemic agent in a population. As Deleuze and Guattari write a few pages later, the resulting abstraction suppresses "[...] that subject's acts of transcendence *capable of constituting new functions of variable or conceptual references.*"[24]

Social Graphs

With social graphs, we move from the contingencies of belief as they might be secured by facts and precise meaning to the contingencies of personal identity as they might be secured through recognitional control over our social surroundings. Harrison White puts the basic dynamic like so:

> An employer, a community, a crowd, oneself, all may be identities. An identity is perceived by others as having an unproblematic continuity. Identities add through contentions to the contingencies faced by other identities. Social organization comes as a by-product of the cumulation of these processes. When contending counteractions result in a dynamic equilibrium, we perceive social structure.[25]

Social graphs trace and observe these equilibrating structures by using the directed graph abstractions of node and edge to represent individuals performing their interpersonal attachments, affinities, and tastes. Relationality is straightforwardly styled as conduct between people, as individuals rely on social graph platforms like Facebook, Spotify, or LinkedIn to perform, associate with, and mark themselves out in groups on the basis of various relational identifications like shared experience, professional and community role, kinship network, sexual identity, cultural taste, or consumer preference. In short, we rely on social graphs to perform our collective belonging and use interface affordances built atop graphs that mobilize illocutionary function and its binding effects toward that belonging, quantifying flows of both one-way and reciprocal affinity along their graph edges at the level of calculation.

Hints take on greater significance here because the desire for and pleasure of social connection need not be expressed in language; it can be merely about a kind phatic communion through the platform. Qualification of emotion meets quantification according to any number of performative hinting mechanisms—Likes, hearts, bits of karma—which register our affinity to other people without the need to resort to statements. As we take them up on our devices, hinting on social graph platforms is also about formatting a sense of what it means to collectively influence and to be influenced, according to reactive metrics like esteem and attraction, which in the past have resisted quantification. Following Nancy Baym, performative gestures expressed in hints promote community through an incipient sense of shared space, the establishment of certain rituals, and the exchange of social support.[26] At the same time, however, as Taina Bucher writes, "Affective encounters between people and the Facebook algorithm are not just productive of different moods and sensations, but also play a generative role in moulding the algorithm itself."[27]

Where in the case of the original web stating involved the idiosyncratic association of texts related according to the whims and scenarios of writers and readers, in social graphs, to state is to accept serialization according to the norms of conversational turn taking. Individual statements remain free form in the sense of being post-documentary objects, like Barthes' lexia. They can be of varying size, and one is always free to hyperlink out from a social platform to elsewhere on the web. Nevertheless, the speaker-listener dyad comes to dominate because it is this framework that ensures that any statements made will fit into the structured data slots of a social graph, which follow an assertoric format, but one styled as registering performative or declarative events that mark one's status and position in a community. This structure for stating ensures that anything said is made ready for pairwise analysis, as the interfaces of social graphs translate performative attachments into factual states to produce an empirical overview of one's social position within populations.

The basic difference between knowledge and social graphs seems to be that one is framed in terms of expressing the factual attributes of things in a fairly planned and stable way, while the other is designed to derive factual attributes about people based on the events and encounters that they *undergo*. In terms of Deleuze's paradox of reference, denotation in social graphs defines a common sense that is premised on a web of prior declarative illocutionary points between people, with success or failure in significational reference based in one's position in and across that web. Speakers and hearers reproduce a socially constructed state of affairs through their homophilous relationships to some individuals and not others, with manifestation in reference endlessly troubling those conditions through contention, with an eye to either destabilizing or restabilizing what White calls a social discipline through claims to status and legitimacy.

On what imagined, transcendental basis do social graphs articulate the machinic and the intersubjective together? The seemingly tautological answer here is the social itself, as defined according to a particular and longstanding tradition of Weberian and phenomenological sociology. While the performatively formatted subject may find himself or herself wrapped up in all kinds of different social situations, configurations, and practices as they go through life, for the phenomenological tradition in sociology, all of these situations share common root in communication and the face-to-face encounter. Alfred Schütz writes, for example, that

> I speak of another person as within reach of my direct experience when he shares with me a community of space and a community of time. [...] This spatial and temporal immediacy is essential to the face-to-face situation. All acts of Other-orientation and of affecting-the-other, and therefore all orientations of relationships within the face-to-face situation, derive their own specific flavor and style from this immediacy.[28]

As a kind of transcendental plane shared by all human beings via the face-to-face ideal, this account of the social remains powerful for interrogating processes of datafication. Platform designers are becoming more keenly aware of the problems that social platforms and interfaces may be fomenting, for example, in their failure to account for the Self-Other relation in the fullest possible terms. On the topic of privacy, gender, and relationship status settings on Facebook, designer Andrew Hinton writes, for instance, that "people are not just one thing in all places and all times, among all people," continuing that

> It's only because Facebook has created such a muddle within the shell structure of a singular profile that people have given up on making sense of it, and decided instead to create their own separately defined contexts for their social fronts."[29]

Tactics like these, where users may carefully group audiences through a platform's settings, or even rely on multiple pseudonymous accounts to negotiate their identity online, amount to a certain kind of reaction against, or subversive disposition toward, the formatting logic of commercial social graphs. When it comes to these platforms though, we largely remain hinters and staters. This is not to discount open-source social networking projects, like Elgg and Oxwall, which allow for individual communities to build social graphs on their own terms. But more broadly, as Nick Couldry and Andreas Hepp write, it can be difficult to escape or ignore the deepest tension that we grapple with today, relative to datafication; "between the necessary *openness* of social life, as the space where human life-in-common develops autonomously, and the motivated (and in its own domain, perfectly reasonable) *enclosure* for commercial ends of the spaces where social life is today being conducted."[30]

While extremely sympathetic toward resolving this tension, and having leaned on thinkers in the phenomenological-sociological tradition myself throughout this book, we can nevertheless turn back to Deleuze and Guattari's assemblage perspective to see a certain occlusion of the social going on. Their concerns over the conceptualization of endo and exoreference return, only this time involving a substantialization of the social relation, rather than a substantialization of an empirical knowledge relation. It is certainly true that social graph technology fosters communication, acting as a very efficient means for managing what the social sciences call strong and weak ties. Add to that the digital serialization of affinity on its terms sets up powerful feedback mechanisms in Westernized societies, which have proved useful during times of crisis and conflict as we encounter, understand, empathize with, and want to help others.

But we also need to acknowledge that, as an artifact of its longstanding paradigmatic status in HCI design and computer-supported cooperative work, phenomenological sociology as applied to social graph designs may also be causing a deleterious rationalization of sociality itself. Knowledge graphs give us the benefit of storing interlaced networks of fact, but potentially at the expense of dissensus, as the circle of sense becomes vicious according to *denotation*, and language comes to matter only to the degree to which it is made inferential in empirical terms. Social graphs suffer the reverse problem, on the basis of *manifestation*, where inference matters only relative to the circumstances of its fostering and circulating a kind of social capital in and among groups. Because social graphs are so driven by personal beliefs and preference, as groups and individuals seek to extend, manage, and police their memberships across social situations, charisma, status, and the pleasures of belonging come to dominate the knowledge relation, especially its key element of being able to recognize the importance of breaking with doxa, to force us to think differently.

Decision Trees, Bayesian AI, and Connectionism

In PA graphs, we see a further over-coding of the intersubjective pragmatics that subtend knowledge and social graphs. Because they are mostly an algorithmic structure rather than a data structure, sociality established on the basis of PA graphs produces a more directly behavioral relation, taking for granted achieved correct reference in order to focus on the broader imperatives of action. Grounded in an institutional consensus derived from existing data, PA graphs are designed to run ahead of that consensus, automatically confirming the already-internalized performances of some context. The goal is to free people up from negotiating meaning at a basic level by introducing capacities for inferential action at a higher level of generalization.

Discursive negotiation of meaning through the positions of self and other remains an ostensible performative surface for PA graph interfaces, as when chat bots and artificial intelligence (AI) assistants offer friendly advice for making plans or correcting one's grammar. At the operational level, however, semiotic multiplicity has effectively given way to a much more strategic steering of signs in which the subject is framed more strictly in terms of rational choice within a web of truth-conditional semantic inference. The result is a social context premised on the optimum generalization of past decisions in order to increase a group's collective ability to classify as-yet-unseen things and people in the world. In the case of a group or institution seeking greater productivity, it makes perfect sense to want to derive patterns of greater efficiency from prior decisions in this way. As a model applied to sociality wholesale though, efficiencies around automatically indexing the world and people come at the expense of further rendering one's hetero-semiotic relationship to the world into the homo-semiotic terms of a behavioral signal.

Those involved in the construction of a PA graph remain in a position to discursively negotiate the meaning behind the correlation of different sets of data for training purposes. At the level of the formatted subject though, *all* signs effectively become hints. In the case of decision trees, nodes and edges represent an operational cascade of imperative, either/or questions. In the case of Markov chains, nodes and edges represent decision points that influence one another probabilistically in a more emergent way, as existing networks of relation get parsed as a kind of voting procedure through multiple and iterative random walks along their edges. Connectionist neural nets take a similarly emergent approach, as massive datasets of predigested classification get fed into perceptron-style graphs, which accumulate strength connections along node and edge according to how the PA graph is supervised and trained to decide on our behalf.

In the language of Deleuze and Guattari's mixed semiotic, we can generalize across all three types to say that PA graphs represent a more thoroughly *diagrammatic* procedure. Beyond representing the real as we see it in knowledge and social graphs, diagrammatic machines construct a real that is "yet to come, a new type of reality," by playing a 'piloting' role.[31] Designed to produce new possibilities for both communicating and acting, PA graphs treat language in ways that entirely skip over its basis in an embedded, intersubjective relation; although it would be more accurate to say that PA graphs skip over meaning negotiation by taking on faith the rationalist view. It is only by treating signs in a strictly statistical mode that the technology can allow designers and users to empirically see redundancies and regularities in their behavior, upon which the graph can induce useful optimizations, along the lines of a social physics. By overlaying the formal pragmatics of a private mind making sense of itself onto prior datasets, PA graphs induce a more purely syntactical *ordering*.

In terms of Deleuze's paradox of reference, PA graph developers largely reserve the powers of denotation for themselves; a power he describes as "[...] the association of words themselves with *particular* images *which ought to* 'represent' the state of affairs."[32] A direct example here is Google's Image Labeler, which entreats users to help developers train its image recognition neural network by presenting them with pictures that may or may not denote things like cats, horses, weddings, and mountains. In this arrangement, manifestation serves only to improve denotation, as when we click on 'yes' or 'no' to transmit our anticipatory beliefs to Google. We habituate both ourselves and the PA graph's algorithmic cycle to have common sense on the basis of simple decision by giving over the manifestation of our good sense to control by the neural net's minders: the simple habit of saying 'I' decides that this image indeed contains a bicycle, a belief that will be rigorously tested and statistically compared against the beliefs of others visiting the site until a reasonable referential certainty has been reached by the neural net.

Once the particular features sought by the PA graph have stabilized, the algorithm can become a site for signification because it can now handle the movements of 'implies' and 'therefore' in the circle of reference automatically on our behalf. Telegraphing Deleuze's concerns again here though, when we allow the assertion, and through technical delegation, the predicate calculus, to frame our relationship between words and things so thoroughly in an empirical-rational way, the problem persists that "[...] language no longer has any relation to that which it denotes, but only to that which it expresses, that is, to sense."[33] He means here the Fregean understanding of sense as a descriptive mode for signs, whereas Deleuze wants to hold on to sense as the virtual, incorporeal features of the semiotic to affect and be affected by *bodies*, and not just language isolated logically from its material context.

Extending the criticism, we might say that PA graphs are becoming a powerful technology for aligning our collective incorporeal powers to denote bodies but that this is occurring in such a way that the technology formats *what happens to things* only according to their conceptualization in terms of empirically observed *states of affairs*. For many, this is a point of little critical import, having been leveled at AI at various points in the past and merely restating the symbolic conditions of IS in general. After all, we're not trying to effect the incorporeal transformation of bodies in the world, we're simply trying to select and organize information about them in terms of rules and language.

The problem is that as PA graphs increasingly become material infrastructure, the line between describing and effectuating blurs considerably. As the intersubjective assumptions around stating take on the linearizing qualities of abstract decisional imperative, new potentials and drawbacks emerge. AI interfaces like Apple's Siri or Google Now can act as useful supplements to our practical reason, helping us to negotiate institutional structures of accountability in an increasingly complex and harried social order. In the process though, their logic begins to fold back on our environment and collective sense of self, as one continues to produce more and more fine-grained, asignifying traces of activity and intention through the systems in ways that continuously redefine the individual according to decisionistic pattern.

As institutional norms become more automatic in this way, it can be increasingly difficult to see where critical intervention into the semiotic operations of PA graphs might occur. Sandy Pentland advocates for data-driven cities to be controlled by way of PA graph, for example, where real time flows of behavior will be fed into massive predictive systems in order to give governments a new point of survey.[34] And AI practitioners like Pedro Domingos are bullish on a future where "Everyone will have a detailed model of him- or herself, and these models will talk to each other all the time."[35] At issue though with Pentland's vision is just how much democratic accountability can act as a viable feedback signal in such a vastly data-driven city. At issue with Domingos' vision is that, given all that has just been said, whatever he means by talk is clearly functioning at a level far removed from the traditional poles of a reflexive semiological exchange between two people.

From one angle, it may be that serializing signs on the formal-pragmatic terms of a PA graph augurs a higher degree of evidential and statistical reasoning in society overall, and that we should welcome the development. From another though, the individual who interfaces with the world on these terms now seems twice removed from their singularizing potential to imaginatively conceptualize what is going on around them. As was the case with the other graph-styles, commercial platforms, standardized libraries, and open-source alternatives are mixing together in contemporary PA graph practice, suggesting that wide-ranging experimentation at various scales is underway. But it should come as little surprise that commercial actors with enormous datasets at their disposal will be the ones who will tend to dominate, like Google's TensorFlow platform and Microsoft's Azure Machine Learning.

As an aftereffect of their original conceptualization by people like Warren McCulloch, what all of these platforms seem to share is a formatting based philosophically in Humean association. Perceptron-style connectionist graphs, for example, deploy a formal pragmatics that borrows heavily from his radically subjectivist ideas concerning the transcendental. For Hume, it was ultimately only habits of impression and idea that give one a ground for making causal connections in the world. Rather than assuming, as Immanuel Kant and others like Frege later did, the need for a necessarily dualistic account—a transcendental schema that reconciled objects to the subject through the categories of the understanding—Hume famously asserted that the subject immanently self-objectifies, in what Deleuze calls in his study of Hume a spontaneity of disposition.[36] We may try to describe it in terms of logic, but one's sense of causal connection and self-coherence concretely arises as a product of custom and habit, as we draw correlations of resemblance and contiguity from our impressions in everyday experience, and their ideational copies, sedimented in our memory.

Recall the problem in this account though, which prompted Kant to develop his schema in response to Hume: how can a mind be a collection of distinct impressions and ideas and yet a subject still arises from out of this collection, with a disposition toward it? Roffe gives a succinct account of the consequences; the problem, he writes, "[...] becomes one of defining the nature of the movement of transcendence that will take the mind from passive receptivity to active transcendence."[37] This is the central power of PA graphs as a technics: to define our communicative activity on social platforms in such a way that accumulations of data can be organized into passive flows for an artificial mind seeking its active transcendence. As a guiding principle for the social at the level of communication, knowledge and social graphs help us to negotiate things in the world and one another according to a *universally shared* inference. At the transcendental level of formatting though, what seems to be taken and given in exchange in this sharing is one's passional capacity to self-objectify through one's own *imaginative* inference, as the latter builds up according to singular habits, experiences, and memories.

Deleuze writes that we should not see this duality as epistemically opposing the singular to the universal. Rather, Hume's perspective demands a realization that there is only ever a *practical subject*. Associationism

> [...] does not define a knowing subject; on the contrary, it defines a set of possible means for a practical subject for which all real ends belong to the moral, passional, political, and economic order. Thus, this subordination of association to the passions already manifests within human nature a kind of secondary purposiveness, which prepares us for the problem of the primary purposiveness, that is, for the problem of the agreement between human nature and nature.[38]

Summing up, we might say then that PA graphs present us with a particular solution to the problem of the practical subject. It is one deeply committed to seeing both our relationship to nature and one another on the epistemic terms of empirical, inferential, and statistical reasoning, generally following the model of Peirce's semiotic logic and related ideas from the philosophy of information, like formal ontology and the DIKW pyramid.

On the lights of Deleuze and Guattari's radical reconfiguration of Peirce's schema into their mixed semiotic, social computing technology now seems somewhat blinkered to institutional conditions with respect to the sign as a result though, suggesting that a heavy reliance on socially disembedded, perceptual, and intentional models of the sign-relation is hampering our ability to see how the semiotic folds together with the institutional and the political to produce and support competing types of hegemonic project. We can conclude on this last point by considering a graph platform 'in the wild'—Twitter—as productive of an enunciative mode of relation that has been taken up with clear political investments in mind, at least when mobilizing significance at the level of its everyday use.

The Twitter Graph

Nathan Rambukkana's characterization of Twitter hashtags as a techno-social event picks up well on this last point; his approach has many affinities with the perspective that I have been summarizing. Describing hashtags as a "pragmatic and metapragmatic speech act," he continues that

> hashtag-mediated discursive assemblages are neither simply the re-flection of pre-existing discourse formations nor do they create them out of digital aether. Rather, they are nodes in the becoming of dis-tributed discussions in which their very materiality as performative utterances is deeply implicated.[39]

Rambukkana goes on to assert, correctly in my view, that social com-puting affordances like the hashtag stoke one's political imagination, and, in turn, our imagination projects into the technology to shape the platform's meaning in significant ways. Explicitly positioning them as both technique and technology of the social, for Rambukkana, hashtags operate relative to the particular assemblages in which they circulate, as groups might or might not come to rely on them to constitute publics or communities, or otherwise 'amplify affect' online in support of partic-ular social movements. His perspective is especially useful for making some of the issues that I have been concerned with more concrete while also pointing up limitations around the rather narrow focus that I have adopted throughout.

Noting in passing some of the corporate, governmental, and interper-sonal effects that social computing produces relative to political repre-sentation, I have generally done so at the expense of important details concerning the many human and non-human actors involved in the production and use of graph platforms as material infrastructure. I have also mostly ignored the details of context when it comes to social computing platform use, whether for explicitly political purposes or in the travails of everyday life. Instead, I have been focusing somewhat obsessively on the philosophical and semiotic commitments of graphs themselves as a blueprint for conceptually motivating and guiding infrastructure and practice. Scholars like Rambukkana are absolutely correct to be emphasizing the importance of determining how global graph platforms like Twitter variously relate to *other* assemblages because it is here that the technology has the most concrete, incorporeal effects on subject and subjugated groups, irrespective of debates over the philosophical status of the sign itself.

It is vital to probe the details of how graph platform affordances, like those found in Twitter, function in reciprocal presupposition with the various corporate, state, and community actors that take them up, whether for the purposes of public relation and marketing, state surveillance, or political activism. Sharing Rambukkana's desire to understand social computing technology in terms of its potential for political organization at the level of the techno-social, what I have been trying to do is open up the black box implied in what he above calls a discursive assemblage to see how its underlying formalizations come to select, structure, and store the meaning and organization of things and people in the first place.

First and foremost, Twitter is a social graph. The company reports some three hundred twenty-eight million monthly active users[40] who engage the platform using either their real name or a pseudonym in all manner of symbolic activity—from interacting with chat bots, promoting commercial brands, talking with strangers and friends about culture and politics, or otherwise engaging in networked publics. As with other social graph platforms, hints on Twitter resolve to the basic illocutionary features of interpersonal affinity and disaffinity; one may feel inclined to boost someone's Tweet by giving it a 'like' or feel irritated enough to click on 'I don't like this Tweet', making it disappear from view. In addition, users follow other users but may also mute them. In the terms of activist politics and what Chantal Mouffe calls agonistic struggle, when things get heated, Twitter's hinting affordances are open to manipulation, as in the phenomenon of vote brigading where users gang up en masse to silence a particular user or swamp a particular hashtag.

Relative to stating, the hashtag's pragmatic/meta-pragmatic status is consistent with the influence of ethnomethodology on HCI design, as described in Chapter 3; conversations on Twitter follow an endogenous logic. Like Facebook, the platform deploys a subtle algorithm for serializing Tweets in a user's timeline when they first log in, which takes into account things like the Tweet's overall engagement, how often one interacts with the person who is writing it, and many other factors.[41]

Past the level of casual reading though, Tweets generally serialize according to the model of conversational turn taking. But hashtags introduce a twist: because they are simultaneously a performative statement and an asignifying hint, hashtags take on an ambiguous status of being both indexical expression and linguistic shifter, like 'this', 'here', or 'now'. Hashtags wind up playing multiple roles under these conditions, including the gathering, redrawing, or reinforcing of social categorization among groups, as well as simpler performative emphases, which together play the twinned role of reproducing strategic consensus around meaning and facilitating information retrieval.

Axel Bruns and Jean E. Burgess get at this complexity by defining the hashtag relative to communities, ad hoc publics, and calculated publics. There is an important resonance between their views and White's social physics, as when they write that hashtags must be seen as

embedded and permeable macro-level spaces which overlap both with the meso-level flow of messages across longer-term follower/followee networks and with the micro-level communicative exchanges conducted as @replies between users who may or may not have found one another through the hashtag, as well as with other, related or rival hashtag communities at a similar macro level.[42]

Their complexity represents an enormous opportunity for the social sciences to study groups and communities in better ways along these more dynamic and transparent lines of communication. That said, hashtags are not just intriguing for sociologists, a point that Rambukkana gets at when he writes that for social platforms like Twitter, "events of discourse are coming to *recognize and mark themselves as such.*"[43]

Relative to Deleuze and Guattari's mixed semiotic, hashtags are an especially interesting middle ground. Twitter can indeed be read strictly as an egological social graph, where people pursue their affiliations and affinities by declaring connections with people and transmitting illocutionary signals by way of likes and shares. But hashtags also have something resembling the original flexibility of hypertext in that they generate an idiosyncratically self-organizing field of discourse and reference at the level of their formatting. Different from hypertext though is that reference now involves more than fixing documents to a precise location. While making statements on Twitter, using hashtags also involves a performative *classification,* meaning that groups are directly involved in generating an endogenous social logic both at the semiological level of statements *and* at the asignifying level of hinting.

As a matter of formatting, stating and hinting are linked together in the dimension of what Michael Warner calls stranger-sociability, establishing a 'we/I' relationship that is less tethered to the individual as an ego and more promoting a kind of transcendental field for the event of discourse to occur. It is not just the case that I can link to whatever I want; it is that I can inflect my utterance according to a disposition toward that linking, giving it an extensible and expressive quality that may (or may not) come to pilot and orient others at the level of ad hoc and calculated publics. Heidegger's interest in the ambiguity of belonging-together seems at play here, more so than with the techniques discussed in analytic isolation. Hashtags represent a technical formatting of entities on the traditional metaphysical level of grouping, according to their identity and difference as knowledge-objects in the information system. But this formatting dovetails with a group's phenomenological sense of belonging-together *as* group, too.

In the reconciliation, hashtags propose an interesting theory of the allagmatically formatted subject in which one undergoes semiotic change according to the expression of difference-constituting-identity among people, yet through an open relationship to difference-in-constituting-meaning in discourse, with the system maintaining only a minimally theorized social rationality of their continual overlap. I will pick up this thread in the next and final chapter to develop Simondon's notion of the allagmatic a bit further in relation to future possibilities of social computing.

Notes

1 Day, *The Modern Invention of Information*, 128.
2 Hansen, *Feed-Forward*, 23.
3 Williams, *Gilles Deleuze's Logic of Sense*, 30.
4 Deleuze and Guattari, *A Thousand Plateaus*, 76.
5 Guattari, *The Three Ecologies*, 36.
6 Frohmann, *Deflating Information*, 69.
7 See, for example, Schneider and Scholz, *Ours to Hack and to Own*; Milan and Halleck, *Social Movements and Their Technologies*.
8 Protevi, *Political Affect*, 191.
9 Heidegger, *Identity and Difference*, 29.
10 Bowker and Star, *Sorting Things Out*, 230.
11 Genosko, *Félix Guattari*, 107–8.
12 Bryant, *Difference and Givenness*, 32.
13 Massumi, *Parables for the Virtual*, 30.
14 Massumi, *A User's Guide to Capitalism and Schizophrenia*, 27.
15 Landow, *Hypertext 3.0*, 10.
16 Ibid., 45.
17 Ibid., 16–17.
18 Day, *The Modern Invention of Information*, 11.
19 Berners-Lee, "Web Architecture: Metadata."
20 Sowa, *Knowledge Representation*, 51.
21 Heath, *Communicative Action and Rational Choice*, 24.
22 Deleuze and Guattari, *What Is Philosophy?*, 137.
23 "'Tree of Life' for 2.3 Million Species Released."
24 Deleuze and Guattari, *What Is Philosophy?*, 142.
25 White, *Identity and Control*, 6.

26 Baym, *Personal Connections in the Digital Age*, 96.
27 Bucher, "The Algorithmic Imaginary," 12.
28 Schutz, *The Phenomenology of the Social World*, 163.
29 Hinton, *Understanding Context*, 328.
30 Couldry and Hepp, *The Mediated Construction of Reality*, 223.
31 Deleuze and Guattari, *A Thousand Plateaus*, 142.
32 Deleuze, *The Logic of Sense*, 12.
33 Ibid., 25.
34 Pentland, *Social Physics*, 170.
35 Domingos, *The Master Algorithm*, 269.
36 Deleuze, *Empiricism and Subjectivity*, 97.
37 Roffe, *Gilles Deleuze's Empiricism and Subjectivity*, 106.
38 Deleuze, *Empiricism and Subjectivity*, 121.
39 Rambukkana, "#Introduction: Hashtags as Technosocial Events," 3.
40 Sparks, "How Many Users Does Twitter Have?"
41 Oremus and Grabar, "Twitter's New Order."
42 Bruns and Burgess, "Twitter Hashtags from Ad Hoc to Calculated Publics," 22.
43 Rambukkana, "From #RaceFail to #Ferguson: The Digital Intimacies of Race: Activist Hashtag Publics," 31.

6 Conclusion
Toward an Enunciative Informatics

It is thus the sense [*sens*] of coming-into-being, the ability of technics to engender the coming-into-being of both the natural and the human world, that makes elementary intuition and the intuition of the ensemble compatible; technical intuition at the level of ensembles, expresses coming-into-being as both basis and result obtained; social and political intuition is the integration of tendencies, the expression of virtualities and forces of coming-into-being, in the same reality.
—Gilbert Simondon, *On the Mode of Existence of Technical Objects*, p. 237

We are finally in a position to ask what would a more frankly enunciative graph platform look like? How might we gather together existing data structures and their mixed machinic and semiological commitments toward representation, to rethink the associative practices of social computing wholesale? How might we do so in ways that would productively complicate, and render more frank, the circumstances of how knowledge and communication circulate today? The bulk of this book has been concerned with acknowledging that, in the situation we now find ourselves, the political power of social computing lies far more in what Tim Jordan calls differences that form information, over and above differences that form communication. It is a fact of digital formalization, as he writes, that

To move as a constituent part of information is entirely connected to the difference that is moved and the social and significatory system that allows such a movement. Communication and information are different things and they carry different senses of what 'move' means.[1]

In light of the foregoing chapters, it should by now be clear how the distinction operates. Hints produced at the asignifying level of a social computing platform move us at a certain speed and velocity together in relation to structured data objects, as they rely on calculative difference at the operational level in order to stage the differential movements of subject and object, and self and other, at the level of the communicational. Having explored the strategies for accomplishing this to different effect, it is time to briefly consider what an alternative practice might look like. What we are looking for is a formatting schema that, like original hypertext, would involve free-form control over the conceptual circumstances of indexical reference. But like knowledge and social graphs, it would carry with it some kind of extensible theory of collective individuation. With an eye to the real time agonistics of social platforms like Twitter, insisting on this dimension of formatting is about recognizing that social computing has developed out of the free association of texts, to become a more global model for social-rational association.

Operational and calculative hints produced at the asignifying level of information processing now cross articulate with the affective and the illocutionary features of habit and desire to move us together and apart at certain speeds and velocities on a daily basis. In so doing, they also stage the conditions of discursive meaning and communication. The problem with these models is that they deploy theories of relation that are defined according to some universalizing principle that sits anterior to individuation itself. The idea is to sketch out an account that is articulated to alternative presuppositions about the philosophical role played by difference and identity in the event of imaginative association, while remaining faithful to the material-semiotic necessities of datafication and information theory. Put in light of Gilles Deleuze's atypical reading of David Hume's socius, how might we conceive of an alternative social computing practice that sidesteps the universal organization of knowledge and the social habits of sympathy that accompany it (possessive individualism) in favor of principles of habit that are focused on an autonomizing subjectivity that thrives on disparity and dissensus in its formal model?

What we are looking for is a formatted subject articulated by a different set of conditions and concerns, both at the asignifying and communicative level. The approach should reflect a desire to communicate difference as a function of one's identity, but with a capacity for endo and exoreference that accounts for that individuality according to problematic divergence rather than utilitarian decision. The point is to think carefully about ways of sidestepping the conceptual limitations that arise from appeals to the poles of speaker and hearer.

To put it in more general terms, how might we reverse the conceptual emphasis presumed by Jordan's two styles of movement in today's global graphs such that users could more thoroughly understand and embrace the asignifying conditions of their expressivity and individuality, both in the enunciative assemblages of graph platforms themselves and in the relations that these platforms have with other assemblages who rely on global graphs? Pulling various desiderata from each style discussed in the last chapter can give us some purchase on these questions.

From hypertext, we might want to reinvigorate the distributed power of free association that it established between linked blocks of text. Historically conceived, its power lay in authors being in a position to move readers around to other locations in a textual universe of their own design; relocating them further down a page, from one topic or site to another, or to some related point in a branching narrative. It would be absurd to suggest that this open relationality has disappeared; but people do seem to have been captivated by a redefinition of the link, away from this original power to broadly define the conditions of association on one's own terms and toward a formatting that gives greater collective coherence and expressive purchase to text blocks styled as individualized utterances. That said, the asignifying power of hypertext continues to lie in its capacity for enchaining pages and blocks of text entirely according to one's own investments into the signifier—via the link. This makes it open and transgressive in terms of textual nonlinearity, but also conceptually limited for its comparative lack of a rigorous collectivizing principle of identity and difference. Consistent with its frequent academic interpretation as a Derridean profusion of traces, George Landow sees the power of hypertext as "a montage-like textuality," that "marks or foregrounds the writing process and therefore rejects a deceptive transparency."[2]

For their part, knowledge graphs are desirable for the way they organize the link relation in order to *seek out* such a transparency of reference, although as we have seen, critics do claim this transparency to be deceptive. Despite their shortcomings in rendering the hetero-semiotic conditions of knowing in homo-semiotic terms, knowledge graphs give us a powerful, truth-functional strategy for streamlining out false beliefs on the pragmatic basis of the facts taken for granted by a community of knowers. They give us a framework for rational social accountability by providing us with a set of universalizing conditions for common and good sense. With respect to Deleuze's circle of sense, denotation is their main emphasis, the problem being that as a technique, knowledge graphs do not seem especially capable of registering the forces of dissent that naturally manifest in the concrete negotiation of knowledge.

The reverse seems true with social graphs. Designed to capture and make visible the forces of individuals belonging to different groups, social graphs are focused on the manifestational portion of the circle of sense. Like knowledge graphs, they produce a powerful analytic for judgment. But it is a subjectivist analytic, based in a formatting of social status and group solidarity, as communities police the boundaries of their belonging and not belonging. Because the I and its desires are primary, social graphs can more clearly harness the energies of disagreement and dissensus, given that exo and endoreference are explicitly premised on the fiction of speaker and hearer. But they do so by sacrificing the truth-functional operations of factuality in favor of social performance.

Finally, through their stricter focus on the syntactical connections of conceptual implication and causation, machine-learning graphs close the circle by mobilizing a logic of *signification*, which maintains and automates the overall conditions of truth and error. In Deleuze's schema of sense, machine learning is a way to represent the underlying conditions of meaningfulness for both denotation and manifestation; as he writes of signification, its logics are "[...] only implied (though not expressed) by the I, presenting itself as having signification which is immediately understood and identical to its own manifestation."[3] In other words, machine learning gives us a 'form of the I' that productively reconciles denotation to manifestation, signified to signifier, and common sense to good sense, through the basic relation of premise and conclusion. Certainly we want to hold on to this incredibly powerful capacity for conceptual generalization out of pure syntax. But we might want to jettison its epistemic grounding in a private thinking mind, divorced from sociopolitical context.

When we gather together the strategies in this condensed way, certain important realizations come to light. Social communication largely becomes a matter of being a statistical differential in a calculated population, or one who 'has a voice' only secondarily according to the fictitious poles of speaker and hearer. We can lose sight of this when we focus too much on the power of platforms from a sociological perspective and must remember that many social groupings, especially subjugated ones, want more than just an apparatus for communication. They want their power to organize the world to have effectivity both at the level of sociopolitical change *and* epistemic-conceptual implication. The two should be fused; but when it comes to today's commercial platforms, too often the energies of the former come to matter only as an extracted semantic resource for continued centralized control over the latter, by dominant platforms. Addressing this issue means that we need to rethink the formatted subject's relationship to asignification; holding on to the basic power of exo and endoreference as it is styled in the register of communication, but finally, emptying out its fictitious construction as speaker and hearer and setting new terms of reference.

It would in other words mean more fully embracing our relativization as patterns and signals; formatted bundles of hints who labor under the illusion of stating but who desire to reach a point of improved creative and critical latitude over the organizing principles of that illusion. Following thinkers in the new materialist tradition who take up a 'post-anthropocentric' position toward technology like Rosi Braidotti, the idea would be to venture beyond intersubjective, consensus-based choice of possessive individuals as the dominant paradigm for social computing. A core step toward doing so would involve putting social computing's epistemic understanding of identity and difference into relief against other theorizations of difference, especially those not conceptually beholden to decision or choice in quite the same way. I have relied on Deleuze and Félix Guattari's mixed semiotic throughout as a way to produce this relief, but in this final chapter, I turn to the philosophy of Gilbert Simondon.

Influential upon Deleuze, but also working alongside (and critical of) both the cybernetic tradition as it unfolded and the phenomenological tradition of people like Martin Heidegger and Maurice Merleau-Ponty, Simondon did not define identity in primarily epistemic terms. For him, difference was not based in an objective knowledge principle for resolving identity mechanistically as a relation of probable choice between objective entities. Rather, difference was *ontogenetic* and non-identitary, manifesting in a process that he called *disparation*, a term for describing a tensile difference between an individual's world and its own process of becoming. Insofar as global graph structures have come to form what Simondon called a principle of psychic and collective individuation, the concept is useful for understanding formatted subjects as a process of technical individuation.

Resonant with Deleuze and Guattari's concerns over the dominance of an epistemic-informational paradigm for the semiotic, and connected to his account of choice, for Simondon, information was not just to be defined as exchanged messages between sender and receiver; it was also an internal resonance to being in which an organism individuates in an indeterminate way on the basis of its own *dephasing*.[4] Simondon's thought carefully spanned dimensions of the psychic, the collective, and the technical here, and in light of his work, I want to conclude by gathering the insights of previous chapters in light of his conceptualization of self-organization.

The goal here would be to reconfigure the representational relay between collective passions and reasoning so that, like original hypertext, affects might once again articulate to the understanding on the basis of free association, simultaneously in content, machinic index, and systemic structure. Unlike current machine-learning strategies, this would occur in asignifying ways that are more distributed in order to follow associative principles that are idiomatic to the collectivizing social fields that each one of us inhabits. Asignifying structures should more totally follow shared imagination, in other words, rather than some universal set of associative principles that have been laid out by Google, Facebook, or Microsoft.

Self-Organizing Knowledge Systems

As seen in the discussions on hypertext, it was not so long ago that networks of discourse were mostly a matter for scientific researchers and a cottage industry of web designers with relation defined simply in terms of the associative principle of the hyperlink. Internetworked connections between servers made real the visions of people like Paul Otlet, Vannevar Bush, and Tim Berners-Lee by affording users a capacity for jumping from one document to another at will, following chains of thought collaboratively inscribed as links between texts. With the rise of Web 2.0, linking became more rationalized as sharing, and data exchange began to pivot on the more individualized, attentional value of the link, soon dragging large portions of life into its orbit. As Helmond writes, citing Langlois and others, here, platforms emerged as

> [...] an interface between users, webmasters and search engines and 'arise as sites of articulations between a diverse range of processes and actors'. For the political economy of linking in the era of social media, platforms become important actors in the production and distribution of links while at the same time regulating access to these links for engines.[5]

Acknowledging these and other important themes concerning the political economy of communication and knowledge online, a second important site for the establishment of the social through the technical relation has to do with social computing's philosophical roots in epistemic individualization. Knowledge graphs are indebted to second-order cybernetics and the field's conceptualization of self-organizing systems. Having lived under conditions of 'information overload' since Herbert Simon coined the term in 1970, most of us are all too familiar with what James Gleick describes as that anxious gap between information and knowledge, where a "barrage of data so often fails to tell us what we need to know."[6] Knowledge graph systems theorize effective action as the key for minding that gap. From a systems perspective, it was the physicist-philosopher Heinz von Foerster who first described it as involving a recursive feedback dynamic, or an observer-knowledge relation. As we saw in discussion of Google's PageRank Markov chain strategy, his accompanying notion of the eigenvalue continues to deeply structure technical, algorithmic, and mathematical approaches to social computing, and to information retrieval on the whole as a discipline.

Self-organizing systems are those that, despite striving for operational closure, are structured in such a way as to remain open and adaptable to change as a function of maintaining/postponing that closure. Paradoxically, in these systems, it is the continuous reaction to difference as a force of imbalance that maintains balance. Referring to some contemporary interlocutors along the way, Bruce Clarke sums up von Foerster's approach when he writes that second-order cybernetics

> sees a world so constructed that any single observer's observations may be rendered stable from moment to moment by the structural couplings and recursive conversations of its multiple observers. Just as

all nervous systems and all organisms that possess them within themselves are virtual consortiums of multiple autopoietic systems, so are all observers bound into (what Varela calls) 'observer-communities' within which (what Luhmann calls) social autopoiesis [...] produces (what von Foerster calls) eigenvalues.[7]

These are defined as "stable yet mobile and multiple recursive consensuses about shared environments."[8] Eigenvalues are the objectified knowledge conditions under which meaning is organized into socially coherent identities such that a probabilistically structured 'either/or' choice can occur between them, with the overall system designed to offer coordinating conditions for collective thinking. Each strategy discussed in prior chapters articulates semiotically and philosophically to these coordinating conditions in a different way. As in Jordan's account of informational movement, each has a logic of the significational and the social, which fits together with the probabilistic and recursive strategies of information theory. More plainly in light of the affordances of social computing in the everyday: thanks to my choices being compared to the trails of choice left behind by others before me, I can more quickly discriminate the particular person, thing, or document I am looking for—while also being exposed to related, 'recommended for you'-type information-signs that may also be of interest.

What they share is that all of these global graphs take a constructivist approach to knowledge, in other words, presuming a stable and self-referential user at their center, relied upon to reproduce the 'recursive consensus' that von Foerster first theorized. Knowledge graphs focus on exteriorizing discourse into networks of atomic assertions, capturing relations between things as disembedded, factual webs of correct reference. Social graphs act in a similar way but treat people as the basic atoms, focusing on the more performative and illocutionary dimensions of identity and group affiliation. Finally, predictive-analytic graphs start from large structured and unstructured datasets to analyze relations between their entities statistically, framed as probabilistic choice.

It is on these terms that global graphs establish a self-organizing model for collective thought predicated on rationally individualized choice, with prior selection outputs feeding back into current needs to interactively resolve our sociality through a platform's eigenvalue relations. Especially with the profusion of mobile devices, the major goal seems to be to offer up this rational, self-organizing relation *whenever* and *wherever* something happens to disturb a user's 'operational autonomy' by providing information that addresses the disparities of one's environment. At the level of technique though, these moments of knowledge disparity and resolution are all defined by a rather idealist conception of what a knowledge-relation is and how it is to be resolved: in the terms of probabilistic choice between already-constituted, mutually-exclusive subjects and objects. Under these circumstances, ontogenetic difference, or difference for itself in individuation, comes to matter only "in relation to a conceived identity, a judged analogy, an imagined opposition, a perceived similitude," as Deleuze writes.[9]

Given the freedom and convenience afforded by social computing—to access so much knowledge about the world around us and to manage the organizational complexity of our everyday interactions with others—we clearly attain a certain significant autonomy through such a technical arrangement. And, as suggested earlier, as a matter of the material functionality of computers being beholden to logic, this may be the only possible arrangement. But to conclude in a more speculative register, we can ask whether users lack autonomy with respect to the prior ontological terms of this knowledge-relation; where in its establishment, each user's shifting differentials of part-sign investment to asignifying process is being projected into global graphs too coarsely on the terms of abstract utilitarian choice. By fitting into preexisting coded structures of behavior, which interlace private choice with the essential diagrams of information theory on either epistemic or performative terms, does the formatted subject not forfeit a deeper, prior relation *of* the knowledge relation; access to the grounding or instituting moment of knowledge, as philosophy or metaphysics?

Elaborating the issue along the lines of technics means shifting discussion from epistemology to ontology, to ask: are there other ways of comprehending the 'productive disparity' of the individual beyond utilitarian choice, as one is coupled to the social through an autopoietic relation? A step away from the dominant view would be to say that each approach we've encountered tacitly relies on, but ultimately leaves out, the prior conditions of *singularity* and the hetero-semiotic and heteronomous relations that it involves. The philosopher Alberto Toscano uses the term anomalous individuation to make appeals to this singularity, read as "the unequal or differential ground of production that lies beneath the actual, constituted, individuals which provide the objects of the philosophies of representation."[10] In the last chapter, I referred to these conditions more simply as a relation between *hints* and *statements:* between the affective, perceptual and psychic polarities, or bifurcations of becoming that constitute individuals at the level of unconscious habit, which form a deeper, yet obscured, ground for making entity-attribute-type assertions, as both procedures fold back on our collective behavior as formatted choice through algorithmic aggregation.

The hinting strategies of social computing captivate and envelop our anomalous individuation, redefining it in the asignifying terms of retrieval. In a corporate video describing the evolution of search, for example, Google Fellow Ben Gomes states that,

> Our goal is actually to make improvements to search that just answer the user's informational needs, get them to their answer faster and faster, so that there's almost a seamless connection between their thoughts and informational needs and the search results they find.[11]

Contemporary academic discourse in the information sciences sees retrieval as deeply penetrating the psyche in similar ways. Charles Cole
writes, for example, that "Information need is at its deepest level primarily a human adaptive mechanism—at the level of human perception,
at the level of society and the world in which the individual operates, and
at the level of survival as a species."[12] It was due to similar, positivistic accounts of information as a phenomenon that Simondon sometimes
criticized cybernetic models of the individual, rejecting the represen-
tationalist assumptions we have been interrogating for misconstruing
what he saw information's real role to be: in individuation.[13]

Knowledge as an Ontological Dephasing Relation

Simondon's ontology does not draw hard boundaries between the vital
individuation of life, individual psyches, social collectivities, and evolving technologies. Rather, he conceives of them all as intercalated, each
participating in the formation of individuated interiors and exteriors
of the other's wider systems.[14] In the similar manner that Deleuze and
Guattari speak of concrete assemblages of enunciation, individuals for
Simondon are only one part in the processes of larger entities that he
called technical ensembles. Justifying this definition requires him to invert the relationship typically established between being and becoming
in a way that is instructive when thinking about graphs. While contemporary schemes for information retrieval based in global graphs tend to
define the sign-relation as a cognitive or epistemic lack, whose need is
fulfilled by inductively and deductively selecting one's way to the correct object, Simondon conceived of the sign-relation as an ontological
excess: a being "more-than-individual,"[15] upon whose surplus individuation takes place. His concept of disparation is fundamental here in
designating

> a tension, an incompatibility between two elements of a situation,
> which only a new individuation can resolve by giving birth to a new
> level of reality. Vision, for instance, is described by Simondon as the
> resolution of a disparation between the image perceived by the left
> eye and the image perceived by the right eye. These two disparate
> two-dimensional images call forth a three-dimensional dimension
> as the only way to unify them.[16]

For Simondon, metaphysically substantialist accounts of the individual
(upon which the technicity of social computing is premised) mistakenly
define becoming in the terms of being: the unity of an individual is sus-
tained and its singularity (or *haecceity*) defined by some prior, universalizing principle of difference. We have seen three over the course of the
last few chapters: rationalist assertion, illocutionary force, and Humean

impression. On his understanding, the issue is that "Anything that can serve as the basis for a relation is already of the same mode of being as the individual, whether it be an atom, an external and indivisible particle, prima material or form."[17] In all three strategies, *individual choice* becomes the general social principle of co-becoming and adaptability for both people and media systems. As has been more carefully argued elsewhere, there is a strong resonance with this technical approach and advanced capitalism, whose "perversity," as Braidotti writes, "[...] consists in reattaching the potential for experimentation with new subject formations back to an overinflated notion of possessive individualism, tied to the profit principle."[18]

How is Simondon's approach distinct from these? From a certain perspective, it can be hard to see much difference between his account of individuation and one given for a reflexive subject who finds themselves integrated into a self-organizing structure. Following the ocular analogy of disparation, are we not in some sense one another's 'opposing eye' on social computing platforms, achieving collective disparation through the algorithmic, pairwise superimposition of our differing private choices? Guided by someone like Anthony Giddens' theory of individualization, for example, social computing by global graph would then simply be the latest technology for predicating social order upon a 'gap' at the heart of a self-reflexive subject. Similar to the account given by phenomenological social science, we negotiate subject-object relations via a disequilibriating encounter with our structuring environment, and these encounters resolve for the individual through the acquisition and use of knowledge, as one also receives its 'structurated', consensual norms for behavior.

For Simondon, however, there is a crucial difference between individuation and individualization: in his account of the former, neither the structure nor the operating individual *ever has unity* as a concrete, self-identical being. Where self-organizing systems theory typically understands incompatibility from the perspective of an organism's demands on the environment, Simondon sees incompatibility with an environment in a more Spinozist way, as the default condition of collective individuation—taking life, psyches, sociality, and technology together in a global situation. The environment has its own individuating conditions, which relate to the conditions of the organism through what Simondon calls the pre-individual, modulating a 'double-becoming'. We can see important parallels here to Deleuze and Guattari's notion of reciprocal planes of content and expression, brought together by some diagram: agent and container are effectively a constant flux, never achieving some state of self-similarity, and it's in this light that Simondon asks: how does the organism differ from itself, how does the environment differ from itself, and under what circumstances do they nonetheless *come to relate* in a disjunctive (non-)relation? As Hansen writes, if the global situation is a global perspective, it is not a perspective of the organism but a perspective on the entire process of individuation of which the organism is only one part—a perspective, in short, that situates the organism within the broader context of the preindividual.[19]

To put the point more forcefully, pre-individual being simply *is* this milieu: the given conditions under which a tension between potentials belonging to previously separated orders of magnitude can be resolved via their communication.[20] Bearing Simondon's 'flipped' understanding of being and becoming in mind, in their current incarnation, social computing platforms stage pre-individual being as a decisionistic milieu that individuates people by modulating them together as choice makers with preferential attachments, with platforms serving as real time decision-capture machines for spacing us out into probabilistic fields of 'having chosen something'. It's in this sense that the systems can be charitably read as structuring a disparation individuating the collective, but in a fashion very much focused on *individualization*. By this I mean an individuation imagined on the basis of independent will; one who meaningfully expresses and informs themselves according to an operational logic of being *free from the wills of others*.

This becomes especially consequential when we learn that Simondon's approach suggests that, at its core, individuating relation is only secondarily epistemic; it is primarily ontogenetic. Following discussions of the transcendental in the last chapter, Brian Massumi writes that ontogenesis involves some "self-inventive passing to a new level of existence," meaning that as we resolve problems in the world around us about what to do next, being and thinking are the same as they occur in an individual's milieu.[21] As we turn to social computing platforms to resolve these problems, however, the question is whether and how much we alienate our singularity through habituation according to the transcendental-epistemic diagrams they offer, which stand in for, but then 'cast back' upon, our being. What I am suggesting with a turn to Simondon is that we might push such concerns for the ontogenetic down into the levels of system design; to begin to think of relation as not taking place according to some principle that must appeal to some higher rank of being, like transcendental logic or transcendental sociality. Instead, if being itself becomes by linking together differentially, spacing itself out in an internal milieu, then we may need to accept that differences particular to living cannot be adequately captured by classification. Or at least, we should not be surprised that such an approach might take us toward a certain taxonomic neurosis as societies, because as Muriel Combes describes in a helpful refrain: "knowledge exists in the same mode as the beings that it links together, considered from the point of view of that which constitutes their reality."[22]

Acknowledging that we are moving here into more science-fictional terrain, which may not fit with the extant capacities of information systems, the user-as-individual in Simondon's case might no longer be understood as a discrete agent making choices with autonomous intentionality. Rather, they would be taken more impersonally as an 'it': an individuating process-organism involved in the "local resolution of disparation, as the invention of a compatibility between heterogeneous domains and demands."[23] Perpetually 'coming-into-being' in the sociotechnical manner described by Simondon in the chapter's epigraph, can we imagine a technical relation that would not be so heavily based in some preconceived notion of 'bringing like together with like' through choice as an abstract mechanism? How might we think about a technical relation that would rather emerge between itself in the vital and semiotic resolution of a milieu, with choice conceived as a problem resolved within one's *own* inventive differential capacity, for what Deleuze describes as a paratactical serialization of signifer and signified—one's own power to see things as belonging together, according to contradictions in life that resolve over time in the perpetual reconstitution of what he calls the cracked I. Here individuation would still be a knowledge relation, but one defined by an individual entirely in light of its particular individuating dynamic—the 'pre-individual share' of its life, as Simondon understands it—and thus not admitting of any one, generalized epistemic principle. Conceived in light of his critique of the cybernetic approach to information, Simondon's appeal to a deeper, 'first information' is instructive here.

In discussing Simondon's ideas, Andrew Iliadis returns us to the assumptions of the DIKW pyramid to discern three ways of talking about data and information: as reality, 'e.g. patterns, fingerprints, tree rings;' for reality, 'e.g. commands, algorithms, recipes;' and about reality, 'e.g. train tables, maps, entries in an encyclopedia'. He points out that "Where the cyberneticists thought the interoperability and indeterminacy of information 'about' and 'for' reality, Simondon thought these concepts in terms of information 'as' reality."[24] A focus on the former two has led to the kinds of structured data and algorithmic procedures that motivate current social computing platforms. In theorizing the latter, Simondon believed that the relational difference of choice might be inverted: to becomes less a principle of signification as information 'about' reality—where a dominating subject presides over a neutral object, engaged in its interactive control—and more a compositional principle of signification as invention, with individuation once again thought of as an excess.

As Massumi describes, for Simondon, information "is not susceptible to any stable formalization because it is continually giving rise to new operational solidarities that did not exist before, and therefore exceed all prior formalization."[25] Choice, thus, needs to be better understood more closely in terms of the *advent* of being—information's 'as'—instead of its simple relation as something already organized between sender and receiver.[26] This is the kind of relation that we are after for the formatted subject, insofar as it may have untapped political potential for the formation of subject groups rather than subjugated groups. As Toscano writes, Simondon is attempting to "appropriate the concept of information for a consideration of ontogenesis in terms that would precede and condition the formation and circumscription of these individuated entities and quantities that go by the names sender, receiver and code."[27] To follow his line of thinking, how might this alternative account bear on the functionality of social computing? In the space that remains, I need to look elsewhere than the services themselves to try and indicate a disparational energy of semiotic difference in generic discourse that currently fails to register in the referential techniques already outlined.

As we saw in Chapters 2 and 3, knowledge and social graphs structure the sign according to predication, pivoting around the copula of the 'is' in formal-semantic terms. I have been arguing that this gives a metaphysical account of identity and difference that, based in both logical-empirical approaches to language and the social-autopoietic terms of a second-order cybernetics, organizes particular relations between subjects and objects. In offering an alternative approach that extrapolates from Simondon, I want to hold on to this designative, referential dimension between subjects and object, as it supports our relationship to signs. But I also want to *empty it out*; to indicate a different way to appreciate reason and ratio as a ground for thinking, which does not rely on formal predication. With an eye to the original, open association of hypertext, but *also* the turn to pure machinic association as mobilized in machine learning, the goal would be to mark a more latent, immanent dimension of the sign that people like Heidegger and Deleuze have in the past thematized as the sign's manifestation.

Insofar as social computing is currently too premised on an intersubjective economy of choice, styled as communication and operationalized as mathematized information, it obscures a collective access to the crucial semiotic hints of difference that contribute to the formatting of most platforms. As argued in the last chapter, these hints are worthy of re-inscription into new practices, especially as they might bolster a Simondonian account of the pre-individual. But we need to see them in the first place; their generic presence in discourse. Let me give an example of one way to see a latent illocutionary dimension in discourse that tends to be ignored, and which we might conceptualize as offering some new site for a hinting practice. The examples are taken from two pieces of editorial writing online.

In Table 6.1 are two sets of four statements, published after US President Barack Obama's 2013 proposed gun control legislation was defeated. Taken from politically polarized sites, they have been very tendentiously excerpted for two reasons. First, to preserve their possible circulation as information-signs: to pull them out as entity-like fragments

Table 6.1 These are direct excerpts from two web articles

President Barack Obama on gun control (Breitbart.com 4/17/13)

Claimed that opponents of expanded federal background checks had "no coherent arguments" for their position	<>	Resorted to false claims and statistics about current laws, including the repeatedly debunked argument that 40 percent of gun sales are private
Used the Newtown disaster to make an argument about the urgent need for new laws	<>	Exploited the Newtown disaster to make an argument about the urgent need for new laws
Noted that 90 percent of Americans, and a majority of National Rifle Association members, supported expanded background checks	<>	Ignored the fact that constitutional rights like the Second Amendment exist precisely to protect minorities against majoritarian passions
Showed a reserved, measured response to the Boston Marathon bombings	<>	Attacked his opponents viciously, expressing and evoking such visceral emotions—especially at a time of mourning

---

President Barack Obama on gun control (Slate.com 4/22/13)

Thwarted by partisanship	<>	Lacked the skills to manage the moment
Could have done more	<>	Required a different skill set
Admitted he usually thinks he can do his staff's job better than they can	<>	Had his best shot handing this issue over to Vice President Joe Biden
Master of the art of politics	<>	Hired because he is the anti-politician

---

Contrastive relations immanent to sequential, or nearby, sentences in the articles themselves are being pulled out of context for the purposes of highlighting how they manifest a differential; some kind of (admittedly abstract) analogical ratio of 'more/less'. For the purposes of a more ontogenetically inflected style of information processing, these differentials might be operationalized—by the author or others, over time—through some kind of technical 'hinting' strategy that marks the ratios in a collective practice—a kind of ontogenetic 'hyper-sense' that builds on the strategies of lexia-based hypertext.

of indexical reference, which bear some resemblance to current, post-documentary styles of algorithmic processing in that they rely on the 'is' copula. Second, and more importantly, they have been excerpted to portray Barack Obama's significance as an ongoing problem of collective individuation. They accentuate the sign in terms of a semiotic field of potential concerning the entity in question rather than the fact that they were uttered by the authors who wrote them—respectively, Joel Pollak and John Dickerson. My underlying motive is to suggest that in this example, there is signification based on hetero-semiotic difference, which is operating in a register different from the traditional retrieval relation. To use Simondon's vocabulary, there is a contrastive meta-stability in these excerpts, between incompatible semiotic potentials of becoming, which contribute to, but would otherwise remain obscured by, a relation of choice between them as author-separated articles. Thinking ontologically about what it means to be social around signs involves recuperating and marking such contrastive energies as themselves constructively individuating hints, which might lead to new styles of stating, according to new applications of eigenvalue technique in formatting. Following Simondon, on this perspective, information-signs percolate with a manifestation of becoming and a deictic of individuation, taking place in ways that are as much about the desiring investments of readers and writers than about the consumption of texts. Instead of seeing signs as closed epistemic entities according to some totalizing universal relation, we may opt to see relationality, as Toscano writes, in terms of "the non-identity of being with regard to itself."[28] Think of the arrows in the middle of the table as representing a kind of identitary 'swing' over an abyss of non-meaning, the idea being that the authors themselves might establish them as a kind of tensor, taking the form of an operational hint. Or alternatively, these two authors might engage one another across the web, using tensors of difference that contrast their writing in agonal discourse.

According to the different statistical and taxonomic strategies of global graphs, a formal-semantic approach might differentiate the sign 'President Barack Obama on gun control' in any number of ways: Barack Obama could be parsed as different from other leadership positions, or Nobel prize recipients, as he is in the Wolfram Alpha knowledge graph. Or he might be differentiated in informational retrieval through some statistical 'bag of words' approach, from similar terms like 'baracan' or 'obey'. Perhaps he might be compared according to a social graph, among others who've attended events discussing the issue. To think relation in Simondon's terms though, as both an epistemic-conceptual relation *and* a pre-individual, becoming-manifestation relation, the goal would be to somehow preserve 'Obama on gun control' as persisting in the action of an individuating entity encountering other entities in a problematic field of its paratactical serialization, with immanent ratios between series of signifiers and signifieds being brought into relation by humans and non-humans dynamically animating the sign's meaningfulness in a more frankly operational way.

Some will think that in this characterization I am simply describing how the sign 'Obama on gun control' already circulates. Search services like Google's autocomplete, or its Ngram Viewer, do apply Markov chain strategies in order to surface terms according to their statistical use in overall discourse. What I am much more interested in capturing in the above table though are hints toward a more ontogenetic view of difference where 'Obama on gun control' is repeatedly compared in the writing to *itself* as a sign, through a sequence of intensive moments that indicate a choice, but one read as an *auto-constitutive* differentiation of its signification as an entity in which sociality is emergent from the signs themselves and not based in selection between already-processed entities. As Combes writes, for Simondon, "A substance appears when a term absorbs into itself the relation that gave rise to it, thus obscuring it."[29] There is a potential for incompossibility in the writing, and it is being resolved by the writers through the absorption of prior meanings, which in my sketch here form a basis for the operational projection of new meanings. This is qualitatively different from the taxonomic sorting of concepts and the classificatory strategies that tend to drive social computing.

I am trying to depict signification more immanently, where the wider goal is not to zero in on Obama's 'correct' reference in, or as a closed constellation of, facts. Rather, difference is being mobilized to realize signification according to the immanent conditions of a collective becoming individual, with other psyches, institutions, collectivities, and signs participating in an overall milieu, staged by signs that thematize the world as a set of outstanding questions or problems. These problems continue to involve singular intensive investments, but these investments need not resolve themselves according to some transcendental principle. Read through a Simondonian lens, the two authors face a surfeit of potential meanings and in their writing are looking to resolve signs into compossible relations. After the fact though, these two documents will persist largely according to the differential logics of platforms like Google or Facebook. What I am wondering here is whether, by design, the overall techno-semiotic force of divergent compossibility could begin from the level of the everyday user and their subjectivation. How would things have to be arranged such that participants in an enunciative informatics would act as pure signal processors, registering their individuation not through the fictitious poles of speaker and hearer but by hinting or marking up their discursive utterances directly, specifying the incorporeal effects that they seek to realize, as these flow from the specific, differential tensions of their collective becoming?

Hypertext already does this in one way, Twitter does it in another, and machine learning is fast becoming its latest horizon. I am basically advocating that we continue to press the issue in critical ways, with an eye to the political consequences for our collective relation. Simondon's alternative account of 'first information' is suggestive in every case; whenever someone chains together signs in disparation, they are tacitly relying on different 'more-or-less' operations of affective, perceptual, and conceptual ratios for connecting up disparate fields so as to conjunct or *modulate* signs into stable series of signifiers and signifieds. I have tried to denote this with the symbols in the middle of the table where the inventive tendency toward one relation over another is denoted by the slightly bolder, greater-than symbol, which is meant to point out an alternative, more ontogenetic reading of choice.

The upshot of this final exposition is to wonder: would it be possible to organize a technical practice and a set of computational operations around these ratios, to push current thinking about the potentials and pitfalls of social computing in a new direction? From the perspective of post-documentary form, here, the basic force for differentiating information-signs into visibility would no longer be personal choice between retrieved objects. It would rather be something like an entity's immanent, continual bifurcation into problematics. As we see with phenomena like hashtags, signs matter in the medium of social computing because their status is in question globally, as the platform captures and motivates the energy of people questioning the world around them. But rather than assuming that the formatted subject is simply communicative in their questioning, can we imagine an approach to systems design that would store and organize signs directly according to their problematics? As a principled approach, this would be about seeing social computing less in terms of crowd trends and virality and more in terms of collective-agonistic strategies for representing questioning itself. The idea is that as a matter of underlying technique, social computing might capture, store, and organize signs as a manifestation of their internal asymmetries and polarities *in* thought rather than to impose a polarizing structure upon them, which causes signs to matter mostly as particular instances or tokens of some universalizing account of, or *about*, thought.

The statements of the two writers quoted above are just one example, inflecting and refracting certain perceptual and affective intensities in their relation to Obama's interventions into gun control, but putting these intensities into relation through disjunctive series that remain invisible to current approaches. Instead of encountering the two articles discretely, with one perhaps ranked over top of the other on the basis of what you've read in the past, or on who's recommended one over another to you, the statements themselves might sit more flush with the enchaining together of series of what you will read, respond to, feel, and do next through their more immanent contrastive relation in technical operation. In other words, the example is meant to suggest a set of alternative hints that we might leave behind (and in a sense already are leaving behind as we make statements about things, but in an obscured way), which might still be productively computed into collective eigenvalues through some new formatting strategy. In terms of one's capacities toward these signs, rather than picking the next document to read, you might conceivably add your own contrastive bifurcation to a transversal space of statements around 'Obama on gun control' as a collective process entity, for example.

The Future Is In Formation

At a more basic level, I have tried to indicate that despite their increasing conflation, signification through retrieval is not the same thing as signification through ontogenesis. In the push to make discourse more technically amenable to the optimizing disparation of existing knowledge, social, and PA graph services, we may be unwittingly obscuring important, philosophical dimensions of the semiotic that deserve inclusion in conversations around future design. Individuals are more than abstract epistemic agents; they carry resonant ontogenetic differences within themselves as they become through their affective and discursive bifurcations to *be* one way and not another. This happens on the basis of the collective assemblages of enunciation that frame our reality, through asignifying signs that circulate, motivate, and mix together our desiring investments with a wide variety of techno-material assemblages, through signals that set up ratios of excess and lack in signification, upon which individuals carry out compatibilities of communication in the form of expressive, individuating sign-events.

Social media systems are putting these signals to work in a particular way, serializing our thinking and relationship to one another. In light of this horizon, we need to be asking questions about the conditions under which their representational techniques give an effectuating account of signification, and whether more preferable conditions for the preservation and amplification of collective individuation might require new ways of thinking. From the altered point of view I have sketched out here, the hope is to have shown how certain long-standing accounts of meaning and knowledge reproduce an intersubjective orientation to the sign that, at this point, come at the expense of obscuring a more potent, prior enunciative relation that has been captured by commercial interests.

As the information retrieval relation bleeds into more intimate registers of life in network societies, these interests risk further defining our relationship to signs as such in a way that may foreclose upon other conceptual possibilities. The counterintuitive gambit is that to reimagine social media then, we must suspend a sociological approach to computing; one where, as Bruno Latour remarks, the social is somehow made of some homogeneous stuff.[30] Instead, we need to engage with social media's procedures directly by taking a materialist and mixed semiotic approach to our relationship toward things, institutions, technologies, and power. Thinking in this vein contends that signs always involve more than the performance of shared meaning in a socio-linguistic context. They also involve more than a formalized relation of valid reference, a feature of signs that has nevertheless become crucial for the coordination of life in an information age. Signs have a still-deeper dimension, best understood in terms of an impersonal event, organized by some enunciative assemblage, and from which individuals receive an ordered orientation for living, including an experiential sense of before and after.

When unique Twitter hashtags emerge to orient people around a street conflict or natural disaster, for example, or when Google aggregates real time search queries to predict national flu activity, we have clearly moved beyond the simple denotation and retrieval of information. If the social web is to serve as a future platform for both information retrieval and public expression, then it will be crucial for us to rethink the latter on its own more distinctive socio-technical terms.

Notes

1 Jordan, *Information Politics*, 17.
2 Landow, *Hypertext 3.0*, 55.
3 Deleuze, *The Logic of Sense*, 15.
4 Simondon, *L'individuation psychique et collective*, 328.
5 Helmond, "The Algorithmization of the Hyperlink."
6 Gleick, *The Information*, 403.
7 Clarke and Hansen, *Emergence and Embodiment*, 56.
8 Ibid.
9 Deleuze, *Difference and Repetition*, 138.
10 Toscano, *The Theatre of Production*, 3.
11 "The Evolution of Search in Six Minutes."
12 Cole, "A Theory of Information Need for Information Retrieval That Connects Information to Knowledge," 1227.
13 Toscano, *The Theatre of Production*, 147.
14 Simondon, "The Genesis of the Individual," 300.
15 Combes, *Gilbert Simondon and the Philosophy of the Transindividual*, 35.
16 Ibid., 111.
17 Simondon, "The Position of the Problem of Ontogenesis," 4.
18 Braidotti, *The Posthuman*, 61.
19 Clarke and Hansen, *Emergence and Embodiment*, 134.
20 Combes, *Gilbert Simondon and the Philosophy of the Transindividual*, 4.
21 Massumi, "'Technical Mentality' Revisited," 43.
22 Combes, *Gilbert Simondon and the Philosophy of the Transindividual*, 18.
23 Ibid., 149.
24 Iliadis, "Informational Ontology: The Meaning of Gilbert Simondon's Concept of Individuation," 7.
25 Massumi, "'Technical Mentality' Revisited," 32.
26 Simondon, *L'individuation psychique et collective*, 310.
27 Toscano, *The Theatre of Production*, 143.
28 Ibid., 140.
29 Combes, *Gilbert Simondon and the Philosophy of the Transindividual*, 16.
30 Latour, *Reassembling the Social*, 91.

Works Cited

Abbate, Janet. *Inventing the Internet*. Cambridge, MA: MIT Press, 1999.

Adam, Alison. *Artificial Knowing: Gender and the Thinking Machine*. London; New York: Routledge, 1998.

Andrejevic, Mark. *Infoglut: How Too Much Information Is Changing the Way We Think and Know*. New York: Routledge, 2013.

Atkin, Albert. *Peirce*. Abingdon, Oxon; New York: Routledge, 2016.

Atkins, Kim. *Self and Subjectivity*. Malden, MA; John Wiley & Sons, 2008.

Azarian, Reza. *The General Sociology of Harrison C. White: Chaos and Order in Networks*. New York; Palgrave MacMillan, 2005.

Baym, Nancy. *Personal Connections in the Digital Age*. 2nd ed. Malden, MA: Polity Press, 2015.

Behrenshausen, Bryan. "Information in Formation: Power and Agency in Contemporary Informatic Assemblages." Unpublished dissertation. Chapel Hill, 2015.

Benkler, Yochai. *The Wealth of Networks: How Social Production Transforms Markets and Freedom*. New Haven, CT; London: Yale University Press, 2007.

Berardi, Franco. *Precarious Rhapsody: Semiocapitalism and the Pathologies of Post-Alpha Generation*. Brooklyn, NY; Autonomedia, 2009.

Berners-Lee, Tim. "Web Architecture: Metadata." *The World Wide Web Consortium*. Accessed September 4, 2017. www.w3.org/DesignIssues/Metadata.html.

Berners-Lee, Tim, Jim Hendler, and Lassila, Ora. "The Semantic Web." *Scientific American*, May 2001.

Blair, David. *Wittgenstein, Language and Information: "Back to the Rough Ground!"* New York; Springer Science & Business Media, 2006.

Bowker, Geoffrey C., and Susan Leigh Star. *Sorting Things Out: Classification and Its Consequences*. Cambridge, MA; London: MIT Press, 2000.

Braidotti, Rosi. *The Posthuman*. Cambridge; Malden, MA: Polity Press, 2013.

Bruns, Axel, and Jean Burgess. "Twitter Hashtags from Ad Hoc to Calculated Publics." In *Hashtag Publics: The Power and Politics of Discursive Networks*. New York: Peter Lang Pub Inc, 2015.

Bryant, Levi R. *Difference and Givenness: Deleuze's Transcendental Empiricism and the Ontology of Immanence*. 1st ed. Evanston, IL: Northwestern University Press, 2008.

Brynjolfsson, Erik, and Andrew McAfee. *The Second Machine Age: Work, Progress, and Prosperity in a Time of Brilliant Technologies*. 1st ed. New York: W. W. Norton & Company, 2014.

Bucher, Taina. "The Algorithmic Imaginary: Exploring the Ordinary Affects of Facebook Algorithms." *Information, Communication & Society* 20, no. 1 (January 2, 2017): 30–44. doi:10.1080/1369118X.2016.1154086.

———. "The Friendship Assemblage: Investigating Programmed Sociality on Facebook." *Television & New Media* 14, no. 6 (November 1, 2013): 479–93. doi:10.1177/1527476412452800.

Burchell, Graham, Michel Foucault, Colin Gordon, and Peter Miller. *The Foucault Effect: Studies in Governmentality: With Two Lectures by and an Interview with Michel Foucault.* London: Harvester Wheatsheaf, 1991.

Bush, Vannevar. "As We May Think." *The Atlantic,* July 1945. www.theatlantic.com/magazine/archive/1945/07/as-we-may-think/303881/.

Campbell-Kelly, Martin, William Aspray, Nathan Ensmenger, and Jeffrey R. Yost. *Computer: A History of the Information Machine.* 3rd ed. Boulder, CO: Westview Press, 2013.

Carl, Wolfgang. *Frege's Theory of Sense and Reference: Its Origin and Scope.* Cambridge; New York: Cambridge University Press, 1994.

Carroll, J.M. "Human Computer Interaction - Brief Intro." *The Interaction Design Foundation.* Accessed July 2, 2017. www.interaction-design.org/literature/book/the-encyclopedia-of-human-computer-interaction-2nd-ed/human-computer-interaction-brief-intro.

Ceruzzi, Paul E. *A History of Modern Computing.* 2nd ed. London; Cambridge, MA: MIT Press, 2003.

Chayko, Dr Mary. "The First Web Theorist? Georg Simmel and the Legacy of 'The Web of Group-Affiliations.'" *Information, Communication & Society* 18, no. 12 (December 2, 2015): 1419–22. doi:10.1080/1369118X.2015.1042394.

Chun, Wendy. *Programmed Visions: Software and Memory.* Cambridge, MA: MIT Press, 2011.

Clarke, Bruce, and Mark B. N. (Mark Boris Nicola) Hansen. *Emergence and Embodiment: New Essays on Second-Order Systems Theory.* Durham, NC: Duke University Press, 2009.

Codd, E. F. "A Relational Model of Data for Large Shared Data Banks." *Communications of the ACM* 13, no. 6 (June 1970): 377–87. doi:10.1145/362384.362685.

Cole, Charles. "A Theory of Information Need for Information Retrieval That Connects Information to Knowledge." *Journal of the American Society for Information Science and Technology* 62, no. 7 (2011): 1216–31. doi:10.1002/asi.21541.

Collins, Harry. *Artificial Experts: Social Knowledge and Intelligent Machines.* Cambridge, MA: MIT Press, 1990.

Combes, Muriel. *Gilbert Simondon and the Philosophy of the Transindividual.* Translated by Thomas LaMarre. Cambridge, MA: MIT Press, 2012.

Couldry, Nick, and Andreas Hepp. *The Mediated Construction of Reality.* Cambridge; Malden, MA: Polity Press, 2017.

Coulter, Jeff. "Logic: Ethnomethodology and the Logic of Language." In *Ethnomethodology and the Human Sciences,* edited by Graham Button, 1st ed., 20–50. Cambridge; New York: Cambridge University Press, 1991.

Cramer, Florian. "Failing Universal Classification Schemes from Aristotle to the Semantic Web." Presented at the Quaero Forum, Maastricht, September 29, 2007. www.nettime.org/Lists-Archives/nettime-l-0712/msg00043.html.

Date, Christopher J. *Logic and Databases: The Roots of Relational Theory.* Victoria, BC: Trafford Publishing, 2007.

——. "The Birth of the Relational Model, Part 1." *Intelligent Enterprise,* November, 1998.

Davis, Martin. *Engines of Logic: Mathematicians and the Origin of the Computer.* Reprint ed. New York: W. W. Norton & Company, 2001.

Day, Ronald E. *The Modern Invention of Information: Discourse, History, and Power by Associate Professor Ronald E Day.* Carbondale, IL; Southern Illinois University Press, 2001.

Day, Ronald. *Indexing It All: The Subject in the Age of Documentation, Information, and Data.* Cambridge, MA: MIT Press, 2014.

——. "Sense in Documentary Reference: Documentation, Literature, and the Post-Documentary Perspective." *Proceedings from the Document Academy* 3, no. 1 (June 15, 2016). http://ideaexchange.uakron.edu/docam/vol3/iss1/6.

De Souza, Clarisse. *The Semiotic Engineering of Human-Computer Interaction.* Cambridge, MA: MIT Press, 2005.

Dean, Jodi. *Democracy and Other Neoliberal Fantasies: Communicative Capitalism & Left Politics.* Durham, NC: Duke University Press, 2009.

DeLanda, Manuel. *A New Philosophy of Society: Assemblage Theory and Social Complexity.* Annotated ed. London; New York: Bloomsbury Academic, 2006.

Deleuze, Gilles. *Difference and Repetition.* New York: Columbia University Press, 1994.

——. *Empiricism and Subjectivity.* Translated by Constantin Boundas. New York: Columbia University Press, 2001.

——. *The Logic of Sense.* New York: Columbia University Press, 1990.

Deleuze, Gilles, and Félix Guattari. *A Thousand Plateaus: Capitalism and Schizophrenia.* London: Athlone Press, 1988.

——. *Anti-Oedipus: Capitalism and Schizophrenia.* New York: Viking Press, 1977.

——. *What Is Philosophy?* New York: Columbia University Press, 1994.

Deleuze, Gilles, and Seán Hand. *Foucault.* Minneapolis: University of Minnesota Press, 1988.

Domingos, Pedro. "A Few Useful Things to Know About Machine Learning." *Communications of the ACM* 55, no. 10 (October 2012): 78–87. doi:10.1145/2347736.2347755.

——. *The Master Algorithm: How the Quest for the Ultimate Learning Machine Will Remake Our World.* 1st ed. New York: Basic Books, 2015.

Donath, Judith. *The Social Machine: Designs for Living Online.* Cambridge, MA: MIT Press, 2014.

Dourish, Paul. "What We Talk about When We Talk about Context." *Personal Ubiquitous Computing* 8, no. 1 (February 2004): 19–30. doi:10.1007/s00779-003-0253-8.

——. *Where the Action Is: The Foundations of Embodied Interaction.* Cambridge, MA: MIT Press, 2001.

Dourish, Paul, and Genevieve Bell. *Divining a Digital Future: Mess and Mythology in Ubiquitous Computing.* Cambridge, MA: MIT Press, 2011.

Dreyfus, Hubert, Michel Foucault, and Paul Rabinow. *Michel Foucault, beyond Structuralism and Hermeneutics.* 2nd ed. Chicago, IL: University of Chicago Press, 1983.

Dreyfus, Hubert L. "From Micro-Worlds to Knowledge Representation: AI at an Impasse." In *Mind Design*, edited by J. Haugel, 161–204. Cambridge, MA: MIT Press, 1981.

Durkheim, Emile. *The Division of Labor in Society*. New York; Simon and Schuster, 2014.

Dyer-Witheford, Nick. *Cyber-Marx: Cycles and Circuits of Struggle in High-Technology Capitalism*. Urbana: University of Illinois Press, 1999.

Epstein, Joshua M., and Robert L. Axtell. *Growing Artificial Societies: Social Science from the Bottom Up*. 1st ed. Washington, DC: Brookings Institution Press & MIT Press, 1996.

Feenberg, Andrew. "Critical Theory of Technology: An Overview." *Tailoring Biotechnologies* 1, no. 1 (2005): 47–64.

———. "From Critical Theory of Technology to the Rational Critique of Rationality." *Social Epistemology* 22, no. 1 (January 1, 2008): 5–28. doi:10.1080/02691720701773247.

———. *Questioning Technology*. Routledge, 2012.

"FLI - Future of Life Institute AI Open Letter." Accessed March 1, 2016. http://futureoflife.org/ai-open-letter/.

Floridi, Luciano. *Information: A Very Short Introduction*. Oxford; New York: Oxford University Press, 2010.

Foucault, Michel. "The Subject and Power." *Critical Inquiry* 8, no. 4 (1982): 777–95.

Freeman, Linton. *The Development of Social Network Analysis: A Study in the Sociology of Science*. Vancouver, BC: BookSurge, 2004.

Frege, Gottlob. "Sense and Reference." *The Philosophical Review* 57, no. 3 (1948): 209–30. doi:10.2307/2181485.

Friedman, Michael. "Coordination, Constitution and Convention: The Evolution of the A Priori in Logical Empiricism." In *The Cambridge Companion to Logical Empiricism*, edited by Alan Richardson and Thomas Uebel. New York: Cambridge University Press, 2007.

Frohmann, Bernd. *Deflating Information: From Science Studies to Documentation*. Toronto, ON: University of Toronto Press, 2004.

Fuchs, Christian. *Culture and Economy in the Age of Social Media*. New York: Routledge, 2015.

Fuller, Matthew. *Software Studies: A Lexicon*. Cambridge, MA: MIT Press, 2008.

Galloway, Alexander. *The Interface Effect*. Cambridge; Malden, MA: Polity Press, 2012.

Garfinkel, Harold, and Harvey Sacks. "On Formal Structures of Practical Action." In *Theoretical Sociology: Perspectives and Developments*, edited by John C. McKinney and Edward A. Tiryakian, 1st ed. New York: Appleton-Century-Crofts, Educational Division, 1970.

Genosko, Gary, ed. *Deleuze and Guattari: Critical Assessments of Leading Philosophers*. 1st ed. London; New York: Routledge, 2001.

———. *Félix Guattari: A Critical Introduction*. 1st ed. London; New York; Pluto Press, 2014.

———. *Remodelling Communication: From WWII to the WWW*. 1st ed. Toronto, ON; University of Toronto Press, Scholarly Publishing Division, 2013.

Genosko, Gary, and Paul Bouissac. *Critical Semiotics: Theory, from Information to Affect*. London; New York: Bloomsbury Academic, 2016.

"Giant Global Graph Decentralized Information Group (DIG) Breadcrumbs." Accessed July 2, 2017. http://dig.csail.mit.edu/breadcrumbs/node/215.

Gleick, James. *The Information: A History, a Theory, a Flood.* 1st ed. New York: Pantheon Books, 2011.

Goldberg, David, David Nichols, Brian M. Oki, and Douglas Terry. "Using Collaborative Filtering to Weave an Information Tapestry." *Communications of the ACM* 35, no. 12 (December 1992): 61–70. doi:10.1145/138859.138867.

Granovetter, Mark S. "The Strength of Weak Ties." *American Journal of Sociology* 78, no. 6 (May 1, 1973): 1360–80. doi:10.1086/225469.

Guattari, Felix. *The Three Ecologies.* Translated by Ian Pindar and Paul Sutton. London; New York: Bloomsbury Academic, 2014.

Guattari, Felix, and David Cooper. *Molecular Revolution: Psychiatry and Politics.* Translated by Rosemary Sheed. Reprint ed. Harmondsworth, Middlesex; New York: Penguin, 1984.

Habermas, Jürgen. *On the Pragmatics of Communication.* Edited by Maeve Cooke. 1st ed. Cambridge, MA: MIT Press, 2000.

———. *The Theory of Communicative Action.* Boston, MA: Beacon Press, 1984.

Halpern, Orit. *Beautiful Data: A History of Vision and Reason since 1945.* Durham, NC: Duke University Press, 2014.

Halpin, Harry, and Alexandre Monnin. *Philosophical Engineering: Toward a Philosophy of the Web.* Chichester; Malden, MA; Oxford: Wiley-Blackwell, 2014.

Hansen, Mark B. N. *Feed-Forward: On the Future of Twenty-First-Century Media.* Chicago, IL; London: University of Chicago Press, 2015.

Hardt, Michael, and Antonio Negri. *Multitude: War and Democracy in the Age of Empire.* New York: Penguin Press, 2004.

Harris, David J. "Machine Learning - What Does the Hidden Layer in a Neural Network Compute? - Cross Validated." Accessed September 4, 2017. https://stats.stackexchange.com/questions/63152/what-does-the-hidden-layer-in-a-neural-network-compute.

Heath, Joseph. *Communicative Action and Rational Choice.* Cambridge, MA: MIT Press, 2001.

Heidegger, Martin. *Being and Time.* New York; Harper, 1962.

———. *Identity and Difference.* Chicago, IL: University of Chicago Press, 2002.

Helmond, Anne. "The Algorithmization of the Hyperlink: Computational Culture." Accessed September 4, 2017. http://computationalculture.net/article/the-algorithmization-of-the-hyperlink.

Hendler, Jim, and Tim Berners-Lee. "From the Semantic Web to Social Machines: A Research Challenge for AI on the World Wide Web." *Artificial Intelligence*, Special Review Issue, 174, no. 2 (February 2010): 156–61. doi:10.1016/j.artint.2009.11.010.

Hill, Will, Larry Stead, Mark Rosenstein, and George Furnas. "Recommending and Evaluating Choices in a Virtual Community of Use." In *Proceedings of the SIGCHI Conference on Human Factors in Computing Systems*, 194–201. CHI '95. New York: ACM Press/Addison-Wesley Publishing Co., 1995. doi:10.1145/223904.223929.

Hinton, Andrew. *Understanding Context: Environment, Language, and Information Architecture.* 1st ed. Sebastopol, CA: O'Reilly Media, Inc., 2014.

Hirschheim, R., Heinz K. Klein, and Kalle Lyytinen. *Information Systems Development and Data Modeling [Electronic Resource]: Conceptual and Philosophical Foundations.* Cambridge: Cambridge University Press, 1995.

Hume, David. *An Enquiry Concerning Human Understanding: With Hume's Abstract of a Treatise of Human Nature and a Letter from a Gentleman to His Friend in Edinburgh.* Edited by Eric Steinberg. 2nd ed. Indianapolis, IN: Hackett Publishing Company, Inc., 1993.

Hume, David, David Fate Norton, and Mary J. Norton. *A Treatise of Human Nature: A Critical Edition.* Oxford; New York: Clarendon, 2007.

Iliadis, Andrew. "Informational Ontology: The Meaning of Gilbert Simondon's Concept of Individuation." *Communication +1* 2, no. 5 (September 2013).

Iliadis, Andrew J. "A Black Art: Ontology, Data, and the Tower of Babel Problem." Purdue University, 2016. http://search.proquest.com/openview/3cd8df3e-515ba81464d98f5403a1f928/1?pq-origsite=gscholar&cbl=18750&diss=y.

JESSOP *, BOB. "Critical Semiotic Analysis and Cultural Political Economy." *Critical Discourse Studies* 1, no. 2 (October 1, 2004): 159–74. doi:10.1080/1 7405900410001674506.

Jordan, Tim. *Information Politics: Liberation and Exploitation in the Digital Society.* 1st ed. London: Pluto Press, 2015.

Kaptelinin, Victor, and Bonnie A. Nardi. *Acting with Technology: Activity Theory and Interaction Design.* Cambridge, MA; London: MIT Press, 2009.

Kauffman, Louis H. "Eigenforms — Objects as Tokens for Eigenbehaviours." *Cybernetics and Human Knowing* 10, no. 3/4 (August, 2003): 73–89.

Kelly, Kevin. "The Three Breakthroughs That Have Finally Unleashed AI on the World." *WIRED*, October 27, 2014. www.wired.com/2014/10/future-of-artificial-intelligence/.

Kittler, Friedrich. *Gramophone, Film, Typewriter.* Stanford, CA: Stanford University Press, 1999.

Kosner, Anthony Wing. "Diffbot Bests Google's Knowledge Graph to Feed the Need for Structured Data." *Forbes.* Accessed July 3, 2017. www.forbes.com/sites/anthonykosner/2015/06/04/diffbot-bests-googles-knowledge-graph-to-feed-the-need-for-structured-data/.

Kurzweil, Ray. *The Singularity Is near: When Humans Transcend Biology.* New York: Viking, 2005.

Landow, George P. *Hypertext 3.0: Critical Theory and New Media in an Era of Globalization.* 3rd ed. Baltimore, MD: Johns Hopkins University Press, 2006.

Langville, Amy N., and Carl D. Meyer. *Google's PageRank and Beyond: The Science of Search Engine Rankings.* Princeton, NJ: Princeton University Press, 2012.

Lathia, Neal. "Computing Recommendations with Collaborative Filtering." In *Collaborative and Social Information Retrieval and Access: Techniques for Improved User Modeling*, edited by Max Chevalier, Christine Julien, and Chantal Soule-Dupuy, 1st ed. Hershey, PA: Information Science Reference - Imprint of: IGI Publishing, 2008.

Lathia, Neal, Stephen Hailes, and Licia Capra. "kNN CF: A Temporal Social Network." In *Proceedings of the 2008 ACM Conference on Recommender Systems*, 227–34. RecSys '08. New York: ACM, 2008. doi:10.1145/1454008.1454044.

Latour, Bruno. *Reassembling the Social: An Introduction to Actor-Network-Theory*. Oxford; New York: Oxford University Press, 2005.

Lazzarato, M. *Signs and Machines: Capitalism and the Production of Subjectivity*. Los Angeles, CA: Semiotext(e), 2014.

Liszka, James. *A General Introduction to the Semeiotic of Charles Sanders Peirce*. Bloomington: Indiana University Press, 1996.

Longino, Helen E. *The Fate of Knowledge*. Princeton, NJ: Princeton University Press, 2001.

Mackay, Hugh, Chris Carne, Paul Beynon-Davies, and Doug Tudhope. "Reconfiguring the User: Using Rapid Application Development." *Social Studies of Science* 30, no. 5 (October 1, 2000): 737–57. doi:10.1177/030631200030005004.

Mackenzie, Adrian. *Cutting Code: Software and Sociality*. New York: Peter Lang, 2006.

Manovich, Lev. *The Language of New Media (Leonardo Books) [Paperback] [2002] Lev Manovich*. 1st ed. Cambridge, MA: MIT Press, 2001.

Marazzi, Christian, Gregory Conti, and Michael Hardt. *Capital and Language: From the New Economy to the War Economy*. Los Angeles, CA: MIT Press, 2008.

Marcus, Gary F. *The Algebraic Mind: Integrating Connectionism and Cognitive Science*. Cambridge, MA; London: A Bradford Book, 2003.

Massumi, Brian. *A User's Guide to Capitalism and Schizophrenia: Deviations from Deleuze and Guattari*. A Swerve ed. Cambridge, MA: MIT Press, 1992.

———. *Parables for the Virtual: Movement, Affect, Sensation*. Durham, NC: Duke University Press, 2002.

———. "'Technical Mentality' Revisited." In *Gilbert Simondon: Being and Technology*, edited by Arne De Boever. Edinburgh: Edinburgh University Press, 2012.

McCulloch, Warren. *Embodiments of Mind*. Cambridge, MA: MIT Press, 1988.

Mejias, Ulises. *Off the Network: Disrupting the Digital World*. Minneapolis: University of Minnesota Press, 2013.

Milan, Stefania, and Dee Dee halleck. *Social Movements and Their Technologies: Wiring Social Change*. 1st ed. Basingstoke: Palgrave Macmillan, 2013.

Mingers, John. "Prefiguring Floridi's Theory of Semantic Information." *tripleC: Communication, Capitalism & Critique. Open Access Journal for a Global Sustainable Information Society* 11, no. 2 (August 15, 2013): 388–401.

———. *Realising Systems Thinking: Knowledge and Action in Management Science*. New York; Springer Science & Business Media, 2006.

Mitchell, J. Clyde. *Social Networks in Urban Situations: Analyses of Personal Relationships in Central African Towns*. New Ed ed. Manchester: Manchester University Press, 1971.

Monnin, Alexandre. "Digitality, (Un)knowledge and the Ontological Character of Non-Knowledge," August 2016. https://hal.archives-ouvertes.fr/hal-01397947.

Moreno, Jacob Levy, and Helen Hall Jennings. *Who Shall Survive?: A New Approach to the Problem of Human Interrelations*. Washington, DC; Nervous and Mental Disease Publishing Co., 1934.

Mosco, Vincent. *To the Cloud: Big Data in a Turbulent World*. Boulder, CO: Paradigm Publishers, 2014.

Moulier Boutang, Yann, and Ed Emery. *Cognitive Capitalism*. English ed. Cambridge; Malden, MA: Polity Press, 2011.

Mumford, Stephen, and Rani Lill Anjum. *Causation: A Very Short Introduction*. 1st ed. Oxford; New York: Oxford University Press, 2014.

Nelson, Theodore H., and Stewart Brand. *Computer Lib/Dream Machines*. Revised ed. Redmond, WA: Tempus Books, 1987.

O'Neil, Cathy. *Weapons of Math Destruction: How Big Data Increases Inequality and Threatens Democracy*. 1st ed. New York: Crown, 2016.

O'Regan, Gerard. *A Brief History of Computing*. Softcover reprint of hardcover 1st ed. London: Springer, 2010.

Oremus, Will, and Henry Grabar. "Twitter's New Order." *Slate*, March 5, 2017. www.slate.com/articles/technology/cover_story/2017/03/twitter_s_timeline_algorithm_and_its_effect_on_us_explained.html.

Page, Larry, Sergey Brin, Terry Winograd, and Raghavan Motwani. "The PageRank Citation Ranking: Bringing Order to the Web." In *Proceedings of the 7th International World Wide Web Conference*, 161–72. Brisbane, Australia, 1998.

Parikka, Jussi. "New Materialism as Media Theory: Medianatures and Dirty Matter." *Communication and Critical/Cultural Studies* 9, no. 1 (March 1, 2012): 95–100. doi:10.1080/14791420.2011.626252.

Pariser, Eli. *The Filter Bubble: What the Internet Is Hiding from You*. New York: Penguin Press, 2011.

Pasquinelli, Matteo, ed. *Alleys of Your Mind: Augmented Intelligence and Its Traumas*. Lüneburg, Germany: Meson Press by Hybrid, 2015.

———. "The Number of the Collective Beast: Value in the Age of the New Algorithmic Institutions of Ranking and Rating." Accessed June 14, 2015. http://matteopasquinelli.com/number-of-the-collective-beast/.

Peirce, Charles Sanders. *Collected Papers of Charles Sanders Peirce*. Cambridge, MA; Harvard University Press, 1974.

Pentland, Alex. *Social Physics: How Good Ideas Spread-the Lessons from a New Science*. New York: The Penguin Press, 2014.

Picard, Rosalind. *Affective Computing*. Cambridge, MA: MIT Press, 1997.

Poster, Mark, and David Savat. *Deleuze and New Technology*. Edinburgh: Edinburgh University Press, 2009.

Protevi, John. *Political Affect: Connecting the Social and the Somatic*. Minneapolis: University of Minnesota Press, 2009.

Rambukkana, Nathan. "From #RaceFail to #Ferguson: The Digital Intimacies of Race: Activist Hashtag Publics." In *Hashtag Publics: The Power and Politics of Discursive Networks*. New York: Peter Lang Pub Inc, 2015.

———. "#Introduction: Hashtags as Technosocial Events." In *Hashtag Publics: The Power and Politics of Discursive Networks*. New York: Peter Lang, 2015.

Resnick, Paul, Neophytos Iacovou, Mitesh Suchak, Peter Bergstrom, and John Riedl. "GroupLens: An Open Architecture for Collaborative Filtering of Netnews." In *Proceedings of the 1994 ACM Conference on Computer Supported Cooperative Work*, 175–86. CSCW '94. New York: ACM, 1994. doi:10.1145/192844.192905.

Riordan, Sally. "What Are Eigen Values?" October 19, 2002. http:/www.physlink.com/education/askexperts/ae520.cfm.

Roberts, Julian. *The Logic of Reflection: German Philosophy in the Twentieth Century.* New Haven, CT: Yale University Press, 1992.

Robinson, Ian, Jim Webber, and Emil Eifrem. *Graph Databases.* 1st ed. Beijing; Sebastopol, CA: O'Reilly Media, 2013.

Roffe, Jon. *Gilles Deleuze's Empiricism and Subjectivity: A Critical Introduction and Guide.* 1st ed. Edinburgh: Edinburgh University Press, 2017.

Rorty, Richard. *Essays on Heidegger and Others: Philosophical Papers, Volume 2.* Cambridge; New York: Cambridge University Press, 1991.

Russell, Bertrand. "On Denoting." *Mind* 14, no. 56 (1905): 479–93.

Ruthrof, Horst. *Semantics and the Body: Meaning from Frege to the Postmodern.* Toronto, ON; Bufalo, NY: University of Toronto Press, 1997.

Sampson, Tony D. *Virality: Contagion Theory in the Age of Networks.* Minneapolis: University of Minnesota Press, 2012.

Schiller, Dan. *Digital Depression: Information Technology and Economic Crisis.* Urbana: University of Illinois Press, 2014.

Schneider, Nathan, and Trebor Scholz. *Ours to Hack and to Own: The Rise of Platform Cooperativism, a New Vision for the Future of Work and a Fairer Internet.* New York: OR Books, 2017.

Schutz, Alfred. *The Phenomenology of the Social World.* Northwestern University Press, 1967.

Scott, John. *Social Network Analysis.* 3rd ed. London; Thousand Oaks, CA: Sage, 2013.

Searle, John R. *Speech Acts: An Essay in the Philosophy of Language.* N Reprint ed. Cambridge: Cambridge University Press, 1970.

Shardanand, Upendra, and Pattie Maes. "Social Information Filtering: Algorithms for Automating 'Word of Mouth.'" In *Proceedings of the SIGCHI Conference on Human Factors in Computing Systems,* 210–17. CHI '95. New York: ACM Press/Addison-Wesley Publishing Co., 1995. doi:10.1145/223904.223931.

Shead, Sam. "Google Is Using Its Highly Intelligent Computer Brain to Slash Its Enormous Electricity Bill." *Business Insider.* Accessed September 4, 2017. www. businessinsider.com/google-is-using-deepminds-ai-to-slash-its-enormous-electricity-bill-2016-7.

Shirky, Clay. "Shirky: Ontology Is Overrated — Categories, Links, and Tags." Accessed July 26, 2016. http://shirky.com/writings/ontology_overrated.html.

Simon, Josef. *Philosophy of the Sign.* Albany: State University of New York Press, 1995.

Simondon, Gilbert. *L'individuation psychique et collective: À la lumière des notions de forme, information, potentiel et métastabilité.* Paris: Aubier, 1989.

———. "The Genesis of the Individual." In *Incorporations,* edited by Jonathan Crary and Sanford Kwinter. New York: MIT Press, 1992.

———. "The Position of the Problem of Ontogenesis." *Parrhesia: A Journal of Critical Philosophy,* no. 7 (2009).

Slack, Jennifer, and J. Macgregor (John Macgregor) Wise. *Culture and Technology: A Primer.* 2nd ed. New York: Peter Lang, 2015.

Sowa, John F. *Knowledge Representation: Logical, Philosophical, and Computational Foundations.* 1st ed. Pacific Grove: Brooks/Cole, 1999.

Sparks, Daniel. "How Many Users Does Twitter Have?." *The Motley Fool,* 11:06. www.fool.com/investing/2017/04/27/how-many-users-does-twitter-have.aspx.

Stiegler, Bernard. *Symbolic Misery- Volume 1: The Hyperindustrial Epoch.* 1st ed. Cambridge: Polity Press, 2014.

Suchman, Lucille. *Human-Machine Reconfigurations: Plans and Situated Actions.* 2nd ed. Cambridge; New York: Cambridge University Press, 2007.

Suchman, Lucy. "Do Categories Have Politics?" *Computer Supported Cooperative Work (CSCW)* 2, no. 3 (September 1, 1993): 177–90. doi:10.1007/BF00749015.

———. "Subject Objects." *Feminist Theory* 12, no. 2 (August 1, 2011): 119–45. doi:10.1177/1464700111404205.

Taleb, Nassim Nicholas. *The Black Swan: The Impact of the Highly Improbable by Taleb, Nassim Nicholas.* 1st ed. Random House, 2006.

Taplin, Jonathan. *Move Fast and Break Things: How Facebook, Google, and Amazon Cornered Culture and Undermined Democracy.* New York: Little, Brown and Company, 2017.

Tauberer, Joshua. "JoshData/Rdfabout." *GitHub.* Accessed July 26, 2016. https://github.com/JoshData/rdfabout.

Taylor, Astra. *The People's Platform: Taking Back Power and Culture in the Digital Age.* 1st ed. New York: Metropolitan Books, Henry Holt and Company, 2014.

Terranova, Tiziana. *Network Culture: Politics for the Information Age.* London; Ann Arbor, MI: Pluto Press, 2004.

"The Evolution of Search in Six Minutes." *Official Google Blog.* Accessed September 4, 2017. https://googleblog.blogspot.com/2011/11/evolution-of-search-in-six-minutes.html.

Toscano, Alberto. *The Theatre of Production: Philosophy and Individuation bewteen Kand and Deleuze.* New York: Palgrave Macmillan, 2006.

Traiger, Saul. "Beyond Our Senses: Recasting Book I, Part 3 of Hume's 'Treatise.'" *Hume Studies* 20, no. 2 (n.d.): 241–59.

"'Tree of Life' for 2.3 Million Species Released." *DukeToday*, September 18, 2015. 2015/09/treeoflife.

Tufekci, Zeynep. *Twitter and Tear Gas: The Power and Fragility of Networked Protest.* New Haven, CT; London: Yale University Press, 2017.

Vellodi, Kamini. "Diagrammatic Thought: Two Forms of Constructivism In C.S. Peirce and Gilles Deleuze." *Parrhesia: A Journal of Critical Philosophy*, no. 19 (2014).

White, Harrison C. *Identity and Control: How Social Formations Emerge.* 2nd ed. Princeton, NJ: Princeton University Press, 2008.

Williams, James. *Gilles Deleuze's Logic of Sense: A Critical Introduction and Guide.* Edinburgh: Edinburgh University Press, 2008.

Winograd, Terry, and Fernando Flores. *Understanding Computers and Cognition: A New Foundation for Design.* Reading, MA: Addison-Wesley, 1987.

Wired Staff, Author: Wired Staff Wired Staff. "The Click Heard Round The World." *WIRED.* Accessed July 3, 2017. www.wired.com/2004/01/mouse/.

Wittgenstein, Ludwig, Marc A. Joseph, C. K. (Charles Kay) Ogden, and Frank Plumpton Ramsey. *Tractatus Logico-Philosophicus.* Peterborough, ON: Broadview Press, 2014.

Woolgar, Steve. "Configuring the User: The Case of Usability Trials." *The Sociological Review* 38, no. S1 (May 1, 1990): 58–99. doi:10.1111/j.1467-954X.1990.tb03349.x.

Index

abstract machine 138–139
active reader 139–140
algebraic logic 37–38
algorithm 9, 19–20, 25–26, 96–99, 114, 134, 150–151
allagmatic 28, 132, 156
Amazon 68, 69, 74, 83, 103
anomalous individuation 165
Apple 64, 144
Apple's Siri 18, 31, 46, 102, 151
Arensberg, Conrad 82, 85
arguments 39
artificial intelligence (AI) 21–23, 27, 48, 64, 96–99, 148–153; decision tree 99–102, 148–149; connectionist 110–114; and perceptrons 111–113, 151
asignification 94, 135, 143, 161
asignifying signs 90–92, 123, 134–137
assemblage of enunciation *see* collective assemblage of enunciation
association 116–117, 120, 122, 151, 152, 159
Austin, J.L. 26, 50, 77

Barthes, Roland 139
Bayesian AI 148
Begriffschrift (Concept Script) 34
Berger, Peter L. and Luckmann, Thomas 13
Berners-Lee, Sir Tim 1–3, 32, 44, 49, 54–55, 140, 142
big data 16, 18
Boole, George 32–33
Brin, Sergey 106
Bruns, Axel 155
Bush, Vannevar 67, 105, 139, 142

Cantor, Georg 32
Carnap, Rudolf 31, 41, 43, 111

Cartwright, Dorwin 65, 82
causality 116
Chapple, Eliot 82, 85
Chat bots 149
CIFAR-100 113
citation analysis 106
classification 133, 155, 168
Codd, Edgar 43
cognitive capitalism 21
collaborative filtering (CF) 66–74, 83–84, 93, 96
collective assemblage of enunciation 11, 14, 61, 83, 88–94, 123, 134, 175
collective consciousness 72
collective intelligence 86
common sense and good sense 12, 137, 150, 160, 161
communicative action 143, 144
communicative rationality 50, 89
computer-supported cooperative work (CSCW) 13, 65, 75, 80, 148
Comte, Auguste 66
conduit metaphor 11
connectionist AI 110, 112, 148
constant conjunction 115
contiguity 116
conversation analysis 116
conversations for action 77, 79
Coordinator, the 77–80
CYC project 101

data 16, 17, 18, 135
data traces 136
datafication 15, 92, 159
Day, Ronald E. 11, 126, 141, 142
decision trees *see* artificial intelligence
definite description 31, 37, 42
DeLanda, Manuel 47

Deleuze, Gilles 12, 116, 120–122, 137–138, 144; and Guattari, Félix 7–8, 10–11, 14–16, 40–41, 59–62, 133–134, 150
denotation 59, 137, 138, 146, 150, 161
dicents 39, 81
DIKW pyramid 16–19, 60, 92, 127, 131, 169
directed graphs 18, 77, 83, 88, 99, 101, 111, 137, 145
disparation 162, 166–169
dissensus 50, 144
Domingos, Pedro 99, 102, 151
Dreyfus, Hubert 37, 75, 101
Durkheim, Émile 66, 72, 73

eigenvalue 108, 174
eigenvector 108
embodied experience 11
Engelbart, Douglas 67, 75, 105
enunciative assemblage 14, 103, 127, 131, 133, 135–136 *see also* collective assemblage of enunciation
enunciative graph 134, 158
epistemic as substance 11
ethnomethodology 65, 78–81, 84, 154–155
ethology 74
Euler, Leonhard 18
existential graphs 37, 48
expert systems 101, 102

Facebook 9, 14, 20–22, 27, 65–66; as social graph 78, 84–85, 92–93 145–148
fake news 71, 80
Feenberg, Andrew 25, 51, 58
figurae 88
filter bubbles 104
Firefly, Inc. 70
Flores, Fernando 26, 65, 75–80
Floridi, Luciano 17
formatted subject 126, 161–162, 170, 174; defined 6–10, 19–20, 25–28; and the mixed semiotic 93; and hypertext 140; epistemically formatted subject 56, 143–145; performatively formatted subject 65–66, 147; signaletically formatted subject 115
formatting 135, 139
Foucault, Michel 7–10
frames 100, 101

Freebase 49, 53, 110
Frege, Gottlob 13, 26, 33–37, 46–47, 59–60, 110–111, 118
Future of Life Institute 23

Garfinkel, Harold 26, 65, 78–80
general intellect 20, 25
Genosko, Gary 90, 97, 136
global graphs 1–8, 20–22, 24, 54, 125–126, 130–133, 142, 164–165
Gödel, Kurt 32, 43
Goffman, Erving 26, 65, 81
Google 19, 20, 22–23, 98–99, 103, 165, 172; and PageRank 104–110
    Google Now 114
    Deep Dream Generator 118
    Image Labeler 150
    TensorFlow 151
governmentality 8–9
Granovetter, Marc 83
graph databases 37, 44–49, 127
graph theory 18, 46, 71
GroupLens system 69
Guattari, Félix 90–92, 104, 123, 125; and Deleuze, Gilles 7–8, 10–11, 14–16, 40–41, 59–62, 133–134, 150

Habermas, Jürgen 13, 22, 50–59, 143–144
habit 115, 140
Hansen, Mark 7, 10, 15, 27, 127, 167–168
Harary, Frank 82
hashtags 12, 15, 54, 81, 153, 155, 174
Hawthorne productivity studies 82
Heidegger, Martin 12, 64, 75–76, 132–133, 156, 162
Hendler, James 1–3, 44–45, 49–50, 55
hidden layer 112, 113, 118
hinting 135–136, 140, 155, 158–159
Hjelmslev, Louis 59, 88, 90
Human-computer interaction (HCI) design 2, 4, 22, 79, 130, 148, 154
Hume, David 27, 98, 103, 114–120–122, 152
Husserl, Edmund 13, 59
Hypercard 105
hypertext 105, 134, 140, 141–142, 159–160; hyperlinking 107, 140
Hypertext Markup Language (HTML) 141
Hypertext Transfer Protocol 3, 140

IBM Watson 49, 97
ideas 115
identity and difference 14, 28,
    160–161
illocutionary acts 66, 77; illocutionary
    force 26–27, 78, 89; illocutionary
    mode 141
imagination 115, 120
impressions 115
individualization 8, 17, 163, 167–168
individuation 8, 28, 159, 162,
    166–169
inference 35
information 9, 15–19, 135, 141–142,
    158–159, 169
information retrieval 9, 22
information systems (IS) 2, 11, 14,
    21, 33, 40, 65, 75; design 5, 11,
    16, 129
information theory 11, 17, 159
interface 2, 9, 13, 17
Intermedia system 105
Internet 2–4, 13, 140
interpretant 34, 38–39
intersubjectivity 10, 135, 147, 161, 170

Kant, Immanuel 42, 152
Karinthy, Frigyes 83
Kitchin, Rob 126
Kittler, Friedrich 2
Kleinberg, Jon 106
k-nearest neighbor algorithm (kNN)
    67, 70–72
knowledge engineering 99
knowledge graph 2, 18–20, 51–61,
    80–81, 97, 99–100, 142–145, 160
knowledge representation (KR) 10, 25
knowledge triples (triplestore) 48,
    51, 143
Kurzweil, Ray 22

Lacanian psychoanalysis 87
Landow, George 139–140, 160
Language-Action Perspective 26, 50,
    75–80
Lazarsfeld, Paul 73
Lazzarato, Maurizio 134
Le Bon, Gustave 73
legisigns 38–39
Lenat, Douglas 101
Lewin, Kurt 82
lexia 139
linked data 49, 136
logical atomism 46

logical empiricism 21, 37, 43
Longino, Helen 53

Machine Intelligence Research
    Institute 22
machine learning 7, 20–22, 96–98,
    104, 112, 117–118, 161
machinic 7, 16, 104, 135, 145, 147
manifestation 59, 137, 148, 150, 161
Markov, Andrei 104
Marx, Karl 20, 58
Massumi, Brian 138, 168
matter-purport 88, 90
McCulloch, Warren 99, 111,
    117–118, 151
media studies 6
Memex 67, 105
Merleau-Ponty, Maurice 162
Merton, Robert 73
metadata 21, 54
Microsoft 21, 64, 104, 151
Milgram, Stanley 83
Mill, John Stuart 36
Minsky, Marvin 100–101
Mitchell, Clyde 65
mixed semiotic 14–15, 21–22,
    58–62, 86–94, 123, 149, 153
Monte Carlo Markov chains
    104–105, 110, 115, 149
Moreno, J.L. 65, 74, 81–82, 86
Mouffe, Chantal 154
multi-agent modeling 73–74, 93
MYCIN 101–102

Nelson, Theodore "Ted" 105, 142
Neo4j graph database 45
neo-humanist (subjectivist) paradigm
    65–66, 75
Netflix 68–69
network science 2, 3, 18
networked knowledge representation
    (KR) 16–18
networked publics 25, 154
neural networks 99, 110–115,
    118, 149–150
Newell, Allen 100

objectivity 53
Online System (NLS) 105
Open Graph Stories 84
Open Tree of Life 145
operational autonomy 25
order-words 89
Otlet, Paul 142

Page, Larry 106
PageRank 99, 104–113, 142
paradox of reference 137–139,
  144, 146–147, 150
Parsons, Talcott 73
part-signs 90–93, 129, 134–136
Peirce, Charles Sanders 21, 26,
  32–40, 47, 118
Pentland, Alex "Sandy" 20, 24, 65,
  85–87, 151
perceptrons *see* artificial intelligence
phenomenological sociology 10,
  147–148
phenomenology 5, 11, 12, 75
philosophical engineering 2, 13, 15
Pitts, Walter 99, 111, 117
political representation 153
power 7–10, 25, 41, 51, 88
pragmatics 15
predicate calculus 32, 34, 48, 58, 150
predictive-analytic graphs (PA graphs)
  19–21, 96–99, 102–104, 109,
  112–122, 148–152 *see also* artificial
  intelligence
pre-individual 167–168
protocol 2, 9, 13, 25–27, 134

Quetlet, Adolphe 66
Quine, W.V.O. 44, 82

random walk 107, 108, 113, 149
rationality 17–18, 21, 111, 114; social
  rationality 14, 17, 22, 57, 131
reference *see* sense
relational databases 32–37, 44–47, 55
resemblance 117
Resource Description Framework
  (RDF) 48
rhema 38, 81
Ringo system 69–70, 72
Rosenblatt, Frank 111–112
Russell, Bertrand 26, 37, 41–42, 58, 118
Ruthrof, Horst 40, 127

Sacks, Harvey 26
Sacks, Warren 65, 80
Santa Fe Institute 22
Schank, Roger 100, 101
Schütz, Alfred 13, 147
scripts 100–101
Searle, John 26, 50, 77–78, 89
second-order cybernetics 13, 163
self-organizing knowledge systems 162

Semantic Web 32, 44, 49–50, 54–55
semantics 15, 135
semiocapitalism 21
semiological 137
sense 32–37, 59, 133; and reference
  33–39; and the virtual 137–138,
  150, 158
Shannon, Claude 11, 32
sign 34, 38, 76, 90
signification 11–14, 59, 104, 137–138,
  150, 161, 171, 173, 175
Simmel, Georg 81
Simon, Herbert 100
Simondon, Gilbert 132, 158,
  166–172
singularity (haecceity) 61, 90, 165,
  166, 168
Singularity, The 22, 23
situated action 78
social computing 65–66, 72, 75, 80,
  103, 129–134, 165, 170, 173–174;
  platforms 12, 20, 103, 122–123,
  130, 133
social construction of technology 10
social graph 19–20, 24, 26–27, 80–86,
  92–94, 140, 145–148, 160
social machines 1–3, 18, 22
social media 1, 3, 65, 81, 104, 175
social network analysis 27, 65, 73,
  80–84
social networking 18, 78
social physics 24, 66, 81–86, 150
social platforms 12, 17–18, 97,
  138, 147
social rationality *see* rationality
social as substance 11
social ties 73
sociometry 27, 74, 82
software studies 7
Sowa, John 48, 111, 143
speech acts 65, 75–79, 153
Spotify 69, 145
stating 135–137, 141, 146, 151
steering media 50–53, 56, 66, 100
stories 84
Storyspace 105
stranger-sociability 155
subject and subjugated groups
  103–104, 154, 170
subjectification and subjectivation
  8–10, 104, 131, 133
subjectivity 7–9
Suchman, Lucy 26, 79–80, 100

symbolist AI 100
syntax 15

Tapestry system 67–69
Taylorism 86
teles 82
Thousand Plateaus, A 14–15, 40
Tractatus Logico-Philosophicus 41, 46
Turing, Alan 32
Twitter 9, 27, 153–156, 159

ubiquitous computing 13
Usenet 69
user 4, 5, 14–16, 20

verificationism 37
Videos@bellcore system 69, 72
virality 73
Von Foerster, Heinz 13, 109, 163

Warner, Michael 155
Weaver, Warren 11
web 1.0 140
web 2.0 163
Weber, Max 66
White, Harrison 65, 83–84, 120,
    145, 147
Whitehead, Alfred North 32
Wikidata 49, 131, 144
Winograd, Terry 26, 65, 75–80
Wittgenstein, Ludwig 11, 13, 17, 26,
    41–42, 46, 50, 77
Wolfram Alpha 31, 39, 46, 49,
    113, 172
World Wide Web 1–3, 44, 105, 142
World Wide Web Consortium (W3C)
    3, 49, 131, 142, 144

Xerox PARC 67

Printed in the United States
By Bookmasters